W9-BUY-540

MODERN NOVELISTS

General Editor: Norman Page

MODERN NOVELISTS

Published titles

Forthcoming titles

MODERN NOVELISTS

ALICE WALKER

Maria Lauret

St. Martin's Press
New York

ALICE WALKER

Copyright © 2000 by Maria Lauret

St. Martin's Press, Scholarly and Reference Division, 175 Fifth Avenue, New York, N.Y. 10010

First published in the United States of America in 2000

This book is printed on paper suitable for recycling and made from fully managed and sustained forest sources.

Printed in Hong Kong

ISBN 0–312–22431–1

Library of Congress Cataloging-in-Publication Data
Lauret, Maria.
Alice Walker / Maria Lauret.
p.   cm. — (Modern novelists)
Includes bibliographical references and index.
ISBN 0–312–22431–1 (cloth)
1. Walker, Alice, 1944– —Criticism and interpretation.
2. Women and literature—United States—History—20th century.
3. Afro-American women in literature.   4. Afro-Americans in
literature.   I. Title.   II. Series.
PS3573.A425Z77   1999
813'.54—dc21   99–25773
                                                          CIP

In memory of my mother
and for
Matthew Forster

Contents

General Editor's Preface

The death of the novel has often been announced, and part of the secret of its obstinate vitality must be its capacity for growth, adaptation, self-renewal and self-transformation: like some vigorous organism in a speeded-up Darwinian ecosystem, it adapts itself quickly to a changing world. War and revolution, economic crisis and social change, radically new ideologies such as Marxism and Freudianism, have made this century unprecedented in human history in the speed and extent of change, but the novel has shown an extraordinary capacity to find new forms and techniques and to accommodate new ideas and conceptions of human nature and human experience, and even to take up new positions on the nature of fiction itself.

In the generations immediately preceding and following 1914, the novel underwent a radical redefinition of its nature and possibilities. The present series of monographs is devoted to the novelists who created the modern novel and to those who, in their turn, either continued and extended, or reacted against and rejected, the traditions established during that period of intense exploration and experiment. It includes as number of those who lived and wrote in the nineteenth century but whose innovative contribution to the art of fiction makes it impossible to ignore them in any account of the modern novel; it also includes the so-called 'modernists' and those who in the mid- and late twentieth century have emerged as outstanding practitioners of this genre. The scope is, inevitably, international; not only, in the migratory and exile-haunted world of our century, do writers refuse to heed national boundaries – 'English' literature lays claim to Conrad the Pole, Henry James the American, and Joyce the Irishman – but geniuses such as Flaubert, Dostoevsky and Kafka have had an influence on the fiction of many nations.

Each volume in the series is intended to provide an introduction to the fiction of the writer concerned, both for those approaching him or her for the first time and for those who are already familiar with some parts of the achievement in question and now wish to place it in the context of the total *oeuvre*. Although essential information relating to the writer's life and times is given, usually in an opening chapter, the approach is primarily critical and the emphasis is not upon 'background' or generalisations but upon close examination of important text. Where an author is notably prolific, major texts have been made to convey, more summarily, a sense of the nature and quality of the author's work as a whole. Those who want to read further will find suggestions in the select bibliography included in each volume. Many novelists are, of course, not only novelists but also poets, essayists, biographers, dramatists, travel writers and so forth; many have practised shorter forms of fiction; and many have written letters or kept diaries that constitute a significant part of their literary output. A brief study cannot hope to deal with all of these in detail, but where the shorter fiction and non-fictional writings, private and public, have an important relationship to the novels, some space has been devoted to them.

NORMAN PAGE

Acknowledgements

A part of Chapter 4 was previously published as "'I've Got a Right to Sing the Blues": Alice Walker's Aesthetic', in Richard H. King and Helen Taylor (eds), *Dixie Debates: Perspectives on Southern Cultures* (London: Pluto, 1996), pp. 51–66.

This book has been a long time in the making, and I want to thank the friends, professional and personal, who helped me in their own, many and various ways to see it through to completion. They are: Peter Messent, Margaret Bartley, Tim Armstrong, Sarah MacLachlan, Liam Connell, Nicky Marsh, Hannah Jordan, Jane Bentley, Sue Currell, and the students who took 'Special Author: Alice Walker' with me at the University of Sussex in 1997. Thank you also, and doubly, Sue Dare and Graham Dawson; Peter Nicholls uniquely and as always; Peter Boxall newly and especially; and *mi vida loca*, Paul Roth, simply – for everything.

M. L.

1

Alice Walker's Life and Work: The Essays

You ask about 'preoccupations'. I am preoccupied with the spiritual survival, the survival *whole* of my people. But beyond that, I am committed to exploring the oppressions, the insanities, the loyalties, and the triumphs of black women.... For me, black women are the most fascinating creations in the world.[1]

Anyone who is interested in Alice Walker's work is likely to turn to her essays and interviews as a first port of call, since they – *pace* Zora Neale Hurston – seem to be the ships at a distance which have every reader's wish on board. Walker's non-fictional prose harbours a treasure trove of source materials, from the autobiographical to the political and from the literary to the anecdotal, with everything but the kitchen sink – no, that too – in between. The extract above, from an early interview with John O'Brien, is as good a summary as any that can be given of her writerly concerns in a few lines: here are the ironic scare-quotes around 'preoccupations', signalling her *commitment* to black women rather than a mere personal interest in them, and here is the 'spiritual survival, the survival *whole* of my people' which is so often quoted, and so rarely analysed. Spiritual survival equals wholeness, in this phrase, and it is a hallmark of Walker's work *as* a black woman's writing that the spiritual dimension is always foregrounded, not so much *against* a materialist or more obviously recognisable 'political' stance as necessary and integral to it. 'My people', furthermore, are not only black people but anyone who has suffered and survived with this spiritual dimension intact. The interview continues:

1

Next to them, I place the old people – male and female – who per-
sist in their beauty in spite of everything. How do they do this,
knowing what they do? Having lived what they have lived? It is a
mystery, and so it lures me into their lives. My grandfather, at
eighty-five, never been out of Georgia, looks at me with the glad
eyes of a three year old. The pressures on his life have been
unspeakable. How can he look at me in this way?[2]

Childlike glee which has survived in the eyes of an old man, the
suffering that has not destroyed beauty: these are key themes in all of
Walker's work, and the question of what makes that possible is
explored over and over again. Often, as here, it is done with an autobiographical reference, a personal memory which is the starting
point for an argument, a poem, a story, or a novel. What might otherwise be abstract notions or wishful thinking are brought into the
realm of the possible and the actual when the author puts her own
life experiences into the frame and invites the reader to do the same.

Distinctive as this autobiographical voice is in the non-fictional
prose, and effective as it is once its didactic ramifications become
clear, it is nevertheless not unique to Walker that she draws upon
her own experience in the meandering form that her essays often
take. The editors of *The Politics of the Essay: Feminist Perspectives* define
the essay form, paradoxically, as 'indefinable', an 'anti-genre', because
it is by its very nature 'an effort to approximate, to approach (like the
original meaning of essay (*essai*) itself): to approach and explore and
"attempt"' an act of writing which is neither pure argument nor
mere observation, which sits between short story and academic article, and which seeks to persuade but without making it quite explicit
what the reader is to be persuaded *of*.[3] They cite as characteristics,
besides use of the personal voice, the meandering movement, the
pursuit of subversive and speculative thought, and the fact that
many essays are either akin to or originate in diary-entries, letters
and speeches. All this is true of Walker's essay collections too, as it
is of that other well-known and well-read woman essayist, Virginia
Woolf, of whom more later.

It is thus not the form or the voice of Walker's non-fictional prose
that is particularly unusual, but rather the way in which it relates to
her fiction: as explication and sometimes defence, but more often as
an early articulation of issues and themes which are subsequently
dramatised and concretised in the novels. Unlike Woolf's essays,

Walker's are not conceived, nor do they function as, a sphere separate and discursively distinct from the fiction; if anything, fiction and non-fiction are integral to each other and to Walker's stature as a writer whose activism consists primarily *in* the act of writing across different forms. In the chapters which follow I shall draw on the essays from time to time to show how this tight interrelation with the fiction works, but since this is a book about Walker's novels I also want to discuss the fiction in its own right, even – or sometimes especially – if that means keeping the author's perspective out of it. Keeping the author out is not easy, and this first chapter therefore addresses the *problem* as well as the didactic effectiveness of Walker's essayistic autobiographical voice and the experiential authority it invokes. Roland Barthes has warned us, in his path-breaking essay 'The Death of the Author', of the dangers of biographical interpretation which confine the meanings of what are, after all, texts – that is: linguistic artefacts – to an author's life-events. Literary texts for Barthes, as for me, have lives of their own, and should not be so delimited.[4]

Yet in Walker's case it is quite clear that the author is not dead: she makes herself heard as a commentator on her own work in *In Search of Our Mothers' Gardens* and *Living by the Word*, and increasingly loudly and intrusively so in *Anything We Love Can Be Saved* and *The Same River Twice*. As one who seeks to be, in an important sense, her own first critic, Walker is less a practitioner of auto-critique than an interpreter and defender of her creative freedom, especially where she writes about the more controversial later novels. Since this author's voice insists on being heard and cannot, it seems, be stifled, the best I think we can do while trying to maintain a critical distance nevertheless, is to give it due attention by putting it back in its place *as text*, as a self-representational *strategy* rather than self-evident truth. To begin with I want to extract a biographical sketch from the essays and interviews, in Walker's own words, as it were, and this should serve two purposes: one, to convey the salient facts in the development of this particular writing life and two, to show how the author's construction of that life is part of a self-fashioning which serves her literary–political concerns and tries to control the reception of her work. I am, therefore, interested not in the person that is Alice Walker, but in the *writing* person, the artist. Moreover, I am interested in the way this artist fashions a persona in the essays and interviews through the autobiographical voice, and what kind of critical author-ity that persona then produces for a reader or a critic like you, or me.

Autobiography in the Essays and Interviews: Life/Writing

Born in Eatonton, Georgia in 1944, Alice Walker was the youngest of
eight children in a sharecropper's family. Snippets from her early
life are scattered throughout interviews and essays, particularly in
In Search of Our Mothers' Gardens, where she writes of her parents,
brothers and sisters and of her glamorous aunts, who came to visit
from the North and whom she saw as role models: independent,
sexy, sassy women of whom she refused to believe that they earned
their living by cleaning other people's (white women's) houses.[5]
These aunts, she says, inspired in part her portrayal of Shug in *The
Color Purple* and wealthy Northern relatives also make their appearance in *The Third Life of Grange Copeland*, where they lead Brownfield to dream about a better life in the North. Walker's childhood was
lived in poverty in the rural South, a poverty which she never fails to
mention when she writes about her parents' lives and about dispossessed people all over the world, with whom she feels an automatic
empathy. Both poverty and the South have ambivalent meanings
for Walker, and she articulates these in 'The Black Writer and the
Southern Experience'. On one hand she feels that as a black Southern writer she has inherited a sense of community as part of the
culture, even if that solidarity came out of poverty. As long as the
consciousness of being poor is recognised for what it is, imposed
from outside through 'deliberate humiliation', and does not become
internalised as a feeling of worthlessness, then the community of
poverty can be a positive thing, enabling an interdependence without shame.[6] On the other hand, Walker also notes that Southern
black life is not something to be romanticised, because it was determined by hard work in the fields, poor housing and the greed and
ruthlessness of white employers who worked her parents nearly to
death. For Southern black writers, this means they have a legacy of
love and hate to draw on, but also an 'enormous richness and
beauty'.[7]

This is evident in the way that Walker has passed on some of her
Southern heritage in her fiction. Childhood memories of happiness
come from the stories that her mother told her, the rural environment of Eatonton, and her friendship with the old man Mr Sweet,
who inspired the short story 'To Hell with Dying' which was later
issued as a book for children. One of her mother's stories about life
in the South during the Depression was the source for 'The Revenge

of Hannah Kemhuff'; both stories in turn connect with two of Walker's favourite figures of the Harlem Renaissance, Zora Neale Hurston and Langston Hughes, whose biography Walker wrote, also for children.[8] *Langston Hughes: American Poet* (1974), *Finding the Green Stone* (1991) and *To Hell with Dying* (1988), the latter two illustrated by Catherine Deeter, together constitute Alice Walker's (little known) children's writing, in which she takes on her mother's role as a storyteller and preserver of the cultural heritage of the black South.

Unlike the closeness Walker experienced with her mother, however, the relationship she had with her father and brothers appears to have been much more distant and negative, marked as it was by sexism and violence. It seems that her exposure of domestic abuse in the fiction had its parallels at home. In 'Beauty: When the Other Dancer Is the Self' she divides her memory of childhood in two as a before-and-after experience of violence:

> *It was great fun being cute. But then, one day, it ended.*
> I am eight years old and a tomboy. [....] Then my parents decide to buy my brothers guns. [....] Because I am a girl, I do not get a gun. Instantly I am relegated to the position of Indian. [....] One day... holding my bow and arrow and looking out towards the fields, I feel an incredible blow in my right eye. I look down just in time to see my brother lower his gun.[9]

This event is constructed and reconstructed as a formative experience in various essays and interviews; evidently it changed Walker from being everybody's (and her own) darling into a victim marked by a disfiguring scar. Only when her daughter Rebecca's adoring gaze, years later, identifies the scar tissue as a 'world' in her mother's eye is that disfiguration redefined and the victim transformed into a survivor.[10] Later still, Walker recounts the trauma of being blinded by her brother as her mode of identification with women who have undergone genital mutilation in Africa, and this becomes the central theme of *Possessing the Secret of Joy* and *Warrior Marks*. Because of the shooting then her childhood is effectively over at the age of eight, but the death of the child gives birth to the writer: '[F]rom my solitary, lonely position, the position of an outcast... I began to really see people and things, to really notice relationships and to learn to be patient enough to see how they turned out. [....] I felt old... and read

stories and began to write poems.'[11] Walker's adolescence in the
essays and interviews is largely passed over in silence, but the
implication is that this prematurely 'old' girl now felt more at home
and at ease in the life of the mind than she did in her family and in
her own body. Nevertheless, that family does try to support her fin-
ancially when in 1961 Walker goes to Spelman College, Atlanta. She
finds the institutional environment stifling (in terms reminiscent of
Saxon College in *Meridian*) and two years later she flees to freedom:
Sarah Lawrence College in Westchester, New York.[12] The world
now begins to open up, literally when she travels to Africa in 1964,
and intellectually too. At Sarah Lawrence she is taught by the poet
Muriel Rukeyser, who encourages her writing and passes her poems
on to Langston Hughes; Hughes will be instrumental in the publication of the first collection of poems, *Once*, in 1968.[13] Before that,
another traumatic experience occurs when Walker finds herself
involuntarily pregnant whilst at college. She feels suicidal and
undergoes an illegal abortion, but this second 'scarring' produces
the same creative impulse as the first: 'That week I wrote without
stopping . . . almost all of the poems in *Once*.'[14]

By then, the mid-1960s, Walker is already involved in the Civil
Rights Movement, another experience which she consistently cites
as crucial to her development as a writer. *In Search of Our Mothers'
Gardens* contains several essays on Civil Rights, especially on Dr Martin
Luther King Jr who first appears in her life on the TV news, inter-
rupting the soap opera Alice and her mother are watching. King and
the movement make a big impression:

> Because of the Movement, because of an awakened faith in the
> newness and imagination of the human spirit, because of 'black
> and white together' – for the first time in our history in some
> human relationship on and off tv – because of the beatings, the
> arrests, the hell of battle during the past years, I have fought harder
> for my life and for a chance to be myself . . . than I had ever done
> before. [. . . .] Now there was a chance at that other that Jesus meant
> when He said we could not live by bread alone.[15]

In this early essay, 'The Civil Rights Movement: What Good Was It?'
Walker's allegiance to the movement's Christian, non-violent and
redemptive philosophy still shows in that last line. It is an ethos of
which she will retain the pacifism and the notion of suffering-as-heal-

ing, minus the Christianity which she comes to reject (again, this shift is charted in *Meridian*).
Walker is involved in Civil Rights campaigns from 1965 until 1968. She canvasses for voter-registration in her native Georgia, and is employed by Headstart in Mississippi to teach black history to adults for SNCC, the Student Non-violent Co-ordinating Committee. Teaching, as a form of activism, turns out to be hard work, not least because the white bias of bible stories has been internalised by Southern black people:

> Try to tell a sixty-year old delta woman that black men invented anything, black women wrote sonnets, that black people long ago were every bit the human beings they are today. Try to tell her that kinky hair is delightful. Chances are that she will begin to talk 'Bible' to you, and you will discover to your dismay that the lady still believes in the curse of Ham.[16]

Despite this insight into the pernicious ideological effects of (white) Christianity, 'black and white together' nevertheless remains Walker's creed, and in 1967 she marries the Jewish Civil Rights lawyer Mel Leventhal. Their life together in Jackson, Mississippi at a time when interracial marriage is still illegal, is both strengthened by the comradeship of being involved in the same cause and marred by others' prejudice. In an essay written in 1980 Walker recalls that her literary work in the 1960s 'was often dismissed by black reviewers "because of my life style", a euphemism for my interracial marriage'. Often her critics were themselves interracially married, or they admired the work of writers who were (Wright, Toomer, Hughes, Baldwin, LeRoi Jones) and so, Walker concludes, the 'traitorous union' in itself could not have been the problem, but rather 'that I, a black woman, had dared to exercise the same prerogative as they'.[17] That prerogative, embattled as it was, results in the birth of Rebecca Leventhal Walker in 1969, which was 'miraculous', in Walker's words, both because she helps her father evade the draft and because she arrives three days after the completion of *The Third Life of Grange Copeland* (in which the birth of Ruth – named after Walker's sister – is described as 'miraculous' too).[18] Perhaps because of motherhood, perhaps because of burn-out and the Civil Rights Movement's loss of momentum in the South after Dr King's death, Walker's activism shifts around about this time to the North and to teaching and writing rather than campaigning in the South. As an academic at the upper-class and largely white Wellesley College (for women) in New England she designs a course in black women's writing ('the first one I think, ever'), which includes such authors as Zora Neale Hurston, Nella Larsen, Frances Ellen Watkins Harper, Ann Petry and Paule Marshall.[19] She finds that in such a privileged environment consciousness-raising of students, but primarily of faculty, is badly needed. In '*One* Child of One's Own' Walker writes, famously, of *The Female Imagination*, Patricia Meyer Spacks's book of feminist criticism which doesn't deal with any black women writers at all. Spacks defends this omission by quoting the psychologist Phyllis Chesler, who wrote that she has '"no theory to offer of Third World female psychology in America" [because] "As a white woman, I am reluctant and unable to construct theories about experiences I haven't had."' Spacks agrees with this statement and adds that she is only interested in texts which '"*describe familiar experience, belong to a familiar cultural setting*"' [Alice Walker's italics], but recognises that the matter of why she selected only texts from women in 'the Anglo-American tradition' is not thereby fully settled. Walker then answers Spacks's guilt-ridden question:

> Why only these? Because they are white, and middle class, and because, to Spacks, female imagination is only that. Perhaps, however, this *is* the white female imagination, one that is 'reluctant *and unable* to construct theories about experiences I haven't had.' (Yet Spacks never lived in nineteenth-century Yorkshire, so why theorize about the Brontës?)[20]

This passage offers the most succinct demolition of identity politics in the classroom you could wish for, and one which still applies whenever the notion of experience is invoked as an excuse for ignorance – or indeed, guilt. However mixed Walker's feelings about herself as a teacher may have been, it is clear from this and other examples in the first two essay collections (and in the Zora Neale Hurston reader *I Love Myself When I Am Laughing*, which she edited in 1979) that her didactic sense was sharply honed and, when applied in her literary work, proved extremely effective. Frustration may nevertheless have induced Walker to shift her attention from academic teaching to writing. From the mid-1960s on she had been receiving awards and fellowships which periodically enabled her to find the solitude necessary for sustained creative work, and these become more frequent in the 1970s and 1980s, allowing her to devote herself full time to her art. A Radcliffe Institute Fellowship, for example, enables her to write *In Love and Trouble* and *Meridian*; she obtains Guggenheim and National Endowment for the Arts Fellowships in 1979 to work on *The Color Purple*, which wins her both the Pulitzer Prize and the National Book Award in 1983. *The Color Purple* is a turning point in Walker's career in more ways than one. For the writing of it, she moves to California in 1977, taking up dual residence in San Francisco and in the countryside around Mendocino. The latter, she explains in 'Writing *The Color Purple*', was necessary because her characters demanded to get out of the city and into an environment as close to their native Georgia as possible, 'only it was more beautiful and the local swimming hole was not segregated', she adds archly.[21] At this time she also divorces Mel Leventhal and sets up home with the black writer Robert Allen and her daughter Rebecca. Even bigger changes are afoot now. Publication of *The Color Purple* brings popular and establishment acclaim, which launches her into the public eye in a way that she had not been before. It also brings her into contact with Steven Spielberg and Quincy Jones, who want to make a film of *The Color Purple*, and into critical controversy with Oakland schools and – later – black community groups who object to the novel and the film because of their depiction of lesbianism, sexual violence and domestic abuse.[22] Walker gives a measured riposte to such criticism in the essay 'In the Closet of the Soul':

> An early disappointment to me in some black men's response to my work [*Meridian* and *The Third Life of Grange Copeland*] is their apparent inability to empathize with black women's suffering under sexism. [....] A book and movie that urged us to look at the oppression of women and children by men (and, to a lesser degree, by women) became the opportunity by which black men drew attention to themselves – not in an effort to rid themselves of the desire or the tendency to oppress women and children, but, instead, to claim that inasmuch as a 'negative' picture of them was presented to the world, they were, in fact, the ones *being* oppressed.[23]

In *The Same River Twice* this defence of *The Color Purple* continues, in great detail and at great length: it is a big book entirely devoted to

the making of the film, the critical controversy, correspondence with
Spielberg and Jones, letters and articles of support from friends, and
so on. It may be that the perceived necessity for such a book testifies
to the importance of *The Color Purple* as a catalyst for (African) American cultural debate, but it also seems that from this point on, round
about 1983, Walker's non-fictional writing takes on a different hue.
The autobiographical voice, by now represented in the essays as that
of a self-styled recluse in the northern California foothills, is less
didactically instrumental in the making of a larger social or political
argument, or illustrative of an experiment in creative thinking (an
essai proprement dit) than defensive and sometimes merely self-serv-
ing. Increasingly the personal accounts of the late 1980s and 1990s
concern what can be dismissed as 'lifestyle politics', or more accurately described as the author's awakening to new age thinking.
Clearly, in *Living by the Word* and especially *Anything We Love Can Be
Saved*, California has left its mark. Among the more serious and
enlightening essays are those on Native American culture and history; Walker's identification with the cause of Native Americans is of
long standing, as the childhood memory of her blinding in which she
positioned herself – naively, but in retrospect significantly – as an
'Indian' shows. But children's play is not the only cultural script in
which Indians and little girls are destined to lose. Historically,
slavery and miscegenation bound African- and Native Americans
together:

> We have been slaves *here* and we have been slaves *there*. The white
> great-grandfathers abused and sold us *here* and our black
> great-grandfathers abused and sold us *there*. [....] We are the
> mestizos of North America. We are black, yes, but we are 'white',
> too, and we are red. To attempt to function as only one, when you
> are really two or three, leads, I believe, to psychic illness: 'white'
> people have shown us the madness of that. (Imagine the psychic
> liberation of white people if they understood that probably no one
> on the planet is genetically 'white'.)[24]

In this essay, 'In the Closet of the Soul', Walker characteristically
brings her Cherokee grandmother into the historical picture as well as
her great-great-grandfather, a white slave-owner. Such a view of racial
and cultural hybridity links her, again, to Zora Neale Hurston, who
had very similar ideas, but it also has earned her the opprobrium

of black nationalists for whom this rejection of racial/cultural authenticity is anathema. The poet and writer K. T. H. Cheatwood is
cited, in the same essay, as saying that Walker in effect refuses black
identity and that, moreover, she has consequently become the darling of the liberal establishment (at the expense of Toni Morrison, he
feels – but this is before *Beloved*), because she purportedly seeks to
divide the black community in her criticism of black men.[25] None
of this has deflected Walker, however, from the true path of spiritual
healing as she sees it, guided by a philosophy combining elements of
Native and African American 'folk' belief with ecology, animal rights
and, of course, womanism and bisexuality ('homospirituality').
'Paganism' is what she calls this philosophy, and we find an early
articulation of it in an interview:

> If there is one thing African-Americans have retained of their
> African heritage, it is probably animism: a belief that makes it pos-
> sible to view all creation as living, as being inhabited by spirit. This
> belief encourages knowledge perceived intuitively. It does not sur-
> prise me, personally, that scientists are now discovering that trees,
> plants, flowers have feelings...emotions, that they shrink when
> yelled at; that they faint when an evil person is about to hurt
> them.[26]

This was as early as 1973. In a speech delivered at a Theological
Seminary in 1995, the same ideas are advanced as the result of a personal spiritual quest:

> 'Pagan' means 'of the land, country dweller, peasant', all of which
> my family was. It also means a person whose primary relationship
> is with Nature and the Earth [cf. Native Americans]...[B]ut there
> was no way to ritually express the magical intimacy we felt with
> Creation without being accused of, or ridiculed for, indulging in
> 'heathenism', that other word for paganism. [....] In fact, millions
> of people were broken, physically and spiritually...for nearly two
> millennia, as the orthodox Christian church 'saved' them from
> their traditional worship of the Great Mystery they perceived in
> Nature.[27]

Paganism, which constructs nature as a goddess and the mother of
all life, enables Walker not only to connect her family history with

African and Native American thinking, it also unites her womanist interest in ancient goddess worship with the theory of creativity, gender and childhood trauma that she finds articulated in the work of Carl Jung and that of Jungian analysts such as Alice Miller.[28] Both *The Temple of My Familiar*, where Miss Lissie is its high priestess, and *Possessing the Secret of Joy* preach this hybrid philosophy on virtually every page, as do the two volumes of non-fictional prose writings Walker has published most recently, *The Same River Twice* and *Anything We Love Can Be Saved*. The latter bring us up to date with her life/writing, documenting as they do her domestic life, the split with Robert Allen, her relationship with her daughter, the death of her mother and brother and the depression she suffered after contracting Lyme's disease whilst writing *The Temple of My Familiar*.

Life/Writing and the Author's Persona: What Can a Critic Do?

While 'paganism' puts a name to Walker's thought and gives it a history (as long as humanity, she would say), as well as respectability in the scholarly references mentioned in her fiction and non-fiction alike, this does not mean that every articulation, explanation or dramatisation of what some see as crackpot ideas (notably in *The Temple of My Familiar*) is equally successful. Although the autobiographical voice was always didactic, in the later non-fictional writings the earnestness of conviction and loss of self-irony in that voice undermine its political edge. They signal, in my view, a lack of connection with a readership that cannot be assumed to confine itself to the Bay area or to comfortable middle-class existence; 'not by bread alone' now seems to mean rejecting not just a vapid consumerism, but materialism (in the political sense) altogether. Discursive and cultural distinctions between the privileged and the dispossessed are no longer made in Walker's ever-widening global consciousness, which subsumes the other into the self. Of her campaigning in Africa against female genital mutilation she writes, for example, that 'Presenting my own suffering and psychic healing has been a powerful encouragement, I've found, to victims of mutilation who are ashamed or reluctant to speak of their struggle. Telling my own story in this context has also strengthened me, an unanticipated gift.'[29] In this context, the autobiographically informed empathy may indeed have been useful, but in *Anything We Love Can Be Saved* 'telling my own story' becomes paramount in essay after letter after autobiographical sketch, whether they be ostensibly about Cuba, Winnie Mandela, the Million Man March or the cat Frida. As often as not the reader is left bewildered by this barrage of self-revelation, however much it may have been intended as 'powerful encouragement'. Take, for example, this passage in 'A Letter to President Clinton':

> America at the moment is like a badly wounded parent, the ageing, spent, and scared offspring of all the dysfunctional families of the multitudes of tribes who settled here. It is the medicine of compassionate understanding that must be administered now, immediately, on a daily basis, indiscriminately.[30]

Similar notions or sentiments – for 'sentiment' is what it is here – of the nation as a family and government as a bad parent, are expressed in the later novels where they can work metaphorically because of the visionary qualities of Walker's creative prose. Here, by contrast, they seem simply misplaced and misdirected, especially when Walker ends her letter saying that in spite of her criticism of Clinton's boycott of Cuba, she 'cares about' him, Hillary and their daughter, but also about the Cuban people: 'Whenever you hurt them, or help them, please think of me' – as if that would, or rather *should* make a difference.[31]

The issue is not whether Walker's new age philosophy is valid, useful, interesting or agreeable to her well-nigh global readership or to her critics. I, for one, have no quarrel with paganism *per se* – if anything, it is too all-encompassing, too utopian and right-on culturally diverse to be objectionable, and that is precisely the problem: it would be like objecting to happiness, or sleeping babies. What one *can* be validly critical of, however, is the form it often takes in the later autobiographical writings, as in the instances cited above. Afterwords to *The Color Purple* and *Possessing the Secret of Joy*, essays about *The Temple of My Familiar* in *Anything We Love Can Be Saved*, the book version of *Warrior Marks* and the 'Meditation on Life, Spirit, Art, and the Making of the Film *The Color Purple* Ten Years Later' which is *The Same River Twice* all function as, even if they were not intended to be, authorial interventions in the critical debate that Walker's work has generated. It is as if she is trying to control the reception of her fiction in ways which then will not let that fiction live – as text and as creative work beyond the reach of authorial possession. This, of course, is where literary criticism comes in, for critics are of a far more diverse plumage than single authors can be and therefore bring multiple perspectives to bear on texts without claiming that any one is the final word. Like many creative writers, Walker dislikes criticism because she sees it – not as a forum where meanings are opened up, but as an exercise in closed-mindedness:

> Criticism is something that I don't fully approve of, because I think for the critic it must be very painful to always look at things in a critical way. I think you miss so much. And you have to sort of shape everything you see to the way you're prepared to see it.[32]

This is a bit much coming from the cultural critic which Alice Walker also is; it is as if that aspect of her creative work is here disavowed. Recently, in 'Getting as Black as My Daddy: Thoughts on the Unhelpful Aspects of Destructive Criticism' she has written about criticism when it is abusive and anonymous and comes in the morning post, as 'verbal battering'. When it is simply critical of her autobiographical writing and printed in *The Village Voice*, she represents it as a form of censorship or self-censorship, something which stifles her creativity. The form of 'Getting as Black as My Daddy' enacts this self-censorship; the essay is unfinished 'as a demonstration of what, because of battering rather than constructive criticism, is sometimes lost'.[33] What gets lost as well in this rhetorical ploy, however, is again a sense of perspective and discursive difference: a critical review is not hate mail, just as 'constructive criticism' cannot be equated with fan mail either. Alice Walker's life/writing in the late 1990s seems to have reached a stage where the author's persona is increasingly constructed as that of an 'elder' whose speech brooks no contradiction, however much aware it also is of the fact that 'being human and therefore limited and imperfect', readers' needs of such a persona cannot always be fulfilled.[34]

What, then, can a critic do? Having charted Walker's self-fashioning as victim/survivor, activist/teacher, writer/healer and finally elder through the non-fictional writings, my examination of the novels in the chapters which follow will both draw on and diverge from the author-itative course of explication she has set out in her essays. Taking that course as a starting point rather than the final word, I want to turn to two women whose work has shaped and informed Walker's writing throughout her career. Zora Neale Hurston and

Virginia Woolf enable an understanding of Walker's writing above and beyond what 'influence' the author herself has acknowledged, and this is why a discussion of both may offer a way out of the critical vicious circle which has so far emerged in this chapter.

Walker and Hurston

We are a people. A people do no throw their geniuses away.
And if they are thrown away, it is our duty *as artists and as witnesses for the future* to collect them again for the sake of our children, and, if necessary, bone by bone.[35]

This familiar quotation from 'Zora Neale Hurston: a Cautionary Tale and a Partisan View' is generally used to shore up Walker's claim to rediscovering Zora Neale Hurston in the early 1970s whilst doing research for her short story about voodoo, 'The Revenge of Hannah Kemhuff'. In the essay which follows it, 'Looking for Zora', Walker further recounts her attempt at recovering Hurston almost literally 'bone by bone' by visiting her burial place and marking it with a headstone proclaiming Hurston 'a genius of the South'. Walker's celebration of Hurston, however, is, as Diane Sadoff notes in 'Black Matrilineage: The Case of Walker and Hurston', not without anxiety and we can read this anxiety in the extract above, which brings various uncomfortable questions in its train. Will Walker's own work survive, or who is going to recollect it? What are the forces that conspired against Zora's survival, and to what extent do they still pertain in the culture's disrespect for black women's writing? Sadoff's answer is that Walker *needed* a literary foremother to validate her own writerly identity, she 'virtually invents Hurston before she defines herself as indebted to Hurston's example'.[36] That 'Anything We Love Can Be Saved' is Walker's own, much later rationalisation for the anxiety of loss, as if in saving Zora Neale Hurston's legacy for posterity she was also safeguarding her own. Hurston then is not only a role model and ancestor, but a legitimating presence for Walker in the African American literary tradition. In search of her mother's garden, Walker not only finds the creativity of the woman who gave birth to her; she also *fails* to find Zora's grave in the overgrown piece of land where it is supposed to be. The recollection, then, is by necessity a matter of conjecture or indeed invention; as

Kadiatu Kanneh has said, 'Black cultures of resistance as well as Black self-recognitions are not always, or ever, *simply* inherited. Black/feminist identities, in order to gain a valid political voice, have repeatedly and contextually to reinvent themselves in dialogue and conflict with racism.'[37] In Walker's fear of loss it is not just racism that is the problem, but also sexism and the failure of oppressed people, at times, to honour their own. Kanneh titles her essay 'Mixed Feelings: When My Mother's Garden is Unfamiliar' because she is concerned primarily with matrilineages which are broken because of migration or racial/ cultural differences between mothers and children. The idea of a constructed, rather than simply inherited or found, matrilineage applies to the case of Walker and Hurston as well. Many have written about the similarities between the two; indeed, Lillie P. Howard has devoted a whole book to this literary coupling, yet I cannot help but feel that in this endeavour most critics simply follow Walker's lead rather than interrogate what her *interest* in Hurston actually might be.[38] If we chart the similarities first, they consist ostensibly in a joint commitment to Southern 'folk' culture and more especially the black vernacular; in the self-emancipation of black women like Hurston's Janie Crawford in *Their Eyes Were Watching God* and Walker's Celie; in the struggle, also, for a farmer's daughter like Walker and the granddaughter of a slave like Hurston to live by the word as self-respecting and respected black women intellectuals and writers. Similarities in the work – especially the parallels between *Their Eyes Were Watching God* and *The Color Purple* – are traced by critic after critic in article after article, and rightly put in the African American tradition of one writer's revision of another's work, or of signifying upon it. Yet few dare to ask, as Henry Louis Gates Jr does in 'Color Me Zora', where Hurston's presence in Walker's fiction is to be found other than in *The Color Purple*; as Michael Cooke observes, the two have interests in common but 'Walker operates on a different pitch and scale'.[39] That difference in tone is identified by Walker herself in an interview as Hurston's lightheartedness and optimism by contrast with her own thematics of black women's suffering and struggle. Again, with the exception of *The Color Purple*, Walker is earnest and serious where Hurston's prose is notoriously slippery and *slant* and plays tricks on its readers.[40] The question of Walker's interest or rather *investment* in Hurston is then only partially answered with a need for self-legitimation. Of all the parallels and shared interests cited, many are of Walker's own and conscious making (such as giving Celie the autonomous voice that Janie lacks in *Their Eyes Were Watching God*, due to its framing of the vernacular by the narrator's discourse), whereas others are of her choosing: Hurston's focus on black women is only evident in that one novel and much less prominent in her other texts; Hurston was a political conservative and cultural separatist, whereas Walker is the opposite, and so on. Yet I do think that folk culture and the black vernacular are what Walker 'sees in' Hurston and what she needs from her. Trudier Harris's comparison of some of Hurston and Walker's short stories put me on the trail of thinking about Walker's migration from the South and the distance she has travelled from family and cultural roots, a distance that her work constantly seeks to undo. Harris argues that Hurston and Walker do not occupy the same position when it comes to African American folk culture: '[it] is the difference between intimate knowledge of the culture as usually possessed by the insider, and acquaintance with the culture as usually possessed by those who are to some extent outside'.[41] Harris's point is that Walker uses Hurston to get back to her Southern roots, with varying degrees of success. In stories such as 'To Hell with Dying' it works, but in 'The Revenge of Hannah Kemhuff' and 'Strong Horse Tea' it does not, in Harris's view, because in those two stories Walker in effect discredits rootworking and conjuring. I mentioned earlier that 'The Revenge of Hannah Kemhuff' came out of a story that Walker's mother told her about an incident that happened to *her* mother during the Depression; Walker then went to research rootworking and found the anthropological work on voodoo *Mules and Men* (from which the story quotes the text of a curse collected by Hurston in the course of her research).[42] What this genealogy of the short story shows is Walker's need to verify, to legitimise her mother's discourse with reference to scholarly work; the delight Walker expresses in finding 'this perfect book' [*Mules and Men*] in a library is in large part due to the fact that another Southern black woman's scholarship – Hurston's – can indeed confirm the 'truth' of the first black Southern woman's private and domestic account of history. Something similar goes on in the story 'Everyday Use', where an educated daughter returns to the South to claim her mother's quilts as art, except in this story the narrator is clearly critical of such high-cultural validation (and appropriation) of an indigenous and *useful* folk practice.[43] The argument in 'Everyday Use' and the implication of the essay, where

Walker relates her delight at discovering Hurston's legitimising book, are therefore at odds with each other. Still, it may well be that what Hurston, when Walker first 'recognised' her as a kindred spirit, enabled Walker to do is bridge the distance between her (by then) educated middle-class and predominantly Northern existence and the life of hard rural labour that was her parents' lot in the South. This desire for a 'cultural return' to the South is not unique, nor is it only a personal preoccupation on Walker's part. After all, she shares the experience of migration to the North with many African Americans this century and with many of her generation, who moved away for reasons of education and employment.

In a 1984 interview Walker said in so many words that the vernacular of *The Color Purple* represents a means of recovering Southern black culture:

> This was the way my grandparents spoke, this is the way my mother speaks today, and I want to capture that. Especially for my daughter, who has a very different kind of upbringing and who doesn't get to Georgia very often. I want her to know when she grows up what her grandparents, her great-grandparents, sounded like, because the sound is so amazingly alive.[44]

Celie's vernacular letters also link Walker's mother's speech with Hurston's achievement in *Their Eyes Were Watching God*, for as Walker explains in another interview, '[Zora] saw poetry where other writers saw merely failure to cope with English.'[45] Hurston, in short, binds the private world of Walker's family history and the public one of anthropology and the literary tradition together. The discovery of her work makes it possible for Walker to shift her activism from Civil Rights to teaching and writing without losing touch with Southern culture, at a time when she is geographically and in terms of class and education removed from it. But this is not the only tie that binds. Even more importantly, I think, Hurston's example enables Walker to articulate her critique of race and gender relations in the feminist post-Civil Rights era and to theorise it in the concept of womanism.

Walker's definition of womanism at the beginning of *In Search of Our Mothers' Gardens* presents less a political analysis of black women's oppression, let alone a programme to end it, than a depiction of a positive role model:

Womanist 1. From *womanish*. (Opp. of 'girlish' i.e. frivolous, irre-
sponsible, not serious.) A black feminist or feminist of color. [. . . .]
Usually referring to outrageous, audacious, courageous or *willful*
behavior. Wanting to know more and in greater depth than is considered 'good' for one. [. . . .] Responsible. In charge. *Serious*.

This first set of epithets for the womanist woman does three things: it
invokes the black folk speech ('womanish') that Zora Neale Hurston
liberated from its degraded status as defective English; it posits a
model of black femininity which Hurston's lifestyle and demeanour
embodied perfectly ('outrageous, audacious') – and which is in many
ways antithetical to Walker's own; and it implicitly contrasts this
black femininity with white feminism. In the bracketed reference to
'girlishness' Walker appeals to a notion prevalent in black feminism
of the 1970s that white women's sense of their own oppression was
like the cry of a spoilt child. Echoing Sojourner Truth, they felt that
middle-class white women might protest against feminine passivity
and agitate for their rights to paid employment and reproductive
freedom, but that they should not be left in blissful ignorance of the
active, hard-working lives that most American women (black and
working class) led out of sheer necessity (in *Meridian* such resentment of white women as wide-eyed and un-serious is articulated by
the protagonist herself). In the second section of Walker's definition
of womanism this critique of 1970s white feminism continues:

2. *Also*: A woman who loves other women, sexually and/or
non-sexually. Appreciates and prefers women's culture, women's
emotional flexibility . . . and women's strength. Sometimes loves
individual men, sexually and/or non-sexually. Committed to survival whole of entire people, male *and* female. Not a separatist,
except periodically, for health. Traditionally universalist [= aware
of the fact that] 'the colored race is like a flower garden, with every
color flower represented'. Traditionally capable [= leading slaves
to escape to Canada]

This section draws both on Hurston's notion of African Americans'
diversity and on white radical feminism's valorisation of woman-
bonding and women's culture. But in its refusal of separatism – which
can apply to racial and lesbian separatism – it revises both. Hurston
is reputed to have been against the desegregation of schools in the

1950s, believing that racial health was most likely fostered by separate education, like her own upbringing in an all-black town. Feminist separatists of the 1970s believed that heterosexuality and feminism were incompatible, because to love men meant to 'sleep with the enemy'. Walker's definition refuses such separatism as an ideology but still leaves the door open for temporary autonomous organisation or – significantly – for the validity of Hurston's view as a strategic choice based upon experience. Significant also is Walker's emphasis on the 'traditionally' universalist and the 'traditionally' capable, which again can be read as targeting the naivety of white women's self-styled 'revolutionary' demand to be released from patriarchal bondage. Black women have always been 'revolutionaries', and black women have a long history of struggle against oppression. They have also always been aware of diversity within a common cause, and this lesson white women have yet to learn, Walker implies. The womanist is committed to both her gender and her race on preferential and historical grounds rather than those of biology, and she values the culture that history has given her:

> 3. Loves music. Loves dance. Loves the moon. *Loves* the Spirit. . . . Loves struggle. Loves the Folk. Loves herself. *Regardless*.

Pleasure and sensuality are foregrounded here; womanism is articulated as a political identity which is integrated into everyday life, non-elitist, and positive/active rather than determined by victim-status. Again Zora, who loved the Folk, the Spirit and herself, serves as a model. Walker ends her definition with a clinching of her polemic with white feminists:

> 4. Womanist is to feminist as purple to lavender.[46]

Tuzyline Jita Allan, who has given the concept of womanism more theoretical attention than any other feminist critic, sees this last line in Walker's definition as divisive. 'Walker sets up (black) womanism and (white) feminism in a binary opposition from which the former emerges a privileged, original term and the latter, a devalued, pale replica', she argues.[47] I am not sure that this is quite right. American lesbian feminists took lavender as their colour in the 1970s, well before *The Color Purple* and *In Search of Our Mothers' Gardens*. Walker intensifies this colour, deepens and darkens it by mixing it with black; in this way she not so much rejects white feminism as absorbs it into her project and *radicalises* it to the point of no return. Allan's charge that womanism is an essentialist notion because it pertains to 'black feminists and feminists of color' and thus excludes white women, may seem valid at first but is not, if we read womanism as subsuming (white) feminism in this way.[48] Within the larger scheme of the essays in *In Search of Our Mothers' Gardens* and of the later novels, where Walker frequently revises white feminism for her own purposes, there is much more scope for feminist/womanist integration than it might at first appear. And this makes sense, not only because of Walker's allegiance to the Civil Rights ethos of 'black and white together' but also because her brand of spiritual universalism embraces all who are aware of their hybrid natures – including white women.

If, then, Walker needed Zora Neale Hurston to formulate womanism as a radicalisation of (white) feminist analysis and aspiration, that analysis itself would have had to be in place as a necessary precondition for Walker's critique and revision of it. The Women's Liberation movement of the late 1960s and 70s provided such an analysis, for example in Kate Millett's bestseller *Sexual Politics* – but Millett is never mentioned in Alice Walker's work. It seems that Walker's polemic with white feminism was primarily conducted as a *literary* activism on behalf of African American women's writing, and for that purpose Walker built on the work of Virginia Woolf.

Walker and Woolf

Recently, I read at a college and was asked by one of the audience what I considered the major difference between the literature written by black and by white Americans. I had not spent a lot of time considering this question, since it is not the difference between them that interests me, but, rather, the way that black writers and white writers seem to me to be writing one immense story – the same story, for the most part – with different parts of this immense story coming from a multitude of different perspectives. Until this is generally recognized, literature will always be broken into bits, black and white, and there will always be questions, wanting neat answers, such as this.[49]

By comparison with Hurston, Alice Walker's debt to Virginia Woolf is relatively little acknowledged, either by herself or by the critics who engage with her work. Walker mentions Woolf on two occasions: first in 'Saving the Life That Is Your Own', amongst other writers who have served as models for her, adding that Woolf 'saved so many of us', and second in *The Same River Twice*, where she explains that Olivia in *The Color Purple* was not named after Oliver Twist but for the Olivia of that famous closet-lesbian line 'Chloe liked Olivia' in *A Room of One's Own*, 'a book that made me happy to be a writer, and bolstered and brightened my consciousness about the role other women, often silenced or even long dead, can have in changing the world'.[50] *A Room of One's Own* must indeed have been a key text for Walker, because there Virginia Woolf famously wrote, in the passage that leads up to the one about 'a woman's sentence':

> they [women] had no tradition behind them, or one so short and partial that it was of little help. For we think back through our mothers if we are women. It is useless to go to the great men writers for help, however much one may go to them for pleasure.[51]

The search for predecessors was rather more fruitful for Woolf than it was for Walker; after all, Woolf could choose from a long and relatively continuous line of writing women in the (white) European tradition from medieval times onwards. When Walker takes Woolf at her word and thinks back through her Southern black mother and her Native American grandmother, she finds a long and relatively continuous line of non-writers, illiterate women burdened with domestic and wage-labour, to whom the world of literature was either unknown or barely conceivable. 'How was the creativity of the black woman kept alive, year after year and century after century, when for most of the years black people have been in America, it was a punishable crime for a black person to read or write?' Walker asks pertinently.[52] Other than Phillis Wheatley, the slave who in 1773 had her *Poems* published (anonymously) in London, and a handful of other black women writers – Zora Neale Hurston among them – as well as important role models like Jean Toomer, James Baldwin and Langston Hughes, Walker was left to her own devices. She argues, in her critical revision of *A Room of One's Own*, that artists of another kind (quiltmakers, weavers, cooks, African hut-painters, gardeners, and last but not least storytellers) were the Shakespeare's sisters of the African American tradition. Extrapolating from Woolf's statement that 'Anon, who wrote so many poems without signing them, was often a woman', she concludes: 'And so our mothers and grandmothers have, more often than not anonymously, handed on the creative spark, the seed of the flower they themselves never hoped to see: or like a sealed letter they could not plainly read.'[53] This reference to the sealed letter is reminiscent of *The Color Purple*, where Celie for a long time cannot read Nettie's sealed letters after Mr_____ has confiscated them, but there is another resonance here too: with Hurston, whose writing Walker could not read due to the intervention of a racist and patriarchal literary institution which failed to honour her work. Apart from these unwitting allusions to her own later novels, Walker's use of Woolf here also makes visible the class and racial limitations of Woolf's argument and exposes white feminism's universalist assumption that all women share the concerns of the educated white middle class. Still, since Walker needs Woolf to make this clear, the question arises whether it is possible to forge an interracial tradition of women's writing despite these differences. The relative silence which surrounds the Walker/Woolf nexus in feminist criticism might suggest that it is not; to date, the domains of Woolf criticism and of African American criticism remain largely segregated. White women write of Woolf, at great length and in great quantity, while black feminist critics focus their attention overwhelmingly on African American writing. The one exception I know of, Tuzyline Jita Allan, reads *Mrs Dalloway* and other white women's texts by Walker's womanist lights to productive critical effect, but she is indeed an exception: both black and white feminist critics, however wise they are to the mechanisms of binary logic and essentialist thinking, have tended to stick to (what they see as) their own. Writing itself however, as Alice Walker says in the opening statement to this section, does not work exclusively along lines of racial (or gender) identification in this way, nor can it afford to. Reading does not work in this way either. How, then, can thinking about the relation between Walker and Woolf contribute to the construction of a literary tradition which more accurately reflects 'the immense story' of which Walker feels her work, and that of Woolf, is a part? Recent debates about canon formation tend to recognise – however fraught they may otherwise be – that a segregated canon is unsatisfactory. Walker herself acknowledges this when she writes that she always felt she needed to read Hurston *and* Flannery O'Connor, Nella Larsen

and Carson McCullers, Jean Toomer *and* William Faulkner in order
to even begin to feel well educated at all.[54] Yet the danger is, if we are
not to read Walker's work purely in terms of 'the' African American
tradition as is usually done, but to put it in dialogue with white writers like Woolf, that we may be assuming an indebtedness which is
misplaced. Walker herself is the chief consciousness-raiser of this
phenomenon: '[T]his is what has happened to black culture all these
years: We produce and produce and create and create and it finds its
way into mainstream culture ten years later, white people assuming
they are the source of it.'[55] The 'immense story' that black and white
writers are evidently piecing together like a quilt, may be a collective
and colourful story 'coming from a multitude of different perspectives', but it does not get written in any idealised setting of sisterly
equality and collaboration. In the context of literary institutions such
as prizes, educational establishments, canon formations and the publishing industry, writers and artists compete for recognition and –
indeed – ownership of ideas and creative practices. In thinking
about Woolf as one of Alice Walker's ancestors or foremothers, the
'assumption that whites are at the source of it' would seem to be
reproduced. Or maybe not. It may be, as I think Walker is trying to
say in her statement on the difference between black and white writers, that what parts of the 'immense story' already exist and are legible
as 'mainstream' are therefore also available for revision, appropriation and unexpected identifications on the part of their readers.
Walker's work lends itself – some might say all too easily – to interracial reading; the black and white feminist criticism which her work
has generated testifies to this. Conversely, it is quite conceivable that
black women like Walker might have read *A Room of One's Own* or
Three Guineas at Spelman College in the 1960s, before the flowering of
black women's writing as we know it today had come into being. They
might indeed have felt alienated by it, but they might equally well have
'recognised' Spelman in Woolf's depiction of Newnham and Girton,
and they might have cheered Woolf's pacifist stance in the light of
the Civil Rights movement and protests against the Vietnam War, less
on the grounds of gender *per se* than on those of race.

Woolf's polemical work, in other words, is productive for African
American writers like Alice Walker, whilst at the same time our
engagement with Walker illuminates Woolf, highlighting gaps in
gender analysis as well as the racist assumptions which are embedded in the latter's critique of empire and colonialism.

Reading Walker with Woolf, as with Hurston, can raise our consciousness about what is involved when 'our mother's garden is unfamiliar'. Most obviously, it makes visible those places in Woolf's work where 'race' surfaces, places which usually are overlooked, regarded as insignificant or politely acknowledged as (historically excusable) instances of Woolf's blindness to what is now acknowledged to be just as important a category of historical silencing as gender is. What Toni Morrison calls a search for 'the ghost in the machine', black women's presence in the white woman's text, yields examples like the Moor on the first page of *Orlando*; the mysterious black woman on the beach in *Jacob's Room*; and most startling of all, 'a very fine negress' in *A Room of One's Own*.[56] In the middle of a meditation on women writers' anonymity over the centuries, and their tendency to make themselves invisible for fear of opprobrium, Woolf writes:

> They [women] are not even now as concerned about the health of their fame as men are, and, speaking generally, will pass a tombstone or a signpost without feeling an irresistible desire to cut their names on it, as Alf, Bert or Chas. must do in obedience to their instinct, which murmurs if it sees a fine woman go by, or even a dog, Ce chien est à moi. And, of course, it may not be a dog, I thought, remembering Parliament Square, the Sieges Allee and other avenues; it may be a piece of land or a man with black curly hair. It is one of the great advantages of being a woman that one can pass even a very fine negress without wishing to make an Englishwoman of her.
> That woman, then, who was born with a gift of poetry in the sixteenth century...[57]

(That is an awkward break, I thought when I first read this. It is upsetting to come upon 'a very fine negress' all of a sudden. The continuity is disturbed. One might say, I continued, laying the book down beside *In Search of Our Mothers' Gardens*, that the woman who wrote those pages had more genius in her than Jane Austen, but if one reads them over and marks that jerk in them, that condescension and complacency, one sees that she will never get her genius expressed whole and entire. Her books will be deformed and twisted. She will write blindly where she should have her eyes wide open. She will write patronisingly where she should write critically. She will write of herself where she should write of other women. She is at odds with her sisters. How could she help but die middle-aged, cramped and thwarted?)

If I were a polemicist like Virginia Woolf, or Alice Walker, this is what I would say. Reading them in dialogue with each other we see a peculiar argument in Woolf's gender-based critique of colonialism: the Englishwoman does not wish to make the negress over in her own image, presumably like men want to do with the man with black curly hair, 'civilise him'. But what does she want, then? To leave the negress as she is, a 'very fine' specimen of nature to be gawped at in the street? Or merely to acknowledge cultural difference, without ever even thinking that the black woman is also a woman, and might – indeed – be an Englishwoman as well? The passage is reminiscent of *Three Guineas*, where Woolf similarly disavows (white) women's share in, and responsibility for, the legacy of empire. When writing of the woman as outsider to all the institutions of Englishness, Woolf impersonates the 'educated man's daughter' to interrogate patriarchal and patriotic ideology:

> 'Our country', she will say, 'throughout the greater part of its history has treated me as a slave; it has denied me education or a share in its possessions. 'Our' country still ceases to be mine if I marry a foreigner. [. . . .] 'For', the outsider will say, 'in fact, as a woman, I have no country. As a woman I want no country. As a woman my country is the whole world.'[58]

This statement of Woolf's feminist internationalism is as inclusive and inoffensive as Alice Walker's 'immense story' being written by black and white together, and it obscures differential relations of power in the same way. Woolf's intended solidarity with women all over the world sounds hollow in the light of what we now know about the difficulties of forging a global sisterhood, and we know it in part through the efforts of an Alice Walker, Toni Morrison or the African American critics of more recent vintage, whose internationalism is of a different kind.[59] Walker revises Woolf in this sense in the essay '*One* Child of One's Own', where she writes boldly

Of the need for internationalism, alignment with non-Americans, non-Europeans and non-chauvinists and again male supremacists or white supremacists wherever they exist on the globe, with an appreciation of all white American feminists who know more of

nonwhite women's herstory than 'And Ain't I a Woman' by Sojourner Truth.[60]

Race *and* gender are inscribed here in a more sophisticated global alliance than Woolf proposed, because of Walker's rejection, in the last line, of a rigid identity politics. Her 'appreciation' of white women's self-education about cultural difference echoes Woolf's insistence on women's self-education about gender and literary ancestry, and it invalidates Tuzyline Allan's charge of womanist essentialism in the process.

The picture which emerges is that Walker and Woolf are, in fact, remarkably similar writers. Both wrote in a variety of different forms, ranging from journalism (the *Times Literary Supplement*; *Ms* magazine), novels and essays to biographies of men they admired (Langston Hughes and Roger Fry), diaries and letters. They share the concern not to be confined to a gender- or race-segregated readership *precisely because* of their race and gender critiques. Furthermore, because both feel at home in different forms, they are able to parody or stretch those forms in order to highlight modes of discursive power embedded within, for example, conventional biography (which Woolf satirised in *Jacob's Room* and *Orlando*) or the English epistolary novel (which Walker parodies in *The Color Purple*). This manipulation of form in the service of a race and gender critique is especially effective in Woolf's and Walker's essays, where an often chatty and narrative style (wandering on and off the garden path, as in *A Room of One's Own*) disguises a complex and sophisticated argument. And because this argument is not authoritatively laid down as linear logic, the essay-as-story draws us unsuspecting readers in, turns our heads and by such distraction gets us to exactly the place where Woolf and Walker want to have us. The essays, in other words, are just as much works of creative writing as any of the novels or short fiction, and in Walker's case short stories such as 'Nineteen Fifty-Five' and 'Advancing Luna – and Ida B. Wells' are in turn every bit as critical and argumentative as any of her more overtly political essays.

Thematic parallels derive from such formal similarities. 'Madness' engendered by societal constraints around gender and race is found in the work of both authors (*Mrs Dalloway*, *Meridian*, *The Voyage Out*, *Possessing the Secret of Joy*); critiques of official (that is: male or white Western) historiography and biography, particularly with regard to empire and war, can be read in *Between the Acts*, *Orlando*, and *Jacob's Room* but also in *Meridian* and *The Temple of My Familiar*. Perhaps most strikingly of all, both writers use the family saga to expose the taboo of domestic violence and child abuse (emotional as well as sexual) in *The Years*, *The Color Purple*, *To the Lighthouse* (albeit in very muted form) and *The Third Life of Grange Copeland*. Charting the transition to modernity, both *The Years* and *The Third Life of Grange Copeland* examine the interplay of individual and social histories through the crucible of successive generations of one family living, and being lived by, those histories.

In 'Unspeakable Things Unspoken' Toni Morrison warns against comparisons between African American and white writers,

> because comparisons are a major form of knowledge and flattery. The risks, nevertheless, are twofold: 1) the gathering of a culture's difference into the skirts of the Queen is a neutralization designed and constituted to elevate and maintain hegemony. 2) circumscribing and limiting the literature to a mere reaction to or denial of the Queen, judging the work solely in terms of its reference to Euro-centric criteria, or its sociological accuracy, political correctness or its pretense of having no politics at all, cripple the literature and infantilize the serious work of imaginative writing. [. . . .] Finding or imposing Western influences in/on African-American literature has value, but where its sole purpose is to *place* value only where that influence is located is pernicious.[61]

Heeding Morrison's warning, and Walker's about white appropriation of black culture, should not mean that a comparison such as I have made between Walker and Woolf is ruled out of court. It provides indeed 'a form of knowledge', the more so because putting Walker and Woolf in dialogue with each other works to suggest different readings of both. In fact, such a comparison can demonstrate that – to cite Morrison once more: 'We are not, in fact, "other". We are choices. And to read imaginative literature by and about us is to choose to examine centers of the self and to have the opportunity to compare these centers with the "raceless" one with which we are, all of us, most familiar.'[62] Morrison's 'we', of course, refers to African Americans rather than black and white writers together, but it works for an interracial tradition too. Reading Woolf with Walker and Hurston defamiliarises the 'us' of a white feminism, which can no longer simply assume itself to be the preferred implied reader of 'women's' writing. Along parallel lines, reading Walker with Woolf shows how 'books continue each other' in a literary tradition which is neither entirely male and Eurocentric nor exclusively female or African American. Walker and Woolf and Morrison and Hurston create cultural spaces where few or none has gone before, and juxtaposing them opens up the space of 'a culture's difference' in the very act of ostensibly closing it.

One final example may illustrate this. In *The Same River Twice* Walker recounts her experience working with Steven Spielberg on the set of *The Color Purple*. Spielberg asks her to appear in the film, their film, holding his young son Max. Walker refuses:

> of course I could not. There is just too much history for that to have been possible. It's a very long Southern/South African tradition, after all – black women holding white babies. And yet I felt so sad for us all, that this should be so. And especially moved by you [Spielberg], who had this history as no part of your consciousness.[63]

There are comparisons to be made *and* there are differences to be articulated; the relationships between black women and white babies, black writers and white foremothers, are problematic and difficult – and all the more worthwhile for that. They are one place where different patches of the 'immense story' are stitched together.

2

The Third Life of Grange Copeland

It is always tempting to read an established writer's first novel either as the founding text of what was to become a coherent *oeuvre*, or as a youthful experiment in which the older writer's powers can perhaps be glimpsed, but are not as yet fully realised. By 1970, when her first novel *The Third Life of Grange Copeland* came out, Alice Walker was twenty-six years old and already a published poet and short story writer.[1] Her first reviewers therefore were able to read the novel on its – and their – own terms, unhindered, we might say, by the benefit of hindsight but also unprejudiced by the writer's youth and gender.[2]

Some thirty years later it is not so easy to read *The Third Life of Grange Copeland* in this fresh and open-minded way, partly because of its apparently radical difference in form from such later works as *The Color Purple* or *Possessing the Secret of Joy*, but in part also because Walker's critique of African American gender relations is now so familiar that its erstwhile novelty and daring are easily obscured by the mists of time. There is, then, an element of surprise for the reader who comes to *The Third Life of Grange Copeland* for the first time, after – say – *The Color Purple*. Its ostensible realism surprises, its conventionality, its subject matter too – for here is a novel in which men take centre stage, with women characters in a subordinate role. And yet that very subordination of the women and the violence and brutality of the men, though shocking still, are already known to us from Walker's later work. As we become familiar with the world of Grange Copeland, the awareness that we are reading backwards in

Walker's development becomes more acute, and Grange comes to look like an earlier version of Mr ____ , Ruth like a younger Meridian, and maybe Celie's life in the earlier part of *The Color Purple* echoes Margaret and Mem's despondency. So, reading today and not in the early 1970s, it is almost inevitable that the problems of *The Third Life of Grange Copeland* should be attributed to Walker's youth, at the same time as we also 'recognise' it as a blueprint for the later work. Whether such a practice of 'reading back' is all there is to be said about it is a different question, however, for Walker's first novel was not *just* a first novel, but also an original and in some ways polemical fictional intervention in African American cultural and political debate of the early 1970s. What, then, does it have to say?

A bare-bones account of the plot might read something like this: *The Third Life of Grange Copeland* is a family saga spanning three generations, set between 1920 and the mid-1960s. It tells the story of Grange Copeland's three lives: the first as an exploited sharecropper in the American South, the second in New York where he works as an itinerant labourer, and the third, again set in the South, in which he develops a close relationship with his granddaughter Ruth, whom he raises and educates. In so doing he breaks the cycle of domestic violence and emotional abuse that has ruled his previous two lives and those of his first wife Margaret, their son Brownfield, and Brownfield's wife Mem.

This is, indeed, only the skeleton narrative. A more fleshed-out summary would inevitably engage in some interpretation, because every repetition of a plot is not just a condensation but also a reconstruction of it. My reconstruction centres on the themes of mobility, violence and transformation and introduces the major questions I want to address in this chapter. These questions concern, besides the novel's historical context, also its narrative inconsistencies, its critical revision of the Oedipal story and finally also of some key texts in the African American literary tradition.

An 'Apprentice Novel': (Patriarchal) Plot and (Feminist) Perspective

The novel begins with a visit from the Copelands' Philadelphia relatives, whose apparent wealth (exemplified by their car, a new 1920 Buick) contrasts starkly with the Copelands' abject poverty. For

young Brownfield, the Northern cousins represent the hope of a
better future, a hope which is never to materialise in his own life.
Poverty and racism take their toll on the Copeland family, which is
racked by violence of both a physical and psychological kind. Brownfield's father Grange absconds to the North in search of fortune and
abandons his family. Brownfield's mother, Margaret, kills herself
after long years of abuse by Grange and her white employers.
Brownfield himself wants to follow his father to the North, but stops
with Josie, his father's former mistress, and for a while Brownfield
lives as a kept man. His marriage to Josie's niece Mem, a schoolteacher, provides a brief interlude of happiness and temporary
advancement, but bad housing, insecure jobs and too many children
soon get the better of them, as does Brownfield's masculine pride
which leads him to abuse and eventually to kill Mem. Brownfield
goes to prison for the murder, and temporarily leaves the stage. The
spotlight is now on Grange once again, who returns from the North
(we never see directly what happens to him there, since his second
life is told only in retrospect) and marries Josie. With Mem dead and
Brownfield in prison, their daughter Ruth is left alone and Grange
takes on the role of substitute parent. A strong bond develops
between them which distances Grange from Josie and further alienates Ruth from Brownfield. Grange and Ruth live happily together
until Brownfield comes out of prison to claim his daughter. After a
court case in which Brownfield is awarded custody of Ruth against
her will, Grange kills Brownfield and then is himself killed by the
police. At the end of the novel, some forty years after the Philadelphia relatives left in their Buick, another car appears at the Copelands' farm, but this time the visitors are Civil Rights workers
organising for voter registration. They seem to offer hope of a different kind of better life than that of mere material advancement; committed to non-violence, the Civil Rights workers hold out the
promise of social and political change. Neither Brownfield nor
Grange live to see the era of Civil Rights for African Americans however, and Ruth is left, alone of the Copelands but with the Civil
Rights workers, to fend and fight for herself and the future.

It is significant that the novel starts and ends with cars, because
– as so often in American literature – it is the car which represents
mobility in the literal and metaphorical sense. The car, coupled with
later images of consumer goods which Mem selects from the Sears
catalogue (but which she either cannot have or cannot hold on to)

signals modernity and economic advancement, both of which are crucial to Walker's argument regarding African American emancipation in this novel. More important, perhaps, the image of the car connotes mobility not just to a different region or mode of production, but to a new era in African American Southern history – a shift from the rural existence and exploitative economic relations of slavery and sharecropping to industrialisation and urban migration. It is perhaps significant that the first car, with the Philadelphia cousins, recedes from, whereas the Civil Rights car arrives at, the Copelands' compound. The fate of the Philadelphia relatives later in the narrative illustrates, after all, that economic and geographical mobility are not all they are cracked up to be. As Grange also discovers in New York (cathartically, in his confrontation with the pregnant white woman who refuses his help): neither the North nor urban wage-labour deliver the promise of release from physical, economic and psychic bondage, because Northern whites as well as Southern black people still live with the legacy of slavery in their hearts and minds. Only with the arrival of the Civil Rights movement, Walker seems to suggest, do African Americans have the chance to emancipate themselves from such bondage and to enter modernity on their own terms.

Intra-familial violence plays such a large part in the novel, because it forces the characters in *The Third Life of Grange Copeland* to recognise and work through their history of bondage, which has internal (psychological) as well as external (economic) manifestations. Walker's portrayal of Brownfield, who seems to be the conduit – victim as well as perpetrator – of such violence is particularly illustrative in this regard, as we shall see later on. His development is sharply contrasted with that of Grange and raises the question of what *kind* of historical and personal change can offer a way out of the chains of violence which dominate the narrative. As the critic Klaus Ennslen observes, Grange and Brownfield embody 'diametrically opposed options for the black man under white supremacy', but whether the way out of their dilemma lies simply in individual responsibility, as he believes, or a combination of collective action, material security and individual growth, as I think, depends on our reading of the text's ambiguities.[3]

The Third Life of Grange Copeland is centrally concerned with a rewriting of the interrelationship of (public) history and the (private) family. The novel can almost be read as a political argument on a dialectical model of thesis (the historically determined *stasis* of racial oppression and violence in the South), antithesis (modernity and migration) and synthesis (return to the South and advancement through education and political action). Such a dialectical model may well look too abstract, too neat and too dry for a novel which is messy and bloody as well as contradictory and confused. But it may be that its very contradictions and problems come out of Walker's desire to transcend the ravages of history in a fusion of personal and political change. This desire for transcendence leads to a kind of idealist overreach which does not quite work in the realist terms that the text seems to set up for itself. *The Third Life of Grange Copeland* is, in many ways, incoherent: the chronology reveals itself only in fits and starts, there are many gaps and silences in the narrative development as well as conflicting character portrayals, and the narrative logic is quite difficult to reconstruct. Elliott Butler-Evans presents a useful structural analysis in *Race, Gender and Desire* which highlights the unevenness of narrative development in *The Third Life of Grange Copeland* and explains what another critic, Hortense Spillers, may have meant by calling it 'an apprentice novel':[4]

> The early stages... are clearly focused on the dehumanizing aspects of racial and economic oppression. The novel then proceeds to focus on victims other than Black males [e.g. Margaret and Mem, Daphne and Ornette]. And the characterizations of Grange and Brownfield, two men marked by exaggerated qualities of good and evil, become signs of opposing ideological positions, with the narrator clearly on the side of Grange.[5]

This black-and-white representation of Grange and Brownfield serves all too obviously to illustrate a polemical point that Walker wants to make about good and bad black masculinities. Yet there are ambivalences and inconsistencies in the characters of the women, too. As Butler-Evans notes, Josie is now good, now evil, sometimes held up as a victim who deserves our sympathy and then again vilified in the narrative discourse because of her vindictive alliance with Brownfield. Her daughter Lorene is an even more extreme example of overdetermined characterisation. She is introduced as some kind of monster who would not be out of place in a horror film:

> She was cursed with the beginnings of a thick mustache and beard. Her hard, malevolent eyes were a yellowish flash in her dark hairy

face. She was sinewy as a man. Only her odor and breasts were
female. She reeked of a fishy, oniony smell. 'Yep', said Josie... 'that's
the pride of her mama's heart.' Lorene turned and hissed something
vile, her tongue showing through her lips like a snake's. (34–5)

Not only is this passage poorly written, it is also not at all clear what
motivates such nastiness in the representation of a Southern black
woman. It might be that we get to see Lorene from Brownfield's
point of view, but that impression is belied by Josie's comment which
comes from an impersonal narrator. There is, then, a problem with
the narrative perspective in *The Third Life of Grange Copeland*. Ostensibly it is a linear, chronological novel with an omniscient narrator at
the helm, but it is – as we see here – also the work of a writer who is
not yet entirely in control of her material. Walker herself said in an
interview with John O'Brien that she prefers short literary forms like
the Japanese haiku, which 'express mystery, evoke beauty and pleasure, paint a picture', over more discursive forms which dissect or
analyse.[6] Short forms (the essay, the short story, the episodic novel)
are undoubtedly Walker's forte, and it is as if in *The Third Life of
Grange Copeland* she was attempting a conventional form which simply
did not suit her. The main problem, throughout, lies with a narrator
who is both too directive and unstable; omniscient, but not consistent
in maintaining a transcendent perspective because it sometimes
merges with the characters' own. Brownfield's portrayal in particular
suffers from this oscillation between inside (character) perspective
and outside (narratorial) judgement. In this passage, for example:

His crushed pride, his battered ego, made him drag Mem away
from schoolteaching. Her knowledge reflected badly on a husband who could scarcely read and write. It was his great ignorance
that sent her into white homes as a domestic, his need to bring her
down to his level! [....] His rage could and did blame everything,
everything on her. And she accepted all his burdens along with her
own and dealt with them from her own greater heart and greater
knowledge. He did not begrudge her the greater heart, but he
could not forgive her the greater knowledge. It put her closer, in
power, to *them* than he could ever be. (55)

The first sentence seems to emanate from the omniscient narrator,
but presumably the second reflects Brownfield's own opinion – we

know of Brownfield's deprived childhood and lack of education by
this stage. But in the third sentence it is not at all clear whether
Brownfield judges himself and feels guilty, or whether the narrator
judges him. The same goes for the rest of this extract: in *whose* view
does Mem have 'greater heart and greater knowledge'? Is the whole
passage one which demonstrates Brownfield's awareness of his mistreatment of Mem and his motivation for it (envy – she has more
power than he has, so she is more like *them*, white people), or is it, on
the contrary, an explanation of something which Brownfield does *not*
know and refuses to see, which earns him the narrator's moral condemnation? Klaus Ensslen puts a positive gloss on such confusion by
explaining it as a 'mobile' narrative perspective, but he concedes 'the
veiled dominance of authorial control over distribution of action'
because 'Alice Walker manages to exert considerable influence on the
normative level on her fictional characters and on their reception by
the reader'.[7] Didactic writing often works in this way, and so in itself
that level of control need not be a problem, so long as it is exercised
consistently. Because it isn't – as Ensslen shows in some detail – it
remains unclear how we are to judge Josie, for example, or Brownfield. Grange, by the novel's end, is obviously the moral centre, but he
has not always been so, and his transformation from absent father and
violent husband to kindly grandfather is rather sudden. Significantly,
there is only one character in whom we can consistently invest our
trust: Ruth, because only she remains sheltered from and untainted
by violence and its counterpart, victimisation, throughout.

The publication date of Walker's first novel becomes relevant
here, not just because of Walker's youth but also because of the ways
in which the text draws on – then current – competing ideologies of
race and gender relations. The year 1970 indicates a historical stage
in African American political thought when feminist, black nationalist and Civil Rights discourses are at war with one another, and we
see the traces of this war in *The Third Life of Grange Copeland*. In *Black
Women Novelists and the Nationalist Aesthetic* Madhu Dubey understands Walker's womanism as the integration of black nationalism
and feminism, and her attention to both race and gender enables her
to foreground the specificity of African Americanisms in Walker's
writing (such as Ruth's description as a 'womanish gal'). But
although Dubey is right to identify feminist and black nationalist
strands in this novel, I think she misunderstands quite how these
discourses work – or rather, fail to work, that is: fail to integrate.

Dubey argues that various aspects of the novel contradict each other or are in conflict with nationalist ideology, such as the ending in which the West African ideal of the 'wholistic personality' is collapsed – as she sees it – into an individualist liberal humanist stance; she regards this as an ideological cop-out.[8] But Dubey seems to assume that Grange's nationalist outlook, combined with the novel's critique of violence against women which comes from a feminist perspective, is validated by the narrative. This is not the case: the ending quite clearly shows that Grange's separatist leanings are misguided and have no future – this is why he has to die. Black nationalism and feminism do not womanism make; at this point in her writing career Walker's theory of womanism is not yet developed, and so instead of a coherent analysis we see a working-through of disparate political positions in the novel which do not as yet come together in a new coalition. The contradiction between the representations of Brown-field and the young Grange on one hand, and the older Grange on the other, sets a victimised black masculinity against one which is politically emancipated (indeed, by black nationalism) and which has come into agency through the acceptance *in addition* of personal responsibility. But this contradiction is not just the effect of a fluctuating narrative perspective; it also shadows an ideological shift on the cusp of 1960s (Civil Rights and black nationalist) and 1970s (feminism and womanism) discursive formations. Diffuse narrative technique and the filtering through of conflicting extra-literary discourses thus produce inconsistent characterisation and ideological confusion in *The Third Life of Grange Copeland*. Here, a feminist perspective on 'patriarchy's plot' against women comes up against racism's hold on the economic and psychological agency of black men. Rather than see this conflict simply as a flaw, however, I think it would be more interesting to regard it as a sign of the times, evidence of live debate about African American gender relations both in the wider world and in the aesthetic development of a writer for whom healing the rift between the African American man and woman was to become a major priority.

African American Masculinity and the Black Family

It is not difficult to see, in the light of Walker's later work and her reputation as a womanist writer, why some critics have focused their attention on the representation of women in the novel. Lawrence Hogue, for example, sees in Alice Walker's portrayal of Mem and Margaret as passive victims a desire to solicit 'a sympathetic response from the reader because the reader always identifies with the helpless victim'.[9] He argues that *The Third Life of Grange Copeland* is a feminist novel designed to counter existing stereotypes of domineering black women with new images recognising her oppression. Undoubtedly Walker's women fit the mould of later victims like the young Celie in *The Color Purple*, or the mutilated Tashi before she recovers her traumatic memory in *Possessing the Secret of Joy*, but Celie and Tashi become survivors in a way that Margaret and Mem cannot. At the beginning of this chapter I summarised *The Third Life of Grange Copeland* in the terms set by its title, that is: as being about Grange Copeland. I did this in spite of Walker's own description of the novel as being only ostensibly about Brownfield and Grange, '[but] it is the women and how they are treated that colors everything'.[10] Walker said this in an interview in 1973, and whilst it may be true that what happens to the women 'colors everything' it may also be true that here Walker colours her own development as a writer, to give it a more womanist hue in line with her later work. This womanist overlay can easily obscure Walker's concern with the crucial role of African American men in personal and political change, which also becomes a recurrent theme later on. *The Third Life of Grange Copeland* as a text which is not just ostensibly, but *indeed* about a man and his son brings Truman in *Meridian*, Albert in *The Color Purple* and Suwelo in *The Temple of My Familiar* into focus. Grange Copeland's transformation and self-healing demonstrate the necessity and ability of black men to change the course of history, starting with the most intimate history of all: that of the black family in the American South. In this way the novel rebuts from the outset the kind of criticism which takes Walker to task for her negative portrayal of black men. Reading this first novel for Grange and Brownfield and Ruth, rather than solely for Margaret and Mem, thus prepares the way for reading Walker's work with a sense of continuity in its portrayal of the transformative potential of African American men as well as women. When Grange takes on 'women's work' in raising Ruth, when he takes on the task of educating her in African American history and the ways of a racist world, and finally when he shoots Brownfield, he earns by degrees the wisdom, love and manhood he had been searching for all his life. '"You want to be with your *real* daddy, don't you, Ruth?"', the judge asks her in the trial that will decide whether her future lies with Grange or with Brownfield's guardianship, but Ruth's answer is an unequivocal '"No Sir"' (244). Ruth knows, even if she does not articulate it, that *real* fatherhood has little to do with material provision, and even less with biology. A real father does the work – of caring, of guiding and of loving. Mothering and fathering go together in Grange Copeland's development, as Madhu Dubey points out, and in that limited but important sense his self-education foreshadows Walker's later womanism.[11]

Reasons why Walker should be so concerned about the plight of the black man and woman as to devote a whole historical novel to it can be found, as we have already seen, in the historical moment of its publication as well as in the author's incipient, but not yet developed, womanist agenda. The construction of African American gender relations as pathological goes back further than that, however. The black family was a hotly debated issue in the 1960s, especially so after the publication of the government-commissioned Moynihan report entitled *The Negro Family: the Case for National Action* in 1965. Joyce Ladner explains in her 1971 black feminist classic, *Tomorrow's Tomorrow*, how Moynihan's argument 'that the black family had reached a stage of breakdown because of the high percentage of female households' was used both by some black men and by white society to serve racist and sexist interests. On one hand, the report fell into line with fear of a black matriarchy and legitimised the theory, already circulating amongst black men, that 'Black men [had] been psychologically castrated because of the strong role Black women played in the home and community.'[12] On the other hand that same argument assumed, and in fact shored up, a patriarchal white model of the nuclear family in which men *should* dominate women. Ladner shows convincingly that Moynihan's thesis was damaging to both black men and black women, because it insinuated that the men failed to look after their families, without either questioning the model of the white nuclear family or taking into account the (un-)employment statistics for black men. In exaggerating black women's strength and stressing the failure of the black man as provider and paterfamilias, white society drove a wedge between men and women which usefully deflected the issue of racism and attributed the 'problem' of black family breakdown to 'deviant' gender roles within the black community. Ladner cites Robert Staples's famous article 'The Myth of the Black Matriarchy', published in *The Black Scholar* in 1970, to make this point, but many similar arguments and refutations of that myth on behalf of the black woman can be found in Toni Cade's pathbreaking anthology *The Black Woman* of the same year; both texts further illustrate how much of a live debate the issue of the black family had generated by the turn of the decade.[13]

It is, then, not at all surprising that Walker chose to tell a 'deviant' family saga in *The Third Life of Grange Copeland*, foregrounding the black woman's double jeopardy as victim of racism and sexism rather than as dominatrix of black men. She adds a further dimension to the family debate in her exploration of the fate of children in poor and violent families, and again, this is a theme she would return to in the novels which followed. Walker explains in the interview with John O'Brien that, in first draft, *The Third Life of Grange Copeland* was to be a novel about a Civil Rights lawyer (Ruth) in confrontation with her drunken father (Brownfield). But Walker felt that a novel set in the present would be too superficial, and that instead she should look at 'how it happens that the hatred a child can have for a parent becomes inflexible'.[14] It seems that, in the interview, Walker means Ruth when she speaks of the child, but of course in the finished novel Brownfield also develops an inflexible hatred of his parent – and one which takes up rather more narrative space. Brownfield is the crucial link in the chain of familial violence which unwinds in *The Third Life of Grange Copeland*, and my analysis therefore focuses, to begin with, on him. Two scenes stand out which typify his deprivation. The first is his daydream, as a fifteen-year-old boy, of ideal family life. The second is an image of his actual existence, abandoned as a small child on the steps of the sharecropper's shack while his parents are out working in the fields. These two scenes are at the heart of what Walker has to say – really in all her work – about what is necessary for 'the survival, whole, of my people', and I want to look at them from a psychoanalytic perspective because I think they are most productively read in that way. This may seem somewhat surprising, since psychoanalysis is often regarded as a body of thought which is arguably 'white' rather than universal. Yet in a post-Freudian age, we can expect imaginative writing to be self-conscious about psychoanalysis, and I think that *The Third Life of Grange Copeland* is critically engaged with it because of its insistence on the importance of fantasy and familial models in early childhood for the later development of psychic health *or* pathology. Walker's analysis of black family life in the Jim Crow South of the early twentieth century works to illuminate the relation between personal and political modes of power and violence, and psychoanalysis provides a theoretical model by which that personal/political nexus can be understood. We can approach this from another angle too. The psychoanalytic method of (re-)constructing an individual's history is itself a story, subject to revision and critique in the light of the different historical and cultural, class and racial contexts in which it is 'read'. To look at the way in which Walker draws on Freud and revises him we should begin with the old man himself.

Brownfield's Daydream: Oedipus and a Family Romance

'The liberation of an individual, as he grows up, from the authority of his parents is one of the most necessary though one of the most painful results brought about by the course of his development.'[15] This is how Sigmund Freud begins his famous essay 'Family Romances', in which he explains how small children imagine a better life for themselves in daydreams once they have discovered that their parents are neither as powerful nor as fully available to them as they would like them to be. In such daydreams, writes Freud, 'both his parents are replaced by others of better birth'.[16] The child's wish for a position of absolute privilege within the family is first figured in class terms. Later a sexual dimension is added, which expresses the child's curiosity about – in particular – his mother's sexuality and places her in sexual liaisons with other men. The father is now displaced by other lovers and the child's siblings, fantasised as the product of these secret liaisons, are consequently bastardised. The fantasy thus wreaks revenge upon both the father and younger siblings in order to secure the child's privileged access to the mother's affections.[17] For Freud, the family romance is quite a normal fantasy and one which is likely to resurface in adult life in dreams, without harmfully affecting the adult's 'normal state' (of having liberated himself from the authority of the parents). 'On the other hand', writes Freud, 'there is a class of neurotics whose condition is recognizably determined by their having failed in this task.'[18] We can take Brownfield Copeland to be a fictional example of such failure. This is Brownfield's family romance:

He saw himself grown-up, twenty-one or so, arriving home at sunset in the snow. [. . . .] he pulled up to his house, a stately mansion with cherry-red brick chimneys and matching brick porch and steps, in a long chauffeur-driven car. The chauffeur glided out of the car first and opened the back door, where Brownfield sat puffing on a cigar. Then the chauffeur vanished around the back of the house, where his wife waited for him on the kitchen steps. She was the beloved and very respected cook and had been with the house and the chauffeur and Brownfield's family for many years. Brownfield's wife and children – two children, a girl and a boy – waited anxiously for him just inside the door in the foyer. They jumped all over him, showering him with kisses. While he told his wife of the big deals he'd pushed through that day she fixed him a mint julep. After a splendid dinner, presided over by the cook, dressed in black uniform and white starched cap, he and his wife, their arms around each other, tucked the children in bed and spent the rest of the evening discussing her day (which she had spent walking in the garden), and making love.

There was one thing that was odd about the daydream. The face of Brownfield's wife and that of the cook constantly interchanged. So that his wife was first black and glistening from cooking and then white and powdery to his touch; his dreaming self could not make up its mind. His children's faces were never in focus. (17–18)

Brownfield's fantasy, five years after the visit from his Northern cousins in their large car with which the novel opens, bears a striking similarity to Freud's scenario. He imagines himself arriving home in the snow (the North) in a large, chauffeur-driven car. Cigar smoke, successful business deals, a manor house, a black cook and a white wife, as well as two adorable children, are all props for the Hollywood movie which plays in his head. The *mise en scène*, however, is more problematic; Brownfield's daydream, which clearly is also a masturbatory fantasy, ends in sexual intercourse, but whether he makes love with the cook or the wife is unclear, just as the faces of his children are out of focus. Why should this be? The dream, conceived as a film in black and white, holds him – 'at times it possessed him' – yet it dissolves into shades of grey at the point of narrative climax: sexual union with the cook (the black woman, his mother) is as unimaginable and forbidden as the wife (the white woman, the film star) is unattainable and prohibited as a sexual object. We could say that, in classic Freudian terms, the incest taboo and castration anxiety make their appearance here and account for Brownfield's inability to direct his home movie to its satisfying conclusion, but we are dealing with more than mere infantile fantasy. Brownfield's daydream, after all, significantly desires two women simultaneously, one black and one white, one of a higher and one of a lower class. Castration anxiety in relation to the cook, the image of his mother, would be quite enough to dissolve her image, but such dissolution is exacerbated in his sexual desire for a white woman: in the South of the early twentieth century, black men were being lynched for less. As late as 1955 Emmett Till, then fourteen years old, was killed by white men for whistling at a white woman. The Emmett Till case is notorious, but it is only one of many instances when the pretext for lynching was a black man's (assumed) desire for a white woman.[19] It is understandable, then, that even in fantasy, Brownfield cannot picture the colour of his wife's face nor those of his children, blurred as they are by the twin taboos of incestuous desire and miscegenation.

But there are other kinds of blurring going on too. Brownfield pictures himself not as a privileged child but as an adored father and husband, who receives as an adult what he has never had as a child. At the same time, it is as if he is also fantasising his own conception and childhood, in an ideal world regulated by wealthy *and loving* parents. In real life, conception and parentage are more problematic. Brownfield does not know who fathered Star for example, the odd-coloured baby brother/sister whom he is supposed to look after, but for whom he feels no kinship, let alone affection. Star is the illegitimate offspring of Margaret's liaison with a white man, and this baby elicits Brownfield's hostility (at worst) and indifference (at best), attitudes which he later replicates with his own children. Freud's remedy of revenge against the father by fantasising other lovers for the mother, is no mere fantasy here but a reality ensnared in the convoluted sexual politics of Southern race relations. In the daydream, furthermore, the revenge on father (the chauffeur) and mother fails, because Brownfield cannot resolve his conflicting desires to, on one hand, match his real mother's interracial betrayal by his own marriage to a white woman, and on the other displace his father through a sexual liaison with the cook. For Brownfield, as for the reader, it is impossible to put him in the frame of his own primal scene, and if it is true that we cannot achieve what we cannot imagine, then this may be why he is destined to repeat the script of failure in sexual and parental relations for life.

This same sense of inevitable failure pervades the social mobility element of the fantasy too, for the bitter irony of Brownfield's American daydream is immediately and painfully obvious. Here we are reminded of an earlier vivid scene involving Brownfield as a small child, left alone in the yard because his parents are out to work:

> When he was four he was covered with sores. Tetter sores covered his head, eating out his hair in patches the size of quarters. Tomato sores covered his legs up to the knee – when the tomatoes in his mother's garden were ripe he ate nothing but tomatoes all day long – and pus ran from boils that burst under his armpits. (7)

However many critics have read *The Third Life of Grange Copeland* as a womanist text which is *really* about the victimisation of Margaret and Mem, somehow the image of Brownfield sucking on a sugar-tit while the flies buzz around his face haunts the novel, and his ultimate fate – debased and deserved as it is by the time Grange comes to shoot him like a rabid dog – returns to, or perhaps remains sealed in, this early moment of abuse and neglect. Contrast Brownfield on the porch steps with the Swiss psychotherapist Alice Miller's depiction of a small child's needs in her book *Banished Knowledge*:

> A baby requires the certainty that he will be protected in every situation, that his arrival is desired, that his cries are heard, that the movements of his eyes are responded to and his fears calmed. The baby needs assurance that his hunger and thirst will be satisfied, his body lovingly cared for, and his distress never ignored. Is that asking too much? *Under some circumstances it is much too much, a great burden*, while under others it is a joy and an enrichment. *It all depends on what the parents themselves experienced in the past and what they have to give.* [. . . .] The only possible recourse a baby has when his screams are ignored is to repress his distress, which is tantamount to mutilating his soul, for the result is an interference with his ability to feel, to be aware, and to remember. (my emphasis)[20]

Alice Miller has made it her life's work to criticise and reconstruct Western child-rearing practices, which in their emphasis on harnessing the child's needs to society's (and parents') desires for discipline and order inflict – as she sees it – an habitual form of violence on children. For Miller, this model of child-rearing is one that is universally desirable, and although she does not spell out what, exactly, the circumstances are in which such ideal parenting is obviously 'too much', it is clear, in the phrases I have highlighted, that the family into which Brownfield Copeland is born falls far short of Miller's ideal. This is in large part due to the Copelands' sharecropping existence, which demands the labour of all family members around the clock (Brownfield himself is sent into the fields at the age of six). Proper parenting, in other words, is a luxury the Copelands cannot afford. Because Brownfield never experiences it he grows up with an inability 'to feel, to be aware, and to remember', and this turns him into a cruel husband and father by the time Mem, Daphne, Ornette and Ruth come along. External causes of poverty and exploitation are thus transmuted into internal causes of aggression and self-hatred and in this way Brownfield's daydream and his early abandonment present a case-study, not so much of individual pathology, but of *institutionalised* violence and abuse. These scenes memorably work on the reader to reveal the impossibility, the inconceivability of the 'successful' (by white, middle-class standards) black family in the South before the Civil Rights era.

Brownfield's fantasy is a white fantasy, not just a fantasy of being white but a fantasy which is generated by a white world. It takes over his life, insofar as he is destined to live out what we recognise in Western culture as an Oedipal fixation on the father, here figured as both a literal father and the white father/authority figure/personification of the law in Southern race relations.

Freud describes the Oedipal complex most succinctly in *New Introductory Lectures on Psychoanalysis*:

> The boy's Oedipal complex, in which he desires his mother and wants to get rid of his father as a rival, develops naturally out of the phase of phallic sexuality. The threat of castration [by the father], however, forces him to give up this attitude. Under the influence of the danger of losing his penis, he abandons his Oedipus complex; it is repressed and in the most normal cases entirely destroyed, while a severe super-ego is set up as its heir.[21]

In *Black Skin, White Masks* Frantz Fanon writes that Oedipal neurosis is not the universal phenomenon that white psychoanalysts have

made it out to be, but that neuroses are generated by the particular
cultural situation in which a person finds himself, notably that of a
black person in a white world.[22] Again, Brownfield's plight illustrates
this. He is possessed throughout his fictional life by the twin desires
of hurting or destroying his father and seeking his mother – even
after her death. He does not find her in other women, whom he
therefore wants to destroy: instead of mother he finds Josie, his
father's erstwhile lover and later wife; instead of mother he finds
Mem, whom he kills. This particular Oedipus, then, persists in his
revenge fantasy, replacing Grange as a figure of failed authority with
various incarnations of the father 'of better birth', that is: the white
men Mr Shipley, Captain Davis, Mr J. L. and later, Judge Harry.
This revenge, however, fails for two good reasons, and this is where
Walker critically revises Freud's not-so-universal scenario. First of all
it fails because Brownfield's Oedipal battle is not the war, and the
ultimate cause of his misery lies not in his relationship with his parents but in the wider social environment in which he grows up,
which in turn is the product of Southern history, and particularly of
slavery. Unlike Grange, Brownfield does not have the psychological
and historical understanding to confront that legacy within himself;
unlike Ruth and the Civil Rights workers he also lacks the political
tools to even conceive of taking it on in the outside world. Second,
Brownfield fails to resolve his Oedipal fixation because Grange –
paradoxically – is not a father to him except in the most narrow biological sense. Even when Brownfield is still very little Grange cannot
bear to touch him (21); neither then nor later will Grange recognise
him, or speak to him, let alone function as a figure of manly identification for Brownfield. Recognition is something that Brownfield
yearns for, and – not having had it from his father – he mistakenly
seeks patronage from Judge Harry towards the end of the novel,
invoking the fact that they knew each other as children (222). The
absence of father as role model is counterbalanced by the fact that
Brownfield grows up without any male examples of respect for his
mother, and thus for women in general. This is what he observes
about Grange and Margaret's marriage, when he is ten years old:
'He thought his mother was like their dog in some ways. She didn't
have a thing to say that did not in some way show submission to his
father' (5). Clearly Brownfield here articulates a feminist insight on
Walker's behalf; his perception of his mother's subordinate position
implies a critique of the idea that the redemption of black masculinity

should lie in some version of black patriarchal authority – as proposed by black nationalist participants in the debate around the black family of the 1960s, for example. Instead, Walker shows how the oppression of black women within the family is part of the problem, not the solution, because it is merely a link in a longer chain of mastery and subordination. This becomes clear when Brownfield witnesses for the first time his father's submission to 'the man who drove the truck', the white man, Mr Shipley:

> 'Say "Yessir" to Mr Shipley', [. . . .]
> Brownfield, trembling, said 'Yessir', filled with terror of this man who could, by his presence alone, turn his father into something that might as well have been a pebble or a post or a piece of dirt. (9)

Just such a scene in which a child sees its father reduced to the status of 'a piece of dirt' occurs in Carolyn Steedman's *Landscape for a Good Woman*, but this time because of class rather than race. Steedman recounts a childhood memory in which she is picking bluebells in a wood with her father and sees him humiliated by the forest keeper, who 'snatched the bunch from my father's hand, scattered the flowers over the ground and among the ferns'.[23] 'The scene in the bluebell wood', she writes,

> was a way of thinking about the oedipal account, its relation to the primal act of patricide, the incest taboo and the whole generalised account of human culture built around the position and role of the father. It was a way of wondering about how the myth works when the father is rendered vulnerable by social relations, when a position in a household is not supported by recognition of social status and power outside it. That scene is a way of saying: no: it wasn't like that; he wasn't important; he didn't matter.[24]

I cite this parallel not in order to attribute Brownfield's predicament to class rather than race (both are, in any case, bound up with each other), but as a way of 'wondering about how the myth works' in a different cultural and political context. Black children in a racist society such as that of the American South between the wars do not grow up with an archetypally strong image of father as patriarch, and are only too aware of the power of class and race in holding them back from the American aspirations that the dominant culture at the same time bombards them with. We are drawn back once more to Fanon, who counterposes the Oedipal myth with what he calls the Negro myth: that of racial inferiority. Fanon writes: 'The Negro is unaware of it as long as his existence is limited to his own environment; but the first encounter with a white man oppresses him with the whole weight of his blackness.'[25] This is what happens to Brownfield when he first meets Shipley. Fanon explains it as an existential moment in a footnote with a quotation from Sartre's *Anti-Semite and Jew*: 'Suddenly they [children] perceive that others [white people] know something about them that they do not know, that people apply to them an ugly and upsetting term [Yid; nigger] that is not used in their own families.'[26] Racism cannot be reduced to class relations: the power of white people to hire and fire, to humiliate and hurt, to violate black women and vitiate the lives of black men, and act as judge and jury to the violence that results, is specific to the Jim Crow South in which *The Third Life of Grange Copeland* is set. Racism and poverty, or more specifically the inequities of the sharecropping system, draw a ring-fence around Brownfield Copeland's one life and all the people who figure in it, except for Ruth.

Brownfield's Oedipal trajectory then runs along different lines from that of the classic Freudian account. Psychoanalysis (here Oedipus and the family romance) does not reveal 'the truth' about Brownfield's condition, but it provides useful grounds for comparison between types of cultural stories by which we understand ourselves and the world, including the world of fiction. As Linda Ruth Williams remarks in *Critical Desire: Psychoanalysis and the Literary Subject*: 'psychoanalysis and literature (as well as other forms such as film) interconnect', and psychoanalysis itself should be 'seen as interdependent with the cultural forms it is often said simply to inform'.[27] In reading Brownfield's daydream as a case history, I am not so much analysing him (let alone his author) as the psychic script of cultural violence which Walker presents. Williams puts it succinctly: 'It is not that the analysand makes up the stories of [his] early life, but that the stories have *made up [him]*. The subject is a creation *of* the story.'[28] In *The Third Life of Grange Copeland* we can see what the culture does to a child when the only available stories make him up in such a way that he can have no place in them. The question then remains whether it is true that a person's fate, a culture's development, is *determined* by stories generated to keep the powerful in power, and the others out. The text's answer in the end is clearly 'no', but it would be useful to trace how it gets there. The striking contrast between the early part of the novel, in which the reader's sympathy for Brownfield is engaged in no uncertain terms, and his later development, which is one of increasing depravity and violence, is relevant here. It would be wrong simply to put Brownfield's pathology down to his social position as a black man in white society – clearly the novel has something much more complex to say about him than that. Conversely, it would be wrong to attribute his violence and suffering solely to arrested development, or to his unsuccessful negotiation of his Oedipal relationship with Grange. Both the psychoanalytic and the political explanations for Brownfield's fate, which the text on one hand invites, are deterministic narratives of subject formation which it ultimately *refuses*. They explain why Brownfield is as he is, but they are not – for the novel – excuses. Instead, Walker makes a utopian jump to Grange, and creates an epistemological break in the narrative of Brownfield's victimisation which moves from pity to condemnation, after which individual responsibility and social change are posited as the only hope for personal and political change. Because this hope is personified in Grange and Ruth, we have to turn back to the question of how personal and public histories intersect and look at the way in which Grange Copeland's three lives unfold in parallel with slavery, modernity and the Civil Rights era.

The First Life of Grange Copeland: Slavery and Sharecropping

In *No Crystal Stair: Visions of Race and Sex in Black Women's Fiction*, Gloria Wade-Gayles describes Alice Walker's first novel as 'a southern work of art', not only because of its setting in America's Deep South, but also because of the insularity and violence of its black characters.[29] While the story of Grange Copeland's first and second lives takes place some sixty years after emancipation (roughly between 1920 and 1940), it is clear that slavery casts its shadow long and wide into the twentieth century, both psychologically and in economic terms. This narrative, in effect, re-enacts at an individual level what slavery and reconstruction represent in collective history.

When, at four years old, Ruth Copeland says to her father: 'you nothing but a sonnabit', she speaks the truth about Brownfield in a way that perhaps only she, in her childlike innocence, can (108).

Because *as* a 'sonnabit' Brownfield is named, not as the son-of-a-bitch of contemporary parlance, but as the son of the bit that slaves were forced to wear, the slave who is his Grange in his first life. In this first life, narrated in only twenty pages of the novel, the sharecropper Grange Copeland is to all intents and purposes still enslaved by the white man, Shipley, who keeps him from being able to provide for his wife and family and robs him of his dignity. In *Fictions of Capital*, Richard Godden explains the similarities between sharecropping and slavery as systems of economic ownership of labour.

> Share wages differ substantially from free wages. The owner con-
> tracts to pay his labourer at the close of the growing season; pay-
> ment takes the form of a pre-determined 'share' of the crop.
> Should the yield be low, or the international price of cotton drop,
> or the market be glutted, the cropper may not make enough to
> pay the merchant who has furnished his seed and his sustenance
> on credit for the year, in which case, the tenant becomes a peon
> insofar as he is bound to labour to pay the debt. The debt holder
> . . . exerts an absolute authority over the labourer.[30]

References to slavery are frequent and explicit in the early part of the novel. For example, after Grange has run away Brownfield sees Shipley turning up at Margaret's funeral, hoping to 'catch Grange' like any slave-owner would in order to recover his property. But such figurations of slavery go further than just labour relations. Just as Shipley seems to own his father, young Brownfield assumes that Grange, in turn, owns his mother (22). Unable to understand his fam-ily's poverty by comparison with the wealth of his Northern cousins, he fantasises that 'Maybe he [Grange] had tried to sell her and she wouldn't be sold – which could be why they were still poor and in debt and would die that way' (11). Brownfield's childlike mind both understands and misunderstands his parents' marriage as another incarnation of the relationship between slave and master; he has certainly caught on to Shipley's command not just of Grange's labour but also of Margaret's sexual services, and he 'knows' about the money that she could make from white men as a prostitute. Unlike Grange, who in leaving his wife and children at least liberates him-self, Brownfield internalises the violence done to him, exchanging one white master for another and retaining his view of women (and children) as property to be acquired and dispensed with as it suits him. He repeats the sins of his father both with Josie and with Mem, on whom he is economically and emotionally dependent without wanting to recognise it. Brownfield's world never gets bigger than the porch steps: even after his marriage to Mem, when their circumstances improve and he has gained, through her efforts, literacy, decent housing and employment in the city, he persists in his definition of manhood as the power to dominate and enslave women. Brownfield goes to court to get Ruth back, 'not because he wanted her, but because he didn't want Grange to have her' (227). It is then Brownfield who lives out, in effect, the first life of Grange Copeland after Grange has abandoned it. His *need* for the white men to recognise him keeps him firmly bound within the master/slave dialectic, Hegel's terms for understanding the psychic machinations of power and subordination to it. In the 1987 Afterword to the novel Alice Walker states that she wants the reader to see the connection between the oppression of black women and children on one hand and the oppression of African Americans as a people on the other.[31] This political insight is personified in Brownfield as a slave, living Grange's first life. Yet the overall message of the novel is a different one and marks the contrast between Brownfield, the bad father, and Grange, the absent one, because the latter mends his ways whilst the former cannot. In his second life Grange comes into contact with different stories and different histories which lead him to a new conception of himself, the race, and American society as a whole. Brownfield never gets the benefit of his father's re-education, which is also a personal *reconstruction*, but Ruth does, and it is she who gives Grange his third life, in which he has to learn still more.

The Second Life of Grange Copeland

As the title indicates, it is this third life of Grange Copeland which matters, because only then does he come into his own and does he gain a real presence in the text. Before that, Brownfield dominates the textual space of his first life and Mem that of his second. It is she who, like Grange, tries to move out of the condition of virtual slavery into a modernity which is figured as migration to the city, waged labour and improved material circumstances. Having moved her family to a house in the city in a bid to save them herself if Brownfield cannot, Mem wants to turn Brownfield's dream of a car, a

house, a devoted wife and children, into reality. Enthralled by the
Sears catalogue, Mem dreams of shiny indoor toilets and a 'deep
white bathtub with greenish blue water' (80–1). Her legitimate
aspirations for decent housing and material comfort then chart the
historical transition from an agricultural economy to consumer
capitalism in the South of the 1920s and 1930s, but even this modest
American dream does not last very long. With the changing economic fortunes of Brownfield's family, Walker makes the point that
modernity and progress are not necessarily the same thing; the
Copelands' initial upward mobility proves fragile due to fluctuations
in the labour market of which they are the first casualties. Brownfield, who cannot abide Mem's determination to take advantage of
the economic opportunities that the city affords her as an educated
black woman, sabotages their advancement and decides that they
should go back to the country. 'Moving to Mr J. L.'s place' means, in
effect, moving back to sharecropping and slavery, to an earlier stage
of economic development. Mem does not take this regression lying
down and, in a scene which is reminiscent of Janie's 'cussing out' of
Joe Starks in Zora Neale Hurston's novel *Their Eyes Were Watching
God*, she turns the gun on Brownfield. Unable to pull the trigger, she
eventually succumbs to Brownfield's ploy to subjugate her. Upward
mobility for Mem, unlike Janie, cannot be sustained in a sex/class/
race system which assigns black women the role of (in the words of
Zora Neale Hurston) 'mule of the world'. Mem's period of 'reconstruction' in the city is thus short-lived; defeated, she burns her
dreams together with her books.

Grange Copeland's sojourn in the North ends similarly in a return
to the rural South, but for different reasons and with a different outcome. For him, migration is an education in the discourses of resistance to racism but also a confrontation with its entrenchment in the
de facto segregation of the North. Like the brief period of Reconstruction after the Civil War, Grange's flight to New York does not deliver
what it promised. 'He had come North expecting those streets paved
with that gold', but instead he finds anonymity (144). The only way he
can make a living is as a hustler, selling bootleg whisky, drugs, and black
women to white men. In an oral history of the Great Migration, Len
Davis describes his disillusionment with the North:

> Why do Negroes leave the South? It's just like getting out of
> slavery. When you get to the Promised Land, you free, man. You

can do what you want to and go where you want to, say what you
want to. [....] And it's really a letdown when you get there, man.
Promised Land is just like the old plantation, really. You still
haven't got any more rights. They're all a bunch of phoney rights.
They're a little bit better, but it's not like what you've been thinking. And that's what makes you mad.[32]

Like Len Davis, Grange Copeland gains the political insight in New
York that there is no such thing as the Promised Land. In addition,
after he has 'murdered' the white woman in the park by letting her
drown, he experiences a change in himself which leads him to hate
white people. This change is articulated in terms highly reminiscent
of two classics of African American literature, Richard Wright's *Native Son* and Ralph Elison's *Invisible Man*. In the latter, the nameless
protagonist feels himself to be invisible in Harlem just as Grange
Copeland does: 'The North put him in solitary confinement where
he had to manufacture his own hostile stares in order to see himself.
For why were they pretending he was not there?' (145). And like
Bigger Thomas in *Native Son*, he feels that murder liberates him:
'He believed that, against his will, he had stumbled on the necessary
act that black men must commit to regain, or to manufacture their
manhood, their self-respect. They must kill their oppressors' (153). As
a result of this realisation, Grange then starts to preach his gospel of
hate on the streets of Harlem and adopts a separatist philosophy
which in part echoes the ideas of another major figure in African
American history, Marcus Garvey. Like Garvey, Grange concludes
that the only promised land was the 'forty acres and a mule' of
Reconstruction which should have enabled former slaves to become
economically independent. Unlike Garvey, however, who advocated
emigration to Africa, Grange returns south. With the money he
earned and robbed in New York (and from Josie) he buys a farm and
land to realise his dream of self-sufficiency; the fence which he builds
with Ruth's help functions metaphorically and literally to create an
all-black space in which he can raise Ruth and teach her black history. Ruth's education is, in other words, a lesson in black nationalism, instilling kinship with Africans and other non-white peoples of
the world – just as Garvey in the 1920s and Malcolm X in the 1960s
preached that African Americans should educate themselves. As
Ruth realises, however, in liberating himself from his first life as a slave,
Grange in his second life has become imprisoned in his righteous

hatred of white people. True freedom, for her, comes about through the non-violence and forgiveness brought to their doorstep by the Civil Rights workers, whom Grange grudgingly learns to admire but cannot bring himself to join.

Grange Copeland's second life in New York and Mem's brief sojourn as a city dweller connect with a wider historical narrative insofar as they are representations of African American migration after the First World War. As precarious moves into modernity, they break the insularity of rural existence that Gloria Wade-Gayles identified as typically Southern, but unlike the official version of history, progress, like storytelling, is not linear for Walker but a movement of back and forth and around. *The Third Life of Grange Copeland* is an historical novel in this didactic and transformational sense. As Melissa Walker has noted, it does not follow a rigid chronology of twentieth-century African American history, from post-Reconstruction Jim Crow *via* two world wars and the Depression through to Civil Rights – although the timespan of the novel suggests that. For Melissa Walker, this deviation from chronological order and lack of realist detail in *The Third Life of Grange Copeland* are critical shortcomings:

> In all but the final scenes of the novel, characters show no aware-ness that they might be affected by or affect history. Not one fights in World War I, participates in the Garvey movement, or loses property during the Depression. [. . . .] For the first two-thirds of the novel, the characters have no public existence: no birth certi-ficates, no draft cards, no bank accounts.[33]

Quite apart from the accuracy of this criticism (Garvey is not explicitly mentioned but the ideas are there; the Copelands do not have any property to lose in the Depression) and the question of whether we have to care about characters' birth certificates, I believe that Alice Walker's view of history is rather less simple than Melissa Walker seems to assume. Alice Walker's conception of fiction, exemplified in this novel as in the later ones, is as a re-vision, reinterpretation, restructuring of official historiography. The Copelands' insularity, the fact that they know little of the issues that affected African Amer-icans in the United States at large, let alone of world affairs during this period, is in my view best read as an aspect of this revision. News-papers, in this novel, poignantly cover the walls of a draughty house or line the shoes of a murdered woman; the Copelands' ignorance of the wider world reflects their overall impoverishment and a psychic reality which is bent only on material survival. Mem exemplifies this. An educated woman and a teacher, Mem nonetheless relinquishes her vocation and burns her books when Brownfield decides to 'move back'; in the world of slavery on Mr J. L. 's place she will literally have no use for them. More importantly perhaps, the Copelands' isolation is also a deliberate abstraction from realist detail which enables Walker to zoom in on intra-familial dynamics. In this way, she shows that the oppressed, who do not get to write history, therefore remain invisible to it and in effect live outside it (just as women, in the title of Sheila Rowbotham's famous book, for centuries were 'hidden from history').

The purpose of Grange Copeland's third life is, then, to fulfil the promise of Reconstruction of a century before, and to reintegrate the public and private narratives of African American progress. That fulfilment necessitates a move back to the South and to the past, which has to be confronted before it can be redeemed. Again, we are reminded here of an African American classic: Jean Toomer's *Cane*, which, in the final section, entitled 'Kabnis', dramatises a similar necessity for the protagonist to return to the South in order to confront his history. Kabnis fails to do so, whereas Grange Copeland succeeds; just as Walker revises Richard Wright's existential stance on black manhood, so also does she revise Toomer's despondent image of a vanishing South whose history is too painful for a modern man to work through and then rise above.

The Third Life of Grange Copeland

By the time Grange returns from the North and begins his third life, the characters who hitherto have taken centre stage recede into the background. To Grange, Brownfield is already dead because he is determined to continue on his path of self-hatred and destruction, whereas Mem, having given up her dreams and surrendered her 'educated' speech, is dead to herself even before Brownfield murders her. The second half of the novel (Parts VII–XI) is then almost completely taken up with Ruth's education and the rehabilitation of Grange which it brings in its train. Walker's didacticism is here writ large, because the reader learns, along with Ruth, the lessons in African American history, folklore and the arts of everyday use (such as dancing and winemaking) that Grange chooses to teach her and which bring her into conflict with the official history she learns at school.

When Ruth is born the old man exclaims: 'Lawd knows the *whole* business is something of a miraculous event. Out of all kinds of shit comes something clean, soft and sweet smellin' (71). From the beginning, Grange takes an interest in this child in a way he had never cared for his own, a bitter irony not lost on Brownfield: '"If you think it so *sweet smellin*', you *take* it," said Brownfield, seeing his baby with entirely different, unenchanted and closely economic eyes' (71). For Brownfield, Ruth represents yet another burden on a family already racked by the poverty he is unable to alleviate. And while the men fight over Ruth's crib, Mem lies silent, with the wind howling through the window, 'moving the newspapers under the bed' (71). Ruth's birth in poverty and strife nevertheless proves auspicious. Before Grange Copeland says it in so many words, this birth has been described, a few pages before, as 'miraculous' already, for Ruth 'had popped out by herself', without the help of any (wo)man's hand (67). In the rest of the narrative, Ruth's independent existence, which remains innocent of most, if not all, of the family's history of violence and oppression, enables Grange's transformation into a loving parent and guardian. Sheltered from the 'closely economic eyes' of the white world which has claimed Brownfield's soul and Grange's first and second lives, Ruth grows up to be a woman who is equipped to oppose depression and destruction – whether within or without. As Peter Erickson points out, the relationship between Ruth and Grange is a 'mutually redemptive' one, reminiscent of Walker's short story 'A Sudden Trip Home in the Spring', which is also about a young woman and her love for her grandfather.[34] Ruth's upbringing by the transformed Grange Copeland is completed when, in the final pages, she can teach *him* a lesson in political philosophy: '"If you fight", she said, placing soft black fingers on Grange's arm, "if you fight with all you got, you don't have to *be* bitter"' (242). In *Possessing the Secret of Joy* this same insight is expressed in even stronger terms: resistance is the secret of joy. Without it, oppression leads to the kind of bitter resignation and depravity Brownfield is reduced to, or to depression and suicide, as in Margaret's case. Resignation (compliance with the white order/Brownfield), resentment (black separatism/Grange) and resistance (Civil Rights/Ruth) are the three positions which the characters are forced to take up when confronted with the 'changing same' of white racism in the American South. Mem briefly experiences the joy of resistance when she stands up to Brownfield, but Mem, like Margaret before her, is finally beaten down by her husband's hatred of himself and their family. The gun which she had wielded against him is in the end turned on her to disastrous effect: violence, for women as for men, in the end does not produce liberation. The novel is dedicated to Walker's mother, who 'made a way out of no way' and the miraculous event of something good and whole being born out of 'all kinds of shit' is paradigmatic for all of Walker's work. In this, as well as many other ways, *The Third Life of Grange Copeland* prepares the ground for the later novels, the essays and short stories. The 'shit' of family history, domestic violence, poverty and economic oppression which somehow gives birth to Ruth is parallelled by the shit of Southern history, in which slavery and Jim Crow segregation give way to the Civil Rights Movement, apparently out of nowhere.

Is a 'miracle' good enough to explain such a major historical shift? Here the connection between domestic and collective African American histories is more muted, although it is possible to draw parallels between the personal transformation, the reconstruction which Grange achieves after he returns from the North and the development of the Civil Rights movement in the South. In this sense I think *The Third Life of Grange Copeland* can, at a stretch, be read as a *Bildungsroman* about Grange, not Ruth as Madhu Dubey sees it. There is little support in the novel for Dubey's argument that '*The Third Life* unquestioningly employs the *Bildungsroman* to map Ruth's movement towards maturity, a linear process that culminates in Ruth's enlistment into the regimes of heterosexuality and reproduction', if only because Ruth never gets that far in her fictional life, but Grange's development does evidence something of a critical rewrite of what it means to grow up into responsible adulthood.[35] Despite his separatist leanings, raising Ruth for Grange is also an act of love, and a process of atonement, a way of making a 'no count' life count, and count for two, and this redemptive quality is certainly akin to the spirit of the Civil Rights movement. Sandi Russell echoes this view of Grange and Ruth's relationship as one that redeems the past. She reads the novel as a story of 'regeneration' in which the African American family stands for the 'global family', and the relationship between men and women is conceived as the 'basis for the transformation of society' with self-love as a necessary – but not sufficient – condition.[36]

But in the end even Grange, 'the beautiful old man', as Alice Walker calls him in her Afterword, cannot save himself from his violent past. In killing Brownfield Grange commits a necessary act of murder in order to seal Ruth's fate, a fate which is no longer to be caught in the vicious circle of familial violence. Grange's own death becomes a sacrifice to Ruth as the embodiment of a healing and non-violent future. With Brownfield and Grange, resignation and resentment are buried, and with the arrival of the Civil Rights workers active resistance is born.

The Third Life of Grange Copeland, then, is not a realist novel, in Melissa Walker's sense, which faithfully depicts 'the way it was' for African Americans in the South during the first six decades of the twentieth century. What we have is a fissured text which explores the development of the African American family *from within* as an altern-ative, domestic history. 'In Europe as in every country characterized as civilized or civilizing,' wrote Fanon, 'the family is a miniature of the nation.'[37] Walker's Copelands can, as such, be read not only as a microcosmic representation of the history of African Americans but of America as a whole, and it is, then, a history of violence and oppression which is passed down a chain of racial, class and gender supremacies from which education and the entry into modernity can provide only a partial release. Ultimately that history can be redeemed by the 'miracle' of individual transcendence and collective action, but also – and crucially – *by writing*. As we have seen, Walker's narrative draws on and revises several other narratives of the (African American) family and the formation of (black) subjecthood, notably that of masculinity. The Copeland saga, as an alternative domestic history, is at odds with official historiography, the Moyni-han report, the Oedipal story and also with fictional representations of black male emancipation in Richard Wright's *Native Son*, Jean Toomer's *Cane* and Ralph Elison's *Invisible Man*. Whatever its tech-nical flaws, Walker's first novel is less simple and straightforward than it might at first appear, and in its ambition to 'talk back' to the tradition *The Third Life of Grange Copeland* sets the agenda for Walker's later work. *Meridian*, the second novel, takes up the Civil Rights theme where it was left with Ruth; Mem and Margaret are revived and rehabilitated in the figure of Celie in *The Color Purple*. Grange Copeland's history teaching is echoed in Suwelo, who – like Grange – also learns a spiritual lesson in *The Temple of My Familiar*. And the theme of child abuse is treated with a different inflection and in a different cultural setting in *Possessing the Secret of Joy*, which takes clitoridectomy as its subject. Fragmented and episodic story-telling, likewise, remains a hallmark of Walker's fiction and becomes a strength in the broken-up form of *Meridian* and the epistolary organisation of *The Color Purple*, rather than the structural weakness it is in *The Third Life of Grange Copeland*. Personal transformation, finally, is at the heart of every Alice Walker novel, and in that sense Grange Copeland's third life is only the first of many reincarnations to come.

3

Meridian

Walker's second novel, published in 1976, revisits the question the author asked in her earlier essay 'The Civil Rights Movement: What Good Was It?' by exploring the case of the eponymous Meridian, whose life as a young, black, unhappily married woman with a baby in a small Southern town, is turned upside down by the arrival of voter-registration activists and then transformed beyond recognition.[1] Among those activists is Truman who, with the charm of his conviction that political change is necessary and possible, draws Meridian into the movement. She leaves her husband and gives up her child, distances herself from her devout Christian mother and devotes her life to activism. As a result of her involvement with Civil Rights Meridian has the opportunity to go to Saxon College in Atlanta on a scholarship provided by wealthy white Northern sympathisers. She finds the college environment, designed to make young black women into ladies 'chaste and pure as the driven snow' (89) stifling and hypocritical. An unwanted pregnancy, which she has terminated, clinches her decision to return to the Civil Rights movement and the real world.

When Truman deserts Meridian for the love of a white Northern woman, Lynne, sexual politics and the integrationist ethos of the Civil Rights movement come into conflict with each other. Meridian is baffled, but continues to work in the South, unlike Truman and her college friend Anne-Marion, who have abandoned non-violence and become militants in New York – at least in theory. Eventually Truman and Lynne return to the South and separate after the murder of their daughter Camara. Other deaths in the movement take their toll on Meridian, too: she loses weight, her hair falls out and she is prone to fainting spells, especially after protest actions in which she finds herself increasingly isolated. Anne-Marion tells her that she is carrying on a form of action which has long since become out-dated: 'Meridian . . . like the idea of suffering itself, you have become obsolete' she says (124). Battle fatigue forces Meridian to reconsider Anne-Marion's question of whether she will 'kill for the revolution' and she concludes that perhaps killing is permissible in self-defence. At the same time, she also has to reconsider her relation to Truman and to Lynne, both of whom turn to her after their separation. Witnessing the sexual humiliations Lynne is forced to undergo at the hands of battle-scarred black men who take their anger out on her makes Meridian aware of sexual as well as racial oppression, and this enables her to become more sympathetic to Lynne. Truman, mean-while, realises the error of his black nationalist and sexist ways and, at the end of the novel, takes up Meridian's place in grass-roots com-munity work.

What good the Civil Rights movement did, then, is represented here as a matter of personal as well as political transformation; the movement exposed rifts between black and white and between men and women, which only an integration of its commitment to non-violence with a feminist analysis of sexual politics – *when really lived through* – could heal. Put like this, it is clear that, in this novel, Walker retraces the steps which led former female Civil Rights activists to feminism, and that she affirms the movement's integrationist stance despite – or perhaps because of – the problems that interracial activ-ism entailed.[2] The experience of reading *Meridian*, however, is very different from the linear trajectory that I have just sketched out and which, in many ways, does violence to the novel's aesthetic achieve-ment. What, then, is that experience like, and what did Walker want to achieve by putting the reader through the hoops and loops of its complicated narrative structure?

In 1984 the writer and critic David Bradley published a long article about Alice Walker in *New York Times Magazine*, in which he stated that he had been 'terribly disappointed with "Meridian"':

In this I was, to all appearances, alone. 'Meridian' had been touted by Newsweek as 'ruthless and tender', by Ms. as 'a classic novel of both feminism and the civil rights movement', and by The New York Times Book Review as 'a fine, taut novel that . . . goes down like clear water.' But to me it seemed far more elliptical and episodic (three parts, 34 chapters) than her first novel, without having that novel's warmth and simplicity. The title character, an itinerant civil-rights worker, seems less pacifist than passive. [*sic*]³

It was inevitable that critics like Bradley would draw comparisons between *The Third Life of Grange Copeland* and *Meridian* and find either the one or the other wanting, since they appear to be so different. In contrast with the first novel, *Meridian*'s broken-up form makes for a startling and – apparently – deliberately disorienting reading experience which obviously irritated Bradley. That he found the main character 'passive' – which, after all, is a strange thing for a political activist to be – is also understandable, since the portrayal of Meridian is closer to that of a martyr or a saint than to the media images we have of 1960s Civil Rights workers, tirelessly on the march or getting beaten up in sit-ins and bus boycotts. Yet Bradley overlooked the continuities and similarities between the two novels, which reveal themselves only on a closer reading. In *Meridian* Walker shows, to begin with, a continuing engagement with African American history from the inside, in the novel's exploration of a black woman's experience in the Civil Rights movement 'on the ground', that is: at the grass roots and beyond reach of the media spotlights. This engagement with history goes deeper than Meridian's personal development through the 1960s and 1970s, because the narrative keeps dipping into other layers of history through the interspersed stories of slavery, and the even earlier presence of Native Americans in Mississippi. In this view of the very recent and very distant past *Meridian* both takes up where *The Third Life of Grange Copeland* left off and tells the latter's pre-history in the mutilations and miscegenations of African American people from the fifteenth to nineteenth centuries. Similar to *The Third Life of Grange Copeland* also, *Meridian* has a tripartite structure which moves from the South ('Meridian') to New York ('Truman Held') and back again ('Ending'); like Grange Copeland, Lynne, Meridian and Truman discover that the scars of their time together in the South cannot heal until the original trauma is confronted by returning there. Part of that healing process is an integration of what we can recognise as feminist and black Civil Rights positions, an integration brought about by a Meridian who lives out Ruth Copeland's philosophy of resistance without resentment. More clearly than in the previous novel, Walker is concerned in *Meridian* to work through her relationship to (white) feminism and, as David Bradley also notes, this often takes the form of awkward dialogues in which opposing ideas are voiced by different characters and argued out. Whereas in *The Third Life of Grange Copeland* white people hardly ever get to speak – however importantly they figure as forces of oppression in the background – in *Meridian* the presence of Lynne forces Truman and Meridian to examine and re-examine their political positions in dialogue and through conflict with her. Lynne, in turn, changes from a naive idealist who romanticises black people and the South into a kindred spirit who, after relinquishing her white, middle-class privilege, experiences the cost of resistance and comes to a more realistic appraisal of black people's human flaws as well as her own. Integration, as a political goal of the Civil Rights movement, does not simply mean love and forgiveness, let alone a one-way adaptation to white standards of behaviour and achievement in *Meridian*, but is tentatively posited as a process of struggle and suffering for 'black and white together' and for men and women together. The personal and political are thus intimately bound up with each other.

If *Meridian* is understood like this, Bradley's critique of it can be countered in two ways: what he calls Meridian's 'passivity' can conversely be seen as a mode of action, in the sense that she acts as a catalyst for those around her; she 'leads' by example rather than exhortation or authority. And the question of whether *Meridian* is a novel at all, implicitly posed by Bradley, can be answered positively, for the realist story of Meridian and Truman and Lynne is *meaningfully* interrupted by myths, anecdotes, parables and asides which have a bearing upon the protagonists' gradual self-enlightenment about their place in history.

In contrast with *The Third Life of Grange Copeland*, Walker's mastery of the short form is allowed to shine here in a way that it could not before. Walker explained in an interview with Claudia Tate that she wanted *Meridian* to be like a crazy quilt, similar to the collages that the African American painter Romare Bearden made, or like the patterning of Jean Toomer's *Cane*, which is made up of portraits of Southern women, poems, worksongs, sketches and a play. Bearden was involved in the early 1960s in the 'Spiral' group which wanted to work in support of the Civil Rights movement; *Cane*, first published in 1923, narratively traces a circular movement in its tripartite structure, from the rural deep South to the urban North and

back to Georgia, like *The Third Life of Grange Copeland* and *Meridian*.[4]
Walker's comment on the quilt metaphor is illuminating:

> You know, there's a lot of difference between a crazy quilt and a
> patchwork quilt. [....] A crazy quilt . . . only *looks* crazy. It is not
> 'patched'; it is planned. A patchwork quilt would perhaps be a
> good metaphor for capitalism; a crazy quilt is a metaphor for
> socialism. A crazy quilt story is one that can jump back and forth in
> time, work on many different levels, and one that can include
> myth. It is generally much more evocative of metaphor and sym-
> bolism than a novel that is chronological in structure, or one
> devoted, more or less, to rigorous realism, as is *The Third Life of
> Grange Copeland*.[5]

Meridian certainly is evocative and, like the crazy quilt and Meridian
herself, '*looks* crazy' but is, in fact, purposeful. Yet the plan is by no
means obvious, and my attempt here to draw out a covert plan from
the overt craziness and a politics of form from the apparent formless-
ness, is only one of many possibilities. In 'Art, Action and the Ancestors: Alice Walker's *Meridian* in Its Context', Christine Hall makes a
link between the reader 'as the active maker of meanings' and 'Meridian's own search for an interpretation which will make sense in and
of her life'.[6] *Meridian*'s 'craziness' is, as Walker and Hall both indic-
ate, self-consciously polysemous and every reader, in every reading
of the text, will have to do his or her own work in stitching a meaning
together out of disparate bits. I begin my handiwork with Anne-
Marion's question whether 'killing for the revolution' is justified, a
question which will lead us, first of all, into a Southern black church
and to the ganglands of LA, unexpected as this may seem. It is because
the question of revolutionary killing frames the novel's political and
spiritual concerns that I want to use it as a kind of vignette for the
1990s as much as the 1960s, when the Black Panthers first voiced it.

Gangstas and Angels: African American Music and Politics in the 1960s and 1990s

The setting is New York, some time in the mid-1960s, and a group
of political activists are engaged in a planning and consciousness-
raising meeting. Meridian's friend, Anne-Marion, has pledged her

commitment to the revolution by stating that she is prepared to kill for it, but Meridian is as usual engaged in remembrance of things past:

> Meridian was holding on to something the others had let go. [....] what none of them seemed to understand was that she felt herself to be, not holding on to something from the past, but *held* by something in the past: by the memory of old black men in the South who, caught by surprise in the eye of a camera, never shifted their position but looked directly back; by the sight of young girls singing in a country choir, their hair shining with brushings and grease, their voices the voices of angels. [....] If they committed murder – and to her even revolutionary murder was murder – *what would the music be like?* (15; original emphasis)

Several critics cite this passage, highlighting the importance of music as a motif in the novel and stressing its resonance with African American cultural tradition, of which music is arguably the major form.[7] None has taken the question of what the music of revolutionary murder would be like as more than merely rhetorical, however, and yet reading *Meridian* in the 1990s we know what that music sounds like because it exists: in gangsta' rap, the music of the urban ghettoes of New York, Los Angeles, or Chicago's South Side. This is a music which, in bell hooks's words, glorifies 'sexist, misogynist, patriarchal ways of thinking and behaving' and which is successful because of, not in spite of, these characteristics.[8] As early as 1988, Maya Angelou characterised rap in general as 'unpoetic', merely 'the cheapest way out of saying something about the street', and she laid the blame for this 'literary laziness' at the door of established black (nationalist) writers of the 1960s who 'told any Black person that if you're Black you can write poetry'. In the debate around gangsta' rap, therefore, more is at stake than just misogyny or violence; there is also a division – exemplified here – between black high and popular culture which also articulates political differences.[9] If we are to understand Walker's project in *Meridian*, then I think the question 'what would the music be like?' deserves to be addressed because it presupposes, after all, a diagnostic connection between cultural expression and the health of the body politic which is akin to hooks's and Angelou's views on black popular music.

Meridian is held by the past in a specific personal and in a very general sense, because she is the product not just of her parents' upbringing but also of America's colonising history. Throughout the novel, the question of violence in its multifarious forms is explored in her individual past and in the history of the nation; the issue of killing for the revolution thus brings a host of others in its train, all connected to the theme of violence and the question of whether ends justify means. Slavery and the conquest of Native American lands – both, according to the history books, essential to the historical identity of the South and of the US as a whole – are recalled in the novel as part of a repetitive pattern of violence, supposedly justified in official historiography by the revolutionary project of nation building. Rape, harassment, reproductive control and enforced childbearing are also constituted in the novel as forms of violence, legitimised in various political discourses (including white feminism and black nationalism) as mere means towards greater, liberating and revolutionary ends. Meridian's abortion and subsequent sterilisation, for example, bring on an acute psychic crisis which has everything to do with Meridian's awareness that her mother and previous generations of African American women 'had not lived in an age of choice' (123). The demand for reproductive control, which in white feminism was seen as a means to achieve women's liberation, is not enough of a justification for Meridian, who is mindful of white women's historical role in 'controlling' the reproduction of black women. Neither is Tommy Odds's rape of Lynne justified, in her view, by the black man's need to liberate himself from white oppression by taking revenge upon white women. In both cases, *Meridian* poses no either/or solution but a series of questions which contextualise political and ethical dilemmas in concrete circumstances, aware of historical difference but also of the destructive force that *any* kind of violence exerts – on perpetrators and victims alike. Anne-Marion's question, to Meridian, whether she is prepared to 'kill for the revolution' is therefore not a rhetorical one, but one which is already determined, or perhaps overdetermined, by American history (killing Indians for the revolution), and more particularly that of African American women (who could or could not keep their babies, depending on the nation's needs).

Meridian, like Walker's previous novel, engages in the working-through of such big historical and ethical questions about ends and means, but unlike the occasionally intrusive narrator in *The Third Life of Grange Copeland* this novel lacks a 'voice' telling us what to think, even if Meridian herself is obviously invested with a moral

authority that is hard to refuse. John F. Callahan relates this structural and political 'openness' of *Meridian* to Walker's refusal to be a
storyteller; 'Walker', he says, 'like Meridian, invites "the rest of
them" (and us) to participate in a generation's unfinished personal
and political work.' [10] Attuned to the sounds of her age, of the Civil
Rights movement and the more distant past, Meridian finds her own
voice only after her journey of self-exploration, in which actions (and
her body) speak louder than words, is completed. Then she vows to
mop up the blood behind the 'real' revolutionaries, but also to

> come forward and sing from memory songs they will need once
> more to hear. For it is the song of the people, transformed by the
> experience of each generation, that holds them together and if
> any part of it is lost the people suffer and are without soul. (205–6)

These songs 'from memory' are not just the famous Civil Rights
songs such as 'We Shall Overcome', but also the older spirituals
which date back to slavery. Meridian's music, the music of the choir-
girls and the black church, is gospel music. The black Southern
church has always drawn upon slavery in its interpretations of
biblical teaching, and gospel music reflects that legacy still. One of
Howell Raines's informants in *My Soul Is Rested*, an oral history of the
Civil Rights movement, describes the black church as a brand of
Christianity which

> has always seen God as being identified with the downcast and the
> suffering. Jesus' first text he used when he preached his first ser-
> mon was taken from Isaiah, which is 'The Lord has anointed me to
> preach the gospel to the poor, to deliver the oppressed, to free
> the captive ...'.[11]

That Christianity is a far cry from Meridian's mother's authoritarian
(and 'whitified') faith, typified by her statement that 'All He asks is
that we acknowledge him as our Master', which is challenged by the
end of *Meridian* and rejected altogether in *The Color Purple* (16).
Unlike the 'white' church music which accompanies this authoritarian Christianity, gospel music is not a form of high culture designed to
inspire fear and awe in the presence of God, but a mode of creating
the Beloved Community by means of active participation. And unlike
the blues, the 'devil's music' which is central to *The Color Purple*,

gospel is not merely *of* this world but *for* this world: it is not so much, or not only, a matter of ends (salvation, freedom) but equally of means: creating a community of spirit. The Civil Rights activist and womanist musician Bernice Johnson Reagon remembers how Fannie Lou Hamer, fellow activist and songleader in the movement during the 1960s, could transform a mass meeting into a 'community of singing'. For Hamer, for Reagon and for the Civil Rights movement as a whole, communal singing had a ritualistic and redeeming function, creating a sense of strength, resolve and resistance all at once. James Farmer recounts, for example, how communal singing became a mode of resistance in prison, when Civil Rights workers would drive their jailers to distraction with their freedom songs.[12] And Reagon explains:

> There is something I feel when sound runs through my body. I cannot sing without experiencing a change in my mood, a change in the way I feel. In the African-American culture, that is a major function of singing. [....] the aim is to be sure that whatever shape you were in before you started to produce this sound is transformed when the singing is over.[13]

But times have changed, and the singing *is* over. Meridian's rhetorical question – *what would the music be like?* – is answered in the 1990s in a way which could not have been anticipated. Perhaps it is significant that rap is not sung but spoken, that it is not the 'flight of doves' which Meridian and Bernice Johnson Reagon hear in choir song, but the rhythmically punctuated rat-tat-tat of gunshots. Anne-Marion's infatuation with armed resistance, when she tries to get Meridian to pledge that she will 'kill for the revolution', is of a piece with the Black Panther thinking of the late 1960s which has since fed into gangsta rap. Andrew Ross notes that 'just as the Black Panthers made theatrical appearances with guns in public, rap's romance with the gangsta has consciously tested the official taboo against images of armed black men (with the exception of black policemen)'.[14] For Meridian, however, there is no theatricality in that image. She considers, instead, its revolutionary reality: 'Would they ever be face to face with the enemy, guns drawn? Perhaps. Perhaps not. [....] the point was, she could not think lightly of shedding blood. And the question of killing did not impress her as rhetorical at all' (15). Both questions, then – the one about music and the one about killing – are serious, and both are explored rather than directly answered in the novel. Re-entering a church after a long period of renunciation of Christianity and all it stands for, Meridian witnesses a memorial service for a 'martyred son' of the (armed) black struggle of the late 1960s. She finds that the church has changed; faced with the dead man's father, who is distraught and almost speechless with grief, the preacher gives a brief political sermon. Short on words, long on silent mourning, this service is one in which Meridian can feel free to contemplate the question of killing for the revolution once again. The stained-glass window of B. B. King, 'With Sword', sums up how the music has changed: it is electrified, infused with a righteous anger which enables her to believe, at last, that 'yes, indeed she *would* kill, before she allowed anyone to murder his son again' (204). The New Testament overtones of this last sentence, 'before she would allow anyone to murder his (God's) son (Jesus) again', are obvious, but there is a difference too, for this is a *real* father, no religious abstraction, and a *real* son who died 'for his talk alone (as far as his father knew, or believed, or wanted to know)', at the hands of the state (201). At this moment of enlightenment, then, Meridian realises that the question of killing for the revolution cannot always, unconditionally, be refused, if the outcome of such refusal is that people *get* killed for what they believe. Unconditional non-violence is as much an abstraction as 'the revolution' or recognising 'God as your Master'; instead, Meridian concludes that 'the contemplation of murder required incredible delicacy as it required incredible spiritual work, and *the historical background and present setting must be right*' (my emphasis) (205).

On the face of it, 1990s rap music, which draws on the 1960s rhetoric of 'killing for the revolution', does not meet these conditions. Spiritual work, never mind historical background, seems diametrically opposed to the glorification of 'killing for sport' that bell hooks identifies in gangsta rap. Then again, rapper Ice Cube explains the 'present setting' in an interview with hooks:

Killin' has become a way of life. Very little talkin', a lot of shootin'. And, I mean, that really has a big effect on us, you know. Television ... [....] Now they can show an actual murder on TV, you know what I'm sayin'? [....] And it's like, it wasn't even shocking. It's a thin line between reality and the fake movie stuff.[15]

We can still wonder what would have happened, what the present setting would look like, if non-violence had carried the day in 1960s African American activism. But the reasons why it didn't are good historical reasons, as Ice Cube is well aware, because black non-violence was met with every conceivable kind of violent resistance to change on the part of American society at large, from the outright murder of political leaders to subversion of Civil Rights organisations as well as the intimidation, humiliation and ridicule of individuals. Gangsta rap and gang warfare are partly the legacy of white intransigence in the 1960s: rap articulates, in the idiom of the African American oral tradition, all-American values of masculine dignity and the right to bear arms, whilst rival gangs act out those values in a (mostly intra-racial) 'killing for sport'. Since the logical end of such killing is self-destruction, it is clear that in gangsta culture means have overtaken ends. *Meridian*, by contrast, explores the other side of that 1960s legacy, that of non-violence: what would it be like if, as in the singing of gospel music, means and ends evolved together? 'The present you are constructing should be the future you want', Ola says in *The Temple of My Familiar*. We see the same philosophy of prefigurative action dramatised in *Meridian*, but before we get to it we must look at the way in which the novel constructs the history that in turn produces such presents and futures.[16]

Historical Background and Present Setting

Meridian is often described as a Civil Rights novel, yet if it is that, it is surely in a class of its own. Unlike Thulani Davis's *1959*, which tells in realist terms of the campaigns for school desegregation and voter registration in the mid- to late 1950s, and unlike the assessment of the aftermath of the Civil Rights movement in Toni Cade Bambara's *The Salt Eaters*, *Meridian* is perhaps less a novel *about* the Civil Rights era than *of* it, in the sense that it embodies and explores the long-term costs and benefits of non-violent direct action.[17] *Meridian*'s 'present setting', at the very end of the novel when Truman takes Meridian's place, is some time in the 1970s, long after Civil Rights as a movement has ceased to be a viable force of significant legal, political and social change in the American South. Its 'historical background' is, however, much more fragmented and difficult to identify; as noted above, this background embraces American history right back to the conquest and settlement of Native lands, before the Civil War and even before the Revolution. This treatment of 'deep history' is perhaps best understood as a series of layers superimposed upon one another, such as an archaeologist might systematically uncover in the course of excavation, as Alan Nadel puts it.[18] Meridian's father's interest in Native Americans, the serpent-shaped burial mound, and Meridian's great-grandmother Feather Mae's mystical experiences are all part of the deepest, most ancient layer. The next contains Crispus Attucks, the first martyr to the American Revolution. Truman makes a sculpture of him out of a sense of kinship with this black man who was killed for his allegiance to a revolutionary ideal. Another layer is formed by three women: the slave Louvinie, the liberator of slaves Harriet Tubman, and the preacher and former slave Sojourner Truth, in their own way sisters and resisters like Meridian. And just as Meridian's grass-roots work follows in the footsteps of these foremothers, so also is Crispus Attucks's martyrdom echoed in the Civil Rights movement, because the town of Meridian in Mississippi was the birthplace of James Chaney, a black man killed in 1965 along with fellow white Civil Rights workers Andrew Goodman and Michael Schwerner, as Greil Marcus reminds us.[19] By now we have reached the present, where yet more political martyrs are buried. John F. Kennedy and Dr Martin Luther King Jr's funerals are represented in the novel, and there is one untitled chapter which – like a headstone – simply bears the names of selected dead from black and post-colonial struggles of the 1960s. The well-known names of Malcolm X , Medgar Evers, Che Guevara and Patrice Lumumba, amongst other male leaders, are listed there alongside the lesser-known names of the four black girls who died in the bombing of a Birmingham church and a white woman who was killed while driving Civil Rights workers home from a political meeting. This catalogue of names, along with the Native American references and remembrances of slavery and the American Revolution, serves to show how the period which has become known as the 'swinging sixties' is in fact riddled with dead bodies, willing and unwilling martyrs to revolutions of various kinds.

Historical background, then, is not so much background as deep space and time which *foregrounds* the cost in human lives of the African American social and political struggle. Consequently *Meridian*'s present setting is suffused with history in various ways: actual in the sense that it makes reference to real historical events, discursive in that it borrows from African American women's texts and speeches, and spiritual in its use of myth and religious symbolism. We shall look at each of these in turn.

Insofar as we get a potted history of the Civil Rights movement in *Meridian*, that history is confined to events and campaigns in Mississippi from the early to mid-1960s. In *This Little Light of Mine: The Life of Fannie Lou Hamer* we find many parallels with Meridian's efforts at voter registration as represented in the chapters entitled 'Travels' and 'Treasure'. Hamer's biography shows that such work of going from door to door trying to persuade people to register to vote, was not just laborious but often frustrating. Would-be voters had good reason to fear repercussions from their white employers and neighbours: many who persevered in trying to exercise their constitutional rights lost their jobs, their homes or their welfare cheques. For Fannie Lou Hamer, who herself had been evicted from the plantation where she worked and lived and who had been beaten and thrown into jail for her activism, personal experience fuelled political fervour:

> [I]f registering to vote means becoming a first class citizen and changing the structure of our state's Government, then I am determined to get every Negro in the state of Mississippi registered. By doing this, we can get the things we've always been denied the rights to. I can say this, we need a change in Mississippi; I'm sick of being hungry, naked, and looking at my children and so many other children crying for bread.[20]

The kind of intimidation Hamer faced as a prospective voter was also extended to the Civil Rights organisers who worked in interracial groups as the movement demanded. In the summer of 1964 white student volunteers came from the North to help with voter registration because their presence, it was believed, would attract more media attention to the struggle for black Civil Rights. Dave Dennis gives a chilling analysis of the strategic motivation for 'freedom summer', as the summer of 1964 was called: the necessity for white martyrs. He explains that 'the death of a white college student would bring on more attention to what was going on than for a black college student getting it. That's cold, but that was also in another sense speaking the language of this country.'[21] 'Freedom summer' is the setting in which Truman meets Lynne, and their subsequent relationship dramatises some of the problems around sexual politics to which the presence of white people, but of women in particular, gave rise within the Student Non-violent Coordinating Committee (SNCC). It was dangerous, for example, for black and white students to ride in the same car together late at night after the day's work was over, because such interracial fraternising might provoke white racists to violence. More dangerous still were interracial relationships, because the spectre of integration leading to intermarriage and miscegenation ('mongrelization of the races', in the words of white supremacists) aroused a deeply ingrained fear and rage in Southern whites.[22] Because *Meridian* highlights the role of black women in the movement (rather than that of the male leaders with whom we are so familiar), it is less concerned with the danger white supremacists posed to interracial couples than with the pain and loss such relationships entailed for black women activists. Black women felt they were being cast aside by black men in favour of a white ideal of femininity, sanctioned by the culture at large, from which they were by definition excluded and which they themselves did not even want, as Meridian makes clear: 'Who would dream, in her home town, of kissing a white girl? Who would want to? What were they good for?' (105). White women, however unwittingly, thus were a divisive presence in the Civil Rights movement because of what they represented as cultural icons, not just in relation to black women, but also to black men. Lynching is invoked in what is said about Lynne's problematic status in the movement: 'To them [black men] she was a route to Death, pure and simple. They felt her power over them in their bones; their mothers had feared her even before they were born' (135), but of course Lynne's forbidden-ness as a white woman who at the same time is involved in liberation struggle makes her all the more desirable. As Mary Aickin Rothschild explains in an article on the role of white women volunteers in 'freedom summer', for women such as Lynne there was no correct option: refusing black men would be construed as racist, whereas

> The [white] woman who simply accepted the advances [of black men] and 'slept around' faced grave consequences [....] In most cases she was written off as an ineffective worker, and she often became the focal point for a great deal of bitterness for the black women on the project. Additionally, her behaviour was seen as scandalous by many within the black community and this

profoundly inhibited community organizing, one of the main goals of the projects.[23]

It was because of such – and other – problems around white students' presence that by the mid-1960s whites were no longer welcome in SNCC. A position paper put it thus in 1966:

> [T]he form of white participation, as practised in the past, is now obsolete. Some of the reasons are as follows:
> The inability of whites to relate to the cultural aspects of Black society; attitudes that whites, consciously or unconsciously, bring to Black communities about themselves (western superiority) and about Black people (paternalism); [....] insensitivity of both Black and white workers towards the hostility of the Black community on the issue of interracial 'relationships' (sex).[24]

Clearly, interracial sex was not simply a personal, but a deeply political issue in the Civil Rights movement, well before Women's Liberation invented the term 'sexual politics'. It is a political/personal issue in *Meridian* too. Truman agonises over his relationship with Lynne after the shooting of Tommy Odds, who later rapes Lynne as an act of vengeance on white society. For Truman, love transcends colour but not in any naive, absolute, romantic sense. There is always history to be reckoned with:

> By being white Lynne was guilty of whiteness. [....] Then the question was, is it possible to be guilty of a color? Of course black people for years were 'guilty' of being black. Slavery was punishment for their 'crime'. But even if he abandoned this search for Lynne's guilt, because it ended, logically enough, in racism ... he could not ... keep from thinking Lynne was, in fact, guilty. The thing was to find out how. (131)

Truman shows in this passage that he is not the hopelessly unreconstructed male that Meridian sometimes takes him to be, but that he is learning to ask the kinds of questions she incessantly poses to herself. Even so, he never quite finds an answer other than that of Lynne's historic guilt by association, and his reconciliation with Lynne towards the end of the novel can therefore only ever be a partial, non-sexual one. His relationship with Meridian, likewise, cannot be consummated after all that has happened, but here the role of history is rather different. For, as Meridian realises when she is dragged off to jail by the white sheriff, their relationship was not a matter of love, it was 'that they were at a time and place in History that forced the trivial to fall away – and they were absolutely together' (80).

Even more than interracial relationships and co-operation, the question of the uses and abuses of violence was a bone of contention in the Civil Rights movement. In Joanne Grant's documentary collection *Black Protest* the debate over violence can be traced through numerous speeches, articles and position statements, from Howard Zinn's 'The Limits of Non-Violence' of 1965, expressing acute frustration at the ineffectiveness of non-violent direct action in the face of white intransigence in the South, through to James Forman's 1969 'Black Manifesto', which argued that time was running out and liberation could only be gained by any means necessary. Forman predicted a 'revolution, which will be an armed confrontation and long years of sustained guerilla warfare inside this country'.[25] Obviously, this is the view that Anne-Marion subscribes to, and which causes Meridian such moral anguish. We can see, then, that *Meridian*'s ostensibly moral or philosophical questions were not at all abstract but actually very real, day-to-day dilemmas in the experience of working for black Civil Rights in the 1950s and 1960s.

Equally concrete and central to that experience was the phenomenon of burnout, or battle fatigue (as one of the chapters in *Meridian* is entitled). In the interview with Claudia Tate, Walker herself expresses frustration at some critics' view of Meridian's 'illness' (the paralysis, the catatonic states, the hair loss) as somehow exotic or symbolic, when in fact Civil Rights workers were under such enormous strain most of the time that many did suffer such physical symptoms.[26] Anne Moody, for example, writes in her autobiography of Civil Rights activism *Coming of Age in Mississippi*: 'It had gotten to the point where my weight was going down to nothing. I was just skin and bones. My nerves were torn to shreds and I was losing my hair.'[27] Dave Dennis, whom Moody knew in Mississippi, tells of a Civil Rights worker in his early twenties who had heart trouble – it turns out that this man, because of constant fear and danger, had the heart function of a 70-year-old. Dennis speaks of voter registration in Mississippi as a war experience, in which you did not know, when setting out campaigning in the morning, whether you would see your fellow workers alive at the end of the day.[28] And Lawrence Guyot, another voter-registration veteran of Mississippi, describes how he suffered periodic paralysis on the left side of his body as a result of exhaustion and permanent anxiety.[29] Yet despite such extensive documentation of battle fatigue in the Civil Rights movement of the early 1960s, and despite what Alice Walker herself thinks of it, the representation of Meridian's 'illness' in the novel amounts to more than mere realistic portrayal. Her symptoms do have symbolic and spiritual resonances in the novel, and are indeed reminiscent of the mystic's ecstasy which connects her with a long line of African American ancestors, as Deborah E. McDowell also notes.[30]

'Deep History': Black Foremothers and Native Americans

Representations of the Civil Rights movement in this 'crazy quilt' which is the novel, accrue meanings beyond those of their literal and historical referents because of the myths, anecdotes and (very) short stories which are stitched across the main pattern and radiant centre of Meridian's life narrative. Some of these cross-stitchings hark back to the words, visions and ideas of African American women who, like Meridian, took part in political struggles of the past. One such is Amy-Jacques Garvey, the wife of the Back to Africa movement leader Marcus Garvey at the beginning of the century. In a 1925 editorial in *Negro World* entitled 'Women as Leaders', Amy Garvey wrote: 'The doll-baby type of woman is a thing of the past, and the wide-awake woman is forging ahead prepared for all emergencies, and ready to answer any call, *even if it be to face the cannons on the battlefield*' (my emphasis).[31] Compare this with *Meridian*'s opening chapter, where we see her leading a group of black children to view a mummified 'doll baby' white woman with long, red hair; in order to gain access she puts herself in front of a white tank and 'stares it down'. Later this military reference is extended when Meridian is 'thrilled ... to think she belonged to the people who produced Harriet Tubman, the only American woman who'd led troops in battle' (106). Unlike Amy Garvey, whose name is never mentioned in the novel, Harriet Tubman repeatedly figures as a role model for Meridian, since she led slaves to freedom in the North (singing particular songs by way of a password or, if all was not well, warning). Just so does Meridian, in her own way, lead the poor and the young to demand their freedom – whether that means seeing a plastic circus attraction ('The Last

Return') or registering to vote ('Travels'), or reminding the mayor of his responsibilities by presenting the body of a drowned black child at the town hall ('Questions'). There are other resonances, from other texts and other black women leaders as well, which together form a chain of association which leads us ever further into 'deep history'. Anne Moody describes in her autobiography a conversion experience which is remarkably like the one Meridian has when she returns to the black church. Moody writes:

> As I walked in, Reverend Cox was leading the adults in 'Oh Free-dom'. It was so moving that I forgot about the ministers and joined in the singing. [....] When I listened to the older Negroes sing, I knew it was the idea of heaven that kept them going. [....] But lis-tening to the teen-agers, I got an entirely different feeling. They felt that the power to change things was in themselves.[32]

It is entirely possible that Moody and Garvey were sources for Walker, just as Greil Marcus notes that the final chapter in Camus's *The Rebel*, which is about the question of justifiable killing and is entitled 'Thoughts at the Meridian' is also a silent reference in the novel, as is, of course, Jean Toomer's poem 'The Blue Meridian', with its call for the poets to 'spiritualise America'.[33] But whether they are or not does not really matter; the thing is that *Meridian* works as a novel *of* Civil Rights *and* of black feminism through such literary and historical resonances, and particularly through such associative links with African American women leaders.

Of these, the major one is Sojourner Truth, who is cast as Meridian's spiritual and political foremother. The Sojourner is a tree on the Saxon College campus which has grown on the spot where the slave Louvinie's tongue was buried after it was cut out by the slave-master to stop her telling murderous tales to her white charges. When the college authorities refuse permission to bury the Wild Child, a homeless girl who is killed by a car, on Saxon ground, the tree is destroyed by the students in riotous protest at this decision. The Sojourner, also known as the Music Tree, does, however, rise like Phoenix from its own ashes when it grows new branches at the end of the novel, coinciding with the regrowth of Meridian's hair; both are simultaneous marks of regeneration and projection out-wards, to the world. There is a hidden pun in Walker's use of Sojourner in this way, because Sojourner Truth was not born with that name: her slave name was Isabella Baumfree and the German word *Baum* means 'tree'. Truth explained why she changed her name when she embarked on her mission to preach the gospel across America:

> When I left the house of bondage [slavery] I left everything behind. I wa'n't goin' to keep nothin' of Egypt on me, an' so I went to the Lord an' asked him to give me a new name. And the Lord gave me Sojourner because I was to travel up an' down the land showin' the people their sins an' bein' a sign unto them. Afterward I told the Lord I wanted another name 'cause everybody else had two names; and the Lord gave me Truth, because I was to declare the truth to the people.[34]

In 'A Name is Sometimes an Ancestor Saying Hi, I'm with You' Walker furthermore invokes Sojourner Truth's name by analogy with her own: 'Sojourner ("Walker") – in the sense of traveler, journeyer, wanderer) Truth (which "Alice" means in Old Greek) is also my name.'[35] Parallels with *Meridian*, her travelling and 'declaring the truth' and showing Truman and Lynne – well, perhaps not their sins, but certainly their misconceptions – are evident. And like Meridian, Sojourner Truth refused white models of femininity also, because the nineteenth-century cult of True Womanhood did not and could not include her as a black woman, a slave and a worker in the cottonfields. In asking, famously, 'Ain't I a Woman?', Truth insisted on the dignity and strength of black femininity and motherhood, a dignity and strength earned through suffering, the forced loss of her children and hard labour. Her speeches in support of the abolition of slavery and for women's rights, combined with her spiritual work as an itinerant preacher and mystic, make her, in Alice Walker's terms, the first womanist, according to the definition of that term in *In Search of Our Mothers' Gardens*, which I analysed in Chapter 1. Sojourner Truth was illiterate, but she did have a voice; it is as if in *Meridian* and in this definition of womanism Walker put in writing what her foremother a century before had been putting into speech – and practice. But the chain of association going back to 'deep history' does not stop here, because the Sojourner is in turn connected with the sacred tree, of which Black Elk speaks in the dedication to *Meridian*:

When I look back now...I can still see the butchered women and
children lying heaped and scattered all along the crooked gulch as
plain as when I saw them with eyes still young. And I can see that
something else died there in the bloody mud, and was buried in
the blizzard. A people's dream died there. It was a beautiful
dream...the nation's hoop is broken and scattered. There is no
center any longer, and the sacred tree is dead. (n.p.)

Unlike Black Elk's view of the Native American past, which is irrevocably lost and can only be mourned, the Sojourner – the African
American past – does not die. Instead, in using that quotation from
Black Elk's famous book and in making Native Americans part of
Meridian's own history and geographical space, Walker regenerates
a Native American spiritual legacy along with that of black Christianity. This intermingling of cultural and racial histories has again a
basis in the historical record, and again its meanings radiate out-
wards and take on symbolic and mythical significance as well. The
historian Jack Forbes draws attention to the oft-forgotten fact that
the first slaves in America were Native Americans, and that Native
American/black African intermixture was very common in the colonial period, thus creating a mixed race of what he calls 'Red–Black
peoples'.[36] Because of this ancient commonality, Forbes argues,

> It would seem that those many students of North American his-
> tory and society who have been fascinated solely with the Black–
> White nexus or who have conceived of Black and Native American
> history as being two largely separate streams are going to have to
> re-examine their assumptions. This will have great implications
> for the study of the diffusion of central traits in areas as diverse as
> folk-tales, music, social structure, folk language and religion.[37]

In *Meridian* Walker seems to be beginning such a re-examination
of the binary divide between black and Native, a project which is
continued in *The Temple of My Familiar*. The chapters 'Indians and
Ecstasy' and 'Gold', interspersed in the narrative of Meridian's early
life, are therefore not merely of exotic or factual interest, but integral
to the novel's theme of the ravages of history. Black Elk speaks of 'the
butchered women and children lying heaped and scattered all along
the crooked gulch as plain as when I saw them with eyes still young';
Meridian mourns these mothers and children along with Fast Mary,

Louvinie, Sojourner Truth, James Chaney, Lynne and Truman's daughter Camara and the drowned little boy. Mothers and dead children therefore are yet another recurrent motif which can help us discover a pattern in *Meridian*'s crazy quilt.

Mothers as Martyrs: The Politics of Race, Reproduction and Black Leadership

In a speech before the Convention of the American Equal Rights Association in New York in 1867, Sojourner Truth addressed her audience on the issue of black women's rights: 'if colored men get their rights, and not colored women theirs, you see the colored men will be masters over the women, and it will be just as bad as before'.[38] Truth's statement can be read as an early articulation of womanism, combining race consciousness and pride with a feminist awareness that refuses to exempt African American men from the responsibility of granting equality and respect to black women. Sojourner Truth significantly invokes in that speech her authority as a mother as well: 'I want you to consider on that [the question of women's rights], chil'n. I call you chil'n; you are somebody's chil'n, and I am old enough to be mother of all that is here.'[39] It is this legacy of heroic and all-encompassing motherhood, embodied by a woman who bore thirteen children and saw them sold off into slavery, and who then made herself into a spiritual and political 'mother of the race', which haunts Meridian. Unworthy of this legacy, because she cannot love her son Rundi/Eddie Jr and has an abortion when she becomes pregnant by Truman, Meridian lives out a heretic's existence as regards the duties of the black mother. As Christine Hall notes, in fact the theme is already announced in the first chapter, when the mummified white woman Marilene O'Shay is described as 'Devoted Mother Gone Wrong'. Not only did she go wrong as a mother, but also as wife and obedient daughter – just like Meridian, who cannot live by her mother's rules and fails to meet the domestic standard of wifehood that Eddie Sr demands of her.[40] But this does not mean that Meridian's political activity and spiritual soul-searching are merely induced by guilt at this early dereliction of duty, as Martha McGowan seems to think, or that her interest in the question of when killing is justified 'is due to her view of herself as a mother, a creator rather than a destroyer of life', as Barbara Christian puts it.[41] As Susan

Willis has argued, Meridian as 'mother' in this sense ends up with rather a lot of dead children on her hands; in my view she can at best be seen as a *preserver* and defender of life (her son's, the Wild Child's) and as chief mourner and protester against the low price white society sets on black children.[42] That protest is, however, attenuated by an awareness of the damage done to children by mothers who never wanted to have them in the first place, but who are resigned to 'duty' – such as her own mother, Mrs Hill. The question of motherhood, then, is not so simple as some critics make it out to be, and this is because *Meridian* is grappling with conflicting models and discourses of femininity and of the politics of reproduction at the same time, models which do not fall simply into a black–white dichotomy. For example, Christine Hall is right to note that Meridian and the doll-woman Marilene O'Shay have something in common in failing – or perhaps refusing, which is different – to live up to an oppressive ideal of female submission. On the other hand, neither the white ideal of feminine beauty and domesticity, nor the African American model of the heroic, self-sacrificing mother who also works outside the home *and* has a role to play in the collective welfare of the community are viable images for a modern black woman like Meridian. As so often, Meridian's position is awkward: she is caught both ways, because she cannot conform to either standard and has no black feminist discourse available to her to articulate the dilemma – the novel as a whole has to do that for her.

Again we need to look at 'historical background and present setting' to put this in context. The Women's Liberation movement of the 1970s called for the right to abortion and women's bodily self-determination, and mounted a strenuous critique of the nuclear family and of heterosexuality itself as oppressive institutions for women. But African American women's necessary and historic alliance with men and extended kinship and community networks were ignored in this analysis; the history of black women's enforced childbearing *and* sterilisation was temporarily forgotten until black women theorists like Angela Davis and bell hooks resurrected it in their work, revealing the supposedly universal demand for 'women's' reproductive rights to be confined largely to the needs of white women.[43] In *Meridian*, then, we see the issue of reproductive rights dramatised in what seem to be (but are not) contradictory ways; there is neither the celebration of family and community that some black feminists invoke against the white feminist 'attack' upon the family, but nor do we find a defence of women's reproductive rights in the universal abstract. Meridian decides to give her child away and she has an abortion, but the reasons are neither selfless (as Sethe's murder of Beloved is in Toni Morrison's novel of that name) nor selfish.[44] Having 'stolen' her mother's life, as Mrs Hill never fails to remind her, Meridian can barely hold on to her own right to existence, let alone reproduce it. Getting Eddie Jr/Rundi adopted and the pregnancy terminated are thus responsible acts but they are not merely a matter of claiming women's liberation. For Meridian lives in history, is *held by* something in the past which she cannot simply shed but has to come to terms with. That something is the legacy of Sojourner Truth, Harriet Tubman, Ida B. Wells and other black women leaders/mothers of the race, who literally or symbolically looked after their own.

In an article on the dilemmas of black female leadership, Rhetaugh Graves Dumas writes of the crushing weight such symbolic investment in the African American woman as mother imposes upon black women professionals and activists:

> Bad mothers who are white seem to be more easily tolerated than bad mothers who are black; bad mothers who are black and female border on the intolerable. Indeed the rich imagery invoked by black women comes as close to the Great Mother as one might imagine. When the black woman leader fails to give people what they believe they need, she is believed to be deliberately depriving and rejecting, and therefore, hostile and potentially destructive.[45]

The woman leader as Great Mother, then, is always in danger of becoming a martyr to her cause, and is expected to put not just her skills and experience and insight, but also 'her *person* at the disposal of those around her'.[46] Again, this statement resonates strongly with Meridian, who lets ideas penetrate her and whose body is like an archaeological site on which the various traumatic layers of the past become visible. In the Civil Rights movement, women leaders like Fannie Lou Hamer, Ella Baker and Ruby Doris Smith Robinson conformed to this all-encompassing 'mother of all that is here' kind of role, but it took its toll upon their health and sometimes significantly shortened their lives. Kathleen Cleaver, for example, believed that the premature death of Ruby Doris Smith Robinson was due to the combined demands of marriage, motherhood, political organising

and particularly the many conflicts within and between thos
of work, and Fannie Lou Hamer's health was never the same a
she was beaten in jail and could not take the time nor afford the med
ical treatment necessary to recover fully.[47]

Like the question of killing for the revolution, the question of
refusing to be a mother is tied up with moral and political integrity
and potential martyrdom. Meridian realises that her reproductive
decisions are decisions about terminating life, even in self-defence,
and therefore they also need 'spiritual work'. Not because of guilt,
however, but because if mothering is one kind of responsibility for
the passing on of culture and racial pride, then political organising
and consciousness-raising can be another. Martyrdom, which can be
connected with guilt, has to be rejected too since it is a form of self-
destruction. 'The only new thing now', says Meridian, 'would be the
refusal of Christ to accept crucifixion. King . . . should have refused.
Malcolm, too, should have refused. All those characters in all those
novels that require death to end the book should refuse. All saints
should walk away (150–1). And this is indeed what she does – walk
away, leaving Truman and Lynne to get on with their own processes
of enlightenment, after she has shown them how to do it.

Meridian is neither a martyr nor a 'leader', if by 'leadership' we
mean qualities manifested by the likes of Dr Martin Luther King Jr
and Malcolm X, men who had a strong public presence, were in
charge of an organisation, and gained a media prominence which
ultimately led to their violent deaths. Perhaps it is more accurate to
liken her to the kind of *organiser* that Ella Baker was, democratic to
a fault and absolutely committed to grass-roots work rather than
speechmaking and media attention. 'Strong people don't need
strong leaders', Baker said famously, meaning they need organisers
and motivators.[48] This model of female leadership, often combined
with that of the mother which Meridian refuses, was widespread
among black women Civil Rights workers. For many of these
women, political activism naturally arose out of their role in the
church not as ministers but as ministering angels, organisers of
church events, visitors of the sick and dying, 'community mothers'.
Lawrence Guyot asserts that 'It's no secret that young people and
women led organizationally' in the SNCC.[49] But this organisational
'leading' was often not as high-profile as the work of the ministers in
other Civil Rights organisations such as the Southern Christian
Leadership Conference (SCLC, led by Dr Martin Luther King Jr) or

the National Association for the Advancement of Colored People (NAACP). It was often slow, laborious, frustrating toil, demanding a lot of personal as well as political discipline. Guyot describes voter-registration campaigns as collaborative work, in which means and ends often blurred:

> You don't alter the basic format that you walk into. Let's say you're riding past a picnic, and people are cuttin' watermelons. You don't immediately go and say, 'Stop the watermelon cuttin', and let's talk about voter-registration.' You cut some watermelons, or you help somebody else serve 'em. [....] The SNCC organizers were no saints. We asked discretion. We were never able to enforce it.[50]

Guyot's oblique approach to political campaigning, via practical help with whatever poor people need, is represented in *Meridian* in the seemingly anecdotal stories at the end, 'Travels' and 'Treasure', and in Meridian's early organising experiences with Lynne, who does not as yet understand the South and must learn Guyot's 'discretion'. Where *Meridian* espouses non-violence against the call for armed warfare and foregrounds female over male leadership in the Civil Rights movement, there also does it favour grass-roots organising and co-operation with the people over imposition of a party line or any other form of authoritarianism. And this anti-authoritarianism is, I would suggest, applicable to the way we interpret the form of *Meridian* too: like Guyot's fieldworker (and Civil Rights organisers were not called that for nothing), the reader cannot alter 'the basic format you walk into' but has to collaborate with the novel's charac-ters, feel her way around the lie of the land before getting to the heart of the matter and pass critical judgement. Like the Civil Rights worker, then, the reader must exercise discipline and discretion in not drawing premature conclusions, making partial meanings or giving up before the collaborative work, working *with* this Southern text, is done. Until we can appreciate Walker's use of spirituality as a 'fourth dimension' to complement her feminism, socialism and anti-racism, that work will not be completed. Only then will we be able to see how Meridian, as a secular saint, takes up where Sojourner Truth left off and how *Meridian*, as a novel, rewrites the Civil Rights movement as a personal/political transformation and a spiritual leg-acy for the decades to come.

'Hitting Them With Something They Don't Understand':
The Politics of Spirituality

In a 1989 speech which was clearly directed against the New Right's attack on abortion legislation in America, Alice Walker invoked the history of Native American genocide, of forced breeding and sexual abuse of women slaves, of compulsory sterilisations and abortions for women of colour, of environmental pollution, and the lack of adequate support services for poor black children and their mothers, in order to defend abortion as an act of mercy, or even of self-defence. 'I will recall all those who died', she said, 'of broken hearts and broken spirits under the insults of segregation', and this is but one of the crimes she listed that white men have perpetrated against black women. But the upshot of her argument is that until these crimes have been redeemed, and the white man can agree 'to sit quietly for a century or so, and meditate on this', he has no right to speak to the black woman about the right to life.[51] In this speech, as in *Meridian*, Walker performed an ideological tightrope act, typical of her incisive and insightful style of interrogating political dogma. By simultaneously mourning the lost children of the race and yet defending women's right to make their own reproductive decisions, she flew in the face of both black nationalist 'race suicide' prophets and white religious fundamentalists. It is important to realise that Walker's defence of abortion was *not* articulated as a matter of individual self-determination but as a recognition of the difficulty of a black woman's position in a racist, capitalist and profoundly self-destructive society which does not value children. This society, Walker argued in a spiritualist and environmentalist vein, preaches a 'right to life' at the same time that it in fact commits murder of every kind on living things, without thinking, every day of the week, in its defence spending, its advocacy of welfare cuts, its participation in war and its refusal to protect the environment.

It is this political analysis and this kind of historical perspective which Walker, in *Meridian*, brings to other feminist issues such as rape and sexual harassment.[52] The Tommy Odds–Lynne episode about interracial rape again highlights the difficulty of Meridian's position as an activist for whom abstract questions (is rape as an act of the black man's revenge on white society ever justifiable? can black and white women unite as victims of sexual violence no matter who perpetrates it?) always have to be examined in their 'present setting and historical background'. But the interracial rape shows more than that; it is also a key issue in the relationship between Truman and Lynne and Lynne and Meridian, a kind of microcosm of personal/political tensions. Lynne's guilt feelings as a white woman prevent her from valuing her bodily integrity enough to name the event as rape, and Truman's confusion about 'whether one can be guilty of a color', which I noted earlier, is never quite resolved. Meridian's position as confidante of both is that she cannot take sides, since as a black woman she is – yet again – obliterated from a binary structure in which '*All the Men Are Black*, [and] *All the Women Are White*', as the title of a seminal book on black women's studies has it. In that title, however, the follow-up is '*But Some of Us Are Brave*', and Meridian's refusal of binary thinking and living leads her to persevere in her emotional courage to neither reject Truman nor Lynne, to develop her racial solidarity *and* to open herself up to Lynne's friendship.[53] Torn by the demands that both Truman and Lynne make upon her, demands which in political terms would translate as comrade in arms and feminist sister respectively, Meridian is for most of the novel drawn into a *ménage à trois* because the three of them have something to work out together. Neither Truman nor Lynne can quite do without her, as indeed Meridian's erstwhile friend, Anne-Marion, can't either; Anne-Marion keeps writing letters even though the communication is one-sided. In the end, the threesome experience a transformation and enlightenment of a personal/political nature. For Truman and Lynne this entails a shedding of borrowed languages, revolutionary posturing and misconceived ideas. Christine Hall astutely notes a contrast between Meridian who is rooted, like the Sojourner, in the South on one hand and 'Truman, with his spoken French, his African prince performance and his Che Guevara outfit, [who] represents an example of cultural expressions which are not rooted in the community' on the other.[54] Such rootlessness and theatricality are also characteristic of Lynne, who often speaks in borrowed idioms and voices, whether they be those of black street-talk or Hollywood. On the occasion when she confronts Truman in his flat in New York and finds 'a tiny blond girl in a tiny, tiny slip that was so sheer she had time to notice ... that the girl's pubic hair was as blonde as the hair on her head' there, she mimics the Southern speech of *Gone with the Wind*: '"Don't shut up Sugah", she said, "Talk. I wants to hear Miz Scarlet talk"' (172–3). After the death of her and Truman's daughter Camara, who is yet another variation on the theme of murdered children, Lynne learns (in 'Two Women' and 'Lynne') to relinquish her idealisation of black people and her identification as a Northern white woman. Her rootlessness, after she has lost husband, child and home, leads her back to the South and back to Meridian. In jokey conversation with the latter Lynne admits, finally, that 'Black folks aren't so special' and that her marriage to Truman taught her that the time for white women to fall off their pedestals had come – in her case that had happened, after all, a long time before, when she started working for Black Civil Rights (185). Truman, similarly, is affected by the way Meridian lives authentically in a way that he cannot, and learns from her. '"Your ambivalence will always be deplored by people who consider themselves revolutionists, and your unorthodox behavior will cause traditionalists to gnash their teeth", said Truman who was not, himself, concerned about either group. To him, they were practically imaginary' (227). The fact that they have become 'practically imaginary' shows his progress in shedding convention and worry about conforming to revolutionary styles. With the final poem, in which Meridian forgives him his trespasses, he falls to the floor in a re-enactment of Meridian's fainting spells, puts on her cap and gets into her sleeping bag. Truman at that point takes on her mission of making the abstract concrete, working through questions of means and ends, and learning to live with ambivalence.

Walker's essay 'The Civil Rights Movement: What Good Was It?' cites an old lady, a 'legendary freedom fighter in her small town in the Delta' who, to the question of whether the movement was dead, replied: '"if it's dead, it shore ain't ready to lay down!"'[55] This essay was written nine years before *Meridian* was published, but I think that the spirit of that black woman's reply has remained with Walker in her subsequent writing career. The theme of changes in personal lives because of the movement, and of 'a debt we owe to those blameless hostages to the future, our children' has likewise persisted, notably in *Meridian* but also in poems, essays and the later novels.[56] I called *Meridian* earlier in this chapter a novel not so much *about* the Civil Rights movement, but *of* it, and by that I meant that its significance lies primarily in Walker's literary use of Civil Rights values and strategies. This requires some explanation, but we can take as an example the model of the crazy quilt. The quilt which requires piecing together by the reader can be likened to the Civil Rights movement's goal of integration, a joining of 'black and white together' or, as Walker would probably have it, a joining of peoples of all colours within the fabric of society, but with distinct patterns, identities and histories still visible and yet harmoniously combined. Skill and artistry lie in the joining process, which in *Meridian*'s case is the attempt to dissolve traditional ways of thinking in binary oppositions: black/white, male/female, leader/follower, realist/mythical, political/spiritual, sick/healthy, and so forth. These pairs are progressively taken apart by the stitching-in of certain other elements which figure in the novel, such as the Indian motif (which breaks up the black/white dichotomy), Meridian's androgynous appearance and role (challenging gender stereotypes) and her community leadership (dissolves distinction leader/ led). The crazy quilt is not so crazy after all, just as Meridian is not, in fact, either a 'weird gal' nor 'God'. Nor, indeed, is she 'sick'; through letting conflict play havoc with her body and by following its course she is, instead, in the process of healing herself. Concepts and practices like Beloved Community and non-violent resistance intervene in the opposition between the political (socialism) and spiritual (Christianity), by ridding the latter of its institutional hierarchy (the Church) and focus on the hereafter, whilst shedding the former's instrumentalism ('killing for the revolution') and giving its materialism and collectivism a moral grounding. The historical suffering of non-white peoples, of women, and of children provides that moral grounding in a recognition that change cannot be brought about by 'doing onto them as they have done to you', because that would only reverse the binary rather than challenge its destructive logic. Or, as one Civil Rights activist put it in typically less pious, and more tactically astute terms: 'We knew that probably the most powerful weapon that people literally have no defense for is love, kindness. That is, whip the enemy with something that he doesn't understand.'[57] The pattern I am tracing then, in this crazy quilt, is Walker's strategy of 'whipping the enemy with something that he doesn't understand', and the novel's form is as much a part of that deliberate strategy as are its enigmatic heroine and her peculiar story. Meridian and *Meridian* embody this ideal in which means and ends are merged – at enormous physical and psychological cost and artistic as well as didactic gain. For reading *Meridian* is, in many ways, a political and personal education, and whatever good the Civil Rights movement did or did not do – which may be more questionable in the 1990s than it was in 1976 or in 1967 – this novel *of* Civil Rights is a powerful reminder of the movement's imaginative and philosophical legacy. Fannie Lou Hamer puts the question of killing for the revolution in perspective for the last time: 'You can kill a man, but you can't kill ideas. 'Cause that idea's going to be transferred from one generation 'til after a while, if it's not too late for all of us, we'll be free.'[58]

4

The Color Purple

In 1970, two women – one white, one black – got together to collect money for a headstone to mark the grave of Bessie Smith, blues singer extraordinaire, who had died in 1937. One of them, Juanita Green, attended the unveiling of the stone, but the other stayed away so as not to detract attention from the commemoration of 'the Empress of the blues'. That absent white woman was Janis Joplin.[1]

In 1973, Alice Walker flies to Eatonton, the birthplace of Zora Neale Hurston, African American writer and anthropologist extraordinaire, to meet a white woman named Charlotte Hunt. Together they want to find Hurston's grave, in order to put a headstone on it with the inscription 'a genius of the South'. Although they do not succeed in locating the grave precisely, they have the headstone placed in the middle of a circle as a monument to Zora Neale Hurston. Alice Walker later relates this event in 'Looking for Zora', a monument in essay form which occupies a central place in Walker's *oeuvre*.[2]

On page 156 of *The Color Purple*, Celie and Shug look for the burial place of Celie's parents. They find 'nothing but weeds' and in the end they stick a horseshoe in the ground by way of a marker. It is at this point that Shug tells Celie 'Us each other's people now', thus declaring their kinship and sisterhood in place of the family that is irrevocably lost (156).[3]

It may be that Janis and Juanita, Alice and Charlotte, Celie and Shug were simply honouring their ancestors: singers commemorate a singer, writers a writer, daughters their parents. But – like Sethe in Toni Morrison's *Beloved* – they may also have been engaging in an act of redemption for those who had been celebrated in life, but who died in ignominy. According to African American folk belief, people who 'die bad' will haunt the living until their spirits are appeased and their bodies laid properly to rest. Bessie Smith died prematurely in a car accident, Zora Neale Hurston from poverty and illness, and Celie's parents through acts of violence. In (belatedly) honouring them, the daughters performed their filial duty in appeasing the spirits of their ancestors, and paid their artistic debts to those whom posterity had denied recognition and respect.

The Color Purple marks the graves of Bessie Smith and Zora Neale Hurston in a similar way. Both foremothers of Celie and Shug assert their presence in The Color Purple, obliquely through many 'buried' references to their work, but more significantly in the novel's tribute to the spirit of women's blues and African American English, which Zora Neale Hurston celebrated in her writing and Bessie Smith personified in her performances and recordings. As a writer of black speech, Celie shows her indebtedness to Zora, whilst Shug, the singer, embodies Bessie Smith's legacy. But more of the blues and vernacular foremothers later. In order to see the multifarious ties that bind Bessie Smith and Zora Neale Hurston to the characters of The Color Purple, we need to look first at the whole network of textual relations which makes up the fabric of the novel. The Color Purple is more like a shapely garment made of finely textured cloth than a patchwork crazy quilt. Where Meridian advertised its formal artifice, The Color Purple dresses its shocking contents in something like the 'folkspants' that Celie sews: custom made, yet 'one size fits all'. Perhaps it is because of this ironic contrast between Celie's innocent voice and what that voice tells us that critics have found so much to say about The Color Purple and yet have contradicted each other so frequently. One size does, indeed, fit all, but the question is what specifically individual readers see in a novel of abuse, rape, incest, battery and exploitation. What is the pleasure of this text? How is it that The Color Purple has become – with Beloved – the teaching novel of choice in the (still emerging) canon of African American women's writing? And what do Zora, Bessie, the blues and feminism have to do with it?

Reading the Critics: The Substance of Form

Few novels of so recent a vintage as The Color Purple have generated as much critical activity. Scores of articles have been written about it, every critical anthology of feminist literary scholarship contains multiple references to it, and the release of Steven Spielberg's film yielded a whole new crop of journalistic and academic responses, as well as protest marches and public debates.[4] *The Color Purple* seemed a most unlikely text to be adopted by the mainstream, given the controversial nature of its political and sexual content. Did it achieve canonical status despite that? Or was it, as Alan Sinfield has argued, because the novel seemed to promote 'a privatised, essentialist humanism' that made it all too easily co-optable into a liberal humanist ethos?[5] Although the latter seems likely, it is equally possible that the legitimisation of Walker's third novel in educational institutions and the critical industry was due to a genuine shift in teaching practices, as a result of the canon debate which has been raging now for more than twenty years. *The Color Purple* made it possible for that debate to be staged in the classroom, around such questions as what constitutes literary language, who writes it, what historically has been allowed to count as literature – and why. Perhaps Celie's story was one which could be studied and taught and written about, because it was *already being read*. This is bell hooks's view: 'Unlike most novels by any writer it is read across class, race, gender and cultural boundaries. It is truly a popular work – a book of the people – a work that has many different meanings for many different readers.'[6]

The plot of *The Color Purple* gives us some clue to its popularity. It tells the story of a poor, uneducated and 'ugly' African American woman in the American South, who is transformed from a fourteen-year-old rape victim and incest survivor into a successful business-woman in her forties, property owner and 'mother' of an extended family clan who gather around her to live in peace and harmony, celebrating each other for ever after. The familiar script of rags to riches combined with sexual and emotional fulfilment is instantly recognisable to us from popular fiction, and therefore may account for *The Color Purple*'s success. But the intricacies of Celie's progress – and, more importantly, the way they are told – belie the ostensible formulaic simplicity of this narrative. As befits any romantic or, for that matter, feminist heroine, Celie has to go through many trials and tribulations to gain her final victory, but her trials are not of the sort which we usually find in fiction, and neither is her victory of her own individualist making – as the tradition of Harlequin or Mills and Boon romance would demand. After having been repeatedly raped by her father, Celie has her children taken away from her, her mother dies and she is married off (effectively sold) to an older man, Mr ____, who beats and humiliates her. She also loses the one friend and confidante she had in her sister Nettie, who emigrates to Africa to work as a missionary there. Her new friend Sofia ends up in prison after a confrontation with white racists, and Celie is left to look after her husband's children as well as his mistress Shug, who treats her like a doormat. The change in Celie's fortunes comes when she and Shug make common cause with each other against the exploitation (sexual and otherwise) of women by men, and fall in love. Even then, her sorrows are not over because Celie loses Shug to a younger man and finds out that the letters she has been sending to Nettie never arrived, while Nettie's letters to her turn out to have been confiscated and hidden by Mr____ for years. When she finally gets to read the letters, Celie discovers that her children are safe with Nettie and the missionary couple with whom her sister has been working in Africa, and that the man who raped Celie is in fact not their father. When the rapist/stepfather dies, Celie inherits the estate of her real father, a property owner who had been lynched by white people, and that enables her to found 'Folkspants Unlimited', which becomes a successful business. In the meantime Nettie, and Celie's children Adam and Olivia, prepare to return to America, but their voyage home coincides with a war in Europe and they are presumed dead after their ship is reported sunk near Gibraltar. As luck would have it, however, the State Department has made a mistake and at the end of the novel Celie and her sister, her children, Shug and Sofia, as well as Mr____ celebrate a family reunion on the Fourth of July, America's day of liberation from colonial rule and obviously also Celie's day of liberation from all the forces that have oppressed her.

This story, even when told as neutrally as I can tell it, is full of holes, unlikelihoods and strange coincidences and any literal-minded reader would be left with lots of questions. Why did Celie's letters return unopened? How can an abused woman reconcile herself with the husband who treated her like dirt, and come to love his mistress? Why has no one else ever told Celie about her real parents? How likely is it, really, that a black woman is allowed a successful business venture (making unisex trousers, of all things) if we are also asked to accept that her father was lynched for just such an enterprise? And isn't it a little too convenient that an inheritance should arrive just as Celie needs it to make her happiness complete? All

these are questions which arise in the mind of anyone who is looking
for more than merely a sob-story which turns out well in the end, a
reader who wants a mode of telling it which will make it coherent, or
someone who is looking for role models in this feminist fable. After
all, the epigraph to the novel is Stevie Wonder's 'show me how to do
like you/show me how to do it', and seems to invite such an inspirational reading. None of those wishes is on first reading fulfilled.
There is a lot of vagueness too, about time and place and the historical details of the relation between Africa and America. Why does
Nettie go to 'Africa', rather than to a specific country or region of
that vast continent? Did the Olinka really exist? Why is the novel not
apparently set in a real time frame (for example, the first forty-five
years or so of the twentieth century) and in a real place, but are both
collapsed into some fantasy space and history?

Clearly, to a more imaginative and less literal-minded reader such
concerns are beside the point. If we try to read *The Color Purple* in the
terms of what we usually understand by realism, then we simply are
not given enough information in the text to make the story – in that
old-fashioned phrase – remotely 'convincing'. Such vaguenesses,
coincidences and inconsistencies derive from the style and form of
The Color Purple, rather than simply its plot. As in *Meridian*, formal
features demand attention, because it is they which make *The Color
Purple* into an exceptional literary achievement, rather than just a
script which provides all the thrills and frills of popular fiction. In
terms of style, for example, we note even upon first reading that Nettie's letters in standard English are in sharp contrast to Celie's
African American vernacular, which looks like transcribed speech.
The style is therefore uneven, or rather modulated with internal differences of tone and pitch. It is also often sentimental (especially at
the end) and in places didactic, as when Nettie writes about conditions and customs in Africa in order to teach Celie (and us) something which, presumably, she doesn't already know. Rather than
assume that this is a matter of simple inconsistency or sloppy writing
(telling not showing), we might more usefully ask how these modula-
tions function not just within the text but also outside it, as markers
of particular forms of social discourse which are of relevance to the
reader's present rather than Celie's historical reality. Second, we may
wonder why *The Color Purple* is written as an exchange of letters. This
form seems to draw upon the early history of the novel, that of the
epistolary novel of the eighteenth century, and yet its content is at

odds with a time frame of two centuries ago. This anachronistic use of the epistolary form has made *The Color Purple* a veritable goldmine for critics to exercise their wits upon. I think that, in order to read it properly, we have to clear up the question of how epistolary discourse functions here and what other genres Alice Walker has woven into her fabric. Generic conventions, after all, determine *how* we read, *what* we can expect and *why* a text is organised in the way that it is. It may be that the mixture of generic strands which we find in *The Color Purple* has tripped readers up, and as we shall see, this has affected the professionals no less than the amateurs. Let us look at the various possibilities suggested in the critical literature to date.

Most critics regard *The Color Purple* as an historical novel of some sort, because it is set in a time which clearly is not the present, but which is only in a generalised way 'the' past. This past we cannot pin down very accurately except by using historical markers such as the appearance of automobiles and mention of a global war. Because *The Color Purple* does not seem to care too much about historical facticity, Lauren Berlant argues that it offers a critical rewrite of the historical novel. As such it is not concerned with the public history of war and conquest, but with domestic strife and victory: a women's version of the historical novel, in other words.[7] Darryl Pinckney situates its setting in the inter-war period, but adds that '[T]he novel, ... with its flat characters, sudden revelations, and moral tags, has a doggedly nineteenth century quality.'[8] Pinckney, like Berlant, thus notes that there is something strange about *The Color Purple*, but puts this down to accident (Walker's inadequacy as a writer) rather than design. Others, like bell hooks and Melissa Walker, focus on the realism we can expect in an historical novel and find it wanting. In hooks's case this leads to an uncharacteristically crude and literal reading, in which she complains that the portrayal of lesbianism as socially unproblematic ('Homophobia does not exist in the novel') is not only unrealistic but also politically suspect.[9] For Melissa Walker the fact that *The Color Purple* 'does not contain a single date' seems to be a problem. She is troubled by the foregrounding of the domestic sphere that Berlant also noted, because in Melissa Walker's view this focus on home and family implies that public history in the novel is 'something that happens to white people', whereas black people seem to live only in the private domain and are thus effectively placed outside history.[10] A host of other, not primarily literary, critics have also got in on the act of writing about *The Color Purple*. Psychoanalytic readings tend to use Celie's story to illustrate a thesis about the development of individual selfhood, and a number of feminist theologians have found this novel of interest because of its reconception of the biblical Father as an immanent deity, an idea which fits in with post-1960s liberation theology.[11] Apart from Berlant's astute insight into Walker's use of the historical novel, I do not think that these kinds of realist (hooks, Melissa Walker) or instrumental (psychoanalysis, theology) readings yield anything very productive. They tend to flatten the text and rewrite it into something more coherent and rather less provocative than it is if we take its contradictions and confusions more seriously into account. This is not necessarily because critics simply get it wrong – their observations are by and large accurate in their own terms – but because they do not dig deep enough into the novel's metafictional layers. By that I mean that *The Color Purple*, like *Meridian*, has an embedded critical dimension to it which comments on the (white) Western literary tradition itself. Other critics, who recognise the significance of Walker's use of the epistolary form, are therefore able to interpret, for example, the politics of language in the contrast between Celie's and Nettie's letters to better effect, as we shall see.

Signifying Celie: *The Color Purple* as Metafictional Critique

Aware of this critical dimension of the text, Wendy Wall notes how the miscommunication between Celie and Nettie explodes any easy notion of community and mutual understanding between black sisters. This miscommunication, says Wall, has wider repercussions because it also applies to the reader in 'call[ing] attention to the inherent problems within the processes of reading, writing and interpretation'.[12] The sisters' difficulty in connecting through writing over time and between two continents should make us more conscious of what we ourselves are doing as readers trying to connect with a different time, place and culture. Many other critics foreground the theme of orality and literacy in *The Color Purple* and note how Walker emancipates not only Celie, but more importantly the African American vernacular by making Celie's voice *as (written down) speech* the privileged discourse.[13] Frequent reference is made, in particular, to Zora Neale Hurston's novel *Their Eyes Were Watching God*, which also used the black vernacular to spectacular literary effect, but without allowing Janie, its protagonist, to tell her own story in the first person from beginning to end. In that sense, critics note, *The Color Purple* completes a feminist project which Zora Neale Hurston had begun.[14] And wherever orality and literacy are highlighted, silence figures too – as a trope which traditionally has been associated with the sexually abused woman. This adds a further layer of signification to Celie's troubled discourse and allies her with Marguerite in Maya Angelou's *I Know Why the Caged Bird Sings*, who is silent for several years after she has been raped by her stepfather: women writers write what abused girls cannot speak.[15] Christine Froula, in a psychoanalytic reading, sees Celie's letters as a breaking of the patriarchal taboo on women speaking out about abuse and she relates Celie's and Squeak's voices to that of Ovid's Philomela, who in the *Metamorphoses* turns into a nightingale after she has been raped. Surprising as this classical contextualisation may seem, it strikes a chord given the recurring motif of (blues) singing in *The Color Purple*.[16] Froula also argues that it is by no means imperative to see *The Color Purple* as a realist text. If we read it as *part of* (as well as a reflection on) the Western canonical tradition and do not confine its ancestry to women's writing or African American fiction (which has largely been excluded from that tradition), then we would do better to regard it as an epic or classical romance. Molly Hite agrees with this view in an illuminating analysis of Walker's novel according to the conventions of Shakespearean romance, with Celie as a pastoral character who epitomises innocence and with powerful male figures of evil who are redeemed at the end. Most valuable in Hite's reading, I think, is her recognition of *The Color Purple*'s comic impetus which, she says, 'is so powerful that it absorbs questions of probability and motivation' (e.g. realism).[17] Few others have noted the many ways in which *The Color Purple* does not take itself quite seriously, when it plays – especially towards the end – with the conventions of the epistolary novel and the *Bildungsroman* in such a way as to make these forms look slightly ridiculous, and in my view this is the point. Celie's progress is, after all, no more the product of coincidence, remarkable reversals of fortune and miraculous feats of sudden reformation of character than is, to name a favourite novel of Alice Walker's and mine, *Jane Eyre*, as Elizabeth Fifer usefully observes.[18] One way of naming this comic, or rather satirical, tendency is to say, as Linda Abbandonato does, that *The Color Purple* transgresses the genre of epistolary writing by invoking the tradition of Samuel Richardson's *Clarissa* – another novel of female sexual danger and abuse – and then turning it inside out.[19] Another way of understanding the anarchic and metafictional impulses of *The Color Purple* is to read it as a 'pastiche' (meaning: an uncritical mimicry of an earlier text, unlike 'parody', which is a negative, satirical aping of conventions) of Zora Neale Hurston, as Henry Louis Gates suggests, or to put it in the context of postmodern fragmentation, as Wendy Wall does.[20] But for my purposes these terms are too non-specific, and I would prefer to say that *The Color Purple* on one hand 'signifies on' the early history of the novel, the novel of letters as written by Richardson, but also Fanny Burney and other white women. On the other hand, it also pays homage to Hurston and other writers and singers of the black vernacular. What does it mean to characterise Walker's novel in this way, and what do we gain by it?

'Signifying' is one of those features of African American cultural practice which, in recent years, have been identified as distinctive in theoretical as well as critical discourse on black women's writing. 'Signifying', as defined in Henry Louis Gates Jr's *The Signifying Monkey*, the *locus classicus* of the term as a theoretical concept, can take many different forms but basically it comes down to two types of linguistic strategy. It can be a way of covert, indirect communication between members of a group who understand its particular code, and it can be a form of playing tricks on someone outside the group by a devious use of words. In the story of the signifying monkey, the monkey gets the upper hand over the lion by passing on to him an insulting comment which someone ('a bad-assed motherfucker down your way', in a modern version) supposedly has made about him. Outraged, the lion then confronts the elephant, who of course beats him up while the monkey is laughing his head off, high up in the tree. There are hundreds and thousands of versions of 'The Signifying Monkey' and they vary in detail as well as in outcome. In the 1964 version, a toast improvised by a Philadelphia 'Kid' from which I quoted, the Monkey only gains a temporary victory and then falls out of the tree and gets beaten up by the Lion in turn.[21] Whatever the outcome, this is obviously a tale of how the weak can outwit the powerful, and the way it works is what is important. The lion takes the monkey at his word(s), whereas the monkey is speaking figuratively, and it is in the resulting misunderstanding/ miscommunication that the monkey gets the upper hand. 'Signifying', according to Gates, then, has two crucial features: one is its indirect address, and the other its metaphorical nature and its facility with revision of formal conventions.[22] To 'signify on' a text (or a person) is to talk negatively about it, often in hyperbole and with either a light touch (in jest) or a heavier, more serious didactic intention.[23] Misrecognition of a signifying practice can lead to serious mistakes. For example, Marjorie Pryse writes in her introduction to *Conjuring: Black Women, Fiction and Literary Tradition* that

> Without formal education, Celie can't know what Walker does, that the earliest novels in English were also epistolary. Therefore, Celie is not writing an 'epistolary novel'. She has simply found the form in which both to express and share her deepest feeling, which is love for other black women and men like Albert who accept her newly discovered autonomy.[24]

This is an extraordinary dismissal of the novel's use of the epistolary tradition, for surely the point is that *Walker* knows what it means to write in that generic convention. In adopting it in Celie's behalf, Walker 'signifies on' the earliest novels in English, where white women's suffering in trying to protect their most precious commodity – their chastity – motivates plot and form. On reading *The Color Purple* against this background, we see how such suffering pales somewhat in significance when compared with Celie's and that of numerous black women over the last three centuries. This process of 'signifying' in the novel is both heavy and light: heavy, in that it teaches us as readers about dominant assumptions regarding what is great literature and what is not. *Clarissa* and *Jane Eyre*'s legitimacy as canonical novels about (and by) 'our' literary foremothers is taken for granted, whereas Celie's has to be established through a catalogue of suffering and Walker's heavily accented alternating use of standard and non-standard (African, American) English in the epistolary exchange. But it is also light, because some of the familiar motifs of the eighteenth-century epistolary and nineteenth-century realist novel (absent mothers, lost and found relatives on different continents, surprise inheritances and initially recalcitrant lovers) are rewritten in *The Color Purple* to tragi-comic effect. And this is done so obliquely that we cannot even say that this or that feature is clearly comic, whereas another is tragic: both elements criss-cross each other with the tragic dominating at the beginning and the comic at the end. The picture of Celie and Albert sewing together on the porch, for example, makes me laugh because it seems so contrived. Yet there are times when men take on women's work (as when everyone gathers round to nurse the sick child, Henrietta) and *vice versa* which are quite moving and which offer a utopian vision of a future in which gender roles, as such, no longer exist. Or maybe not so utopian, as in this famous passage when Celie and Albert exchange lessons learned, and Walker's didacticism is evident:

> You know Shug will fight, he say. Just like Sofia. She bound to live her life and be herself no matter what.
> Mr.____ think all this is stuff men do. But Harpo not like this, I tell him. You not like this. What Shug got is womanly it seem like to me. Specially since she and Sofia the ones got it. (228)

This works at a literal level, because it sums up what we already know through having observed Shug and Sofia's behaviour. But as a signifying passage this dialogue also rewrites the early epistolary novel's script of rigidly fixed gender roles and compulsory heterosexuality, and it makes of Celie at least as worthy a literary victim/heroine as Clarissa or Jane Eyre. What is more, in *The Color Purple* no female rivals need to be killed off in order to establish Celie's moral superiority, and the love triangle is resolved in, first, a lesbian relationship between the women which bypasses the man and only later, once the villain has redeemed himself, in tripartite respect and harmony.

By now we can see that critics who read *The Color Purple* in predominantly realist terms fall victim to the signifying monkey's trickery, while those who get the message will derive more learning and more fun from the novel. But we have not quite got there yet. Calvin Hernton – finally – regards *The Color Purple* as a twentieth-century slave narrative, in which Walker replaces white/black exploitation with a gendered one in which black women are enslaved by black men.[25] Hernton has a point with regard to the autobiographical slave narrative as the founding genre of African American literature, something which Houston Baker also notes in a more theoretical context. In his book *Workings of the Spirit* Baker contends that

> The most forceful, expressive cultural spokespersons of Afro-America have traditionally been those who have first mastered a master discourse – at its most rarefied metalevels as well as at its quotidian performative levels – and then, autobiographically,

written themselves and their *own* metalevels palimpsestically on the scroll of such mastery.[26]

This is a complicated way of saying that, if we take the slave narrative as our example, the slave who told his or her own story first had to prove that s/he could write and write *in the language of the slave master* (that is, standard American English) in order to then be able to take issue, not just with slavery as an exploitative and dehumanising system, but also with the *slave master's language and discourses*. When Harriet Jacobs ends her story *Incidents in the Life of a Slave Girl* with a direct and wry comment to the reader that this story does not end, as one might expect in a conventional novel, with marriage but with a precarious freedom, what she does in effect is critique a dominant literary genre by showing just what kinds of race-, gender- and class-specific assumptions underlie it.[27] I think we can use Baker's insight, and Jacobs's historical example, to look at *The Color Purple* as a text which is self-aware in this sense. It both shows evidence of mastering a master discourse at Baker's metalevel (its use of the epistolary form) and at his 'quotidian performative' level (Nettie's stilted, 'white' written style), which is subverted by Celie's and Shug's vernacular/blues discourse. Hernton's model of the slave narrative in turn connects neatly with the practice of 'signifying' as the slave's trope, in Henry Louis Gates's term, because it is through his stylistic mastery that the slave (the monkey) can critique the master.[28]

Part of this critique in *The Color Purple* is – paradoxically perhaps – Walker's privileging of speech and other cultural practices (music, needlework, sexuality, spirituality) over writing. An often overlooked passage in *The Color Purple* is the one in which Shug tells Celie that she has fallen in love with a much younger man, Germaine, and that she wants to go away with him for six months. Celie at this point cannot speak, and answers Shug with written notes instead:

> All right, say Shug. It [the affair with Germaine] started when you was down home. I missed you, Celie. And you know I'm a high natured woman.
>
> I went and got a piece of paper that I was using for cutting patterns. I wrote her a note. It said, Shut up. (211)

This episode, as much as the first letter to God, makes it clear that Celie's writing is not in itself an act of liberation or even self-expression, but rather an escape valve when all else fails. Celie writes, in other words, when telling is impossible: 'You better not never tell nobody but God' is how the novel starts, and Celie does not actually break that taboo until about midway through when she tells Shug that Mr＿＿ beats her. 'Telling' is thus confined to spoken, human communication, whereas writing to God does not count as an act of self-empowerment. This seems to me an important distinction to make, because it crucially defines the difference between the dominant (white) culture's valorisation of writing as against speech. Writing letters or notes is as close to speaking as writing can get, and yet we see in *The Color Purple* how writing can malfunction as a mode of communication. This is because writing in its pure form, as it were, is an abstract activity requiring solitude and stillness, whose end product is removed from the circumstances in which it was done. In a literate, technologised culture, writing which is aimed at no one in particular and shows no personal markers (namely print, in the standard language) is prized most highly of all. Speech, by contrast, is a practice of *communication*, a call which only functions if it elicits a response. And call and response is another characteristic of African American cultural practice, whether it takes the form of shouting in church or the audience's interjections of approval in oral storytelling or jazz performance. Speech is not usually regarded as an art form in the way that writing is, *because* of its communal, evanescent and interactive nature.[29] Christine Hall observes that in *Meridian* Walker already seemed 'to be undermining the ground of verbal discourse upon which her own work rests', because Meridian frequently cannot speak, so choked up is she with the violence of history which she has taken into herself. Instead, it is Meridian's body which speaks in physical symptoms – as indeed Celie's does, in an understated way (when her father 'sells' her he informs Mr＿＿ that 'God done fixed her', meaning that she has lost her fertility through sexual trauma and will therefore not get pregnant again (10)). In relation to *The Color Purple* we can revise Hall's statement to say that Walker undermines the ground of *written* discourse upon which her own work rests, and agree that, for Walker, '[I]t is by means of art, whether it is story-telling, performance, the visual arts or music, that history can be transformed', a statement which pointedly refuses to privilege writing over other, non-verbal art forms.[30]

The feminist critical cliché that *The Color Purple* charts Celie's progress through her 'finding a voice' is thus, in my construction, to be taken literally as referring to a speaking voice; the fact that Celie also writes is only of secondary importance in the scheme of cultural difference *and critique* which Walker articulates in the novel. I see the text's insistence on the power and presence of the speaking and singing voice as polemically engaging with white women's literature, which tends to take *writing* as the mark of liberation from patriarchal oppression, in a tradition which ranges from Anne Bradstreet to Charlotte Perkins Gilman and from Virginia Woolf and Tillie Olsen to Hélène Cixous. In Anne Bradstreet's famous poem 'The Prologue' of 1650, for example, the oft-quoted lines are: 'I am obnoxious to each carping tongue/who says my hand a needle better fits [than a pen]' – Celie, obviously, has no such disdain for the needle. Later, Charlotte Perkins Gilman argued for a woman's right to write as a means of doing something useful and keeping herself sane in the novella *The Yellow Wallpaper* of 1892 , and Virginia Woolf's *A Room of One's Own* (1929) was concerned with women's right to education and acceptance into the republic of letters. In the contemporary period, white feminist criticism has taken Tillie Olsen's documentation in *Silences* of all the forces which have held women (and other oppressed people) back from writing as central, and it has applauded the French critic Hélène Cixous, for her exhortation to women to write as a means of self-liberation.[31] Clearly, the assumptions all these feminist and proto-feminist writers made about the availability and validity of literacy over orality are culturally and class-specific. In the exchange of letters between Celie and Nettie, likewise, the salient point is that it is *not* – strictly speaking – an exchange, *not* a correspondence, but a miscommunication, as Tamar Katz shows.[32] Literally so, in that letters aren't received or aren't read until much later, so that the sisters in fact do not actually reconnect until they meet each other again in the flesh. And figuratively there is miscommunication too, in that the two constituents of Celie's and Nettie's hybrid national and cultural identities, Africa and America, do not connect, let alone 'map on to' each other in any easy way. Africa is not the Eden from which slaves were brutally taken away, because slavery, as the novel suggests and the historical record confirms, started in Africa with warring tribes selling their prisoners to each other and later to European slave traders. Therefore, as Graham Connah explains, 'the slave trade has a history in West Africa which goes much further back than the advent of Europeans on the Guinea Coast'.[33] And because patriarchy exists in Africa too, albeit in a different form, Africa can neither be black Americans' homeland nor can America assert its 'civilising' influence over it with any legitimacy: American missionaries are merely trying to replace one patriarchal social system with another, Christian one. This leaves African American women between a rock and a hard place, through which *The Color Purple* attempts to steer a precarious passage. It is not at all clear that the sisters learn anything much from each other, besides African folk remedies (the yam which is used to heal Henrietta) and the relative nature of cultural difference. But *we* certainly do, by reading, as it were, over the sisters' shoulders and between the lines of the ironic juxtaposition of African and American perspectives in their letters. Where Nettie writes about Samuel's Christian teaching on the evils of polygamy, for example, it is clear that her own *ménage à trois* with him and Corinne is not that different. At the same time, such a polygamous arrangement is also mirrored at Celie's end in family structures which incorporate lovers of both sexes as well as spouses and legitimate and illegitimate children. 'Africa', despite its almost mythical presence in the novel, is not celebrated as some idealised space outside the history of women's oppression, but then neither is America held up as a locus of liberation, in spite of the reference to the Fourth of July at the end. Just as Celie's first letters to God echo Sojourner Truth's statement that when she suffered during slavery, 'none but Jesus heard me', so also does the final chapter of the novel reiterate Frederick Douglass's rhetorical question of the mid-nineteenth century: 'What to the slave is the Fourth of July [as long as the American constitution does not grant freedom and equality to all its subjects]?'[34] Harpo's answer is that it is simply a holiday for black people to celebrate each other, and that response signals a continuing disaffection with and alienation from the rituals of American national identity (243). The relation between Africa and America is, then, metaphorised as one of precarious kinship (or even sisterhood), without antecedence or superiority/inferiority. Instead, the kinship means a sharing of some common ground in cultural memory and cultural practices ('And men sew in Africa too, I say' (230)), but one which is not easily recoverable due to the history of European colonialism in Africa and present Euro-American economic imperialism.

   The Color Purple is, then, at least in part, a meta-text which 'signifies on' the (white) history of the epistolary novel and white culture's (including white feminists') valorisation of writing over other cultural practices. It also poses the problematic relationship between two continents, Africa and America, and two cultural traditions (at least) which a hybrid African American identity must negotiate. But it is not Celie who does this in *The Color Purple* so much as Alice Walker, who uses the black tradition of a vernacular art in Celie's story in order to establish an alternative model of cultural production and reception to that of white Western canonicity. That alternative model can be glimpsed in the text through the recurring motif of the blues, and I want to explore that motif at some length to see what the conventions of the blues can tell us about the way in which Alice Walker interweaves the African American oral tradition with that of the white-identified epistolary novel. This detour into the history of the blues and into other Walker texts where the blues make an appearance will then lead us back to my earlier questions about the pleasure of the text, the spectre of Zora Neale Hurston and Bessie Smith in it and some further questions relating to teaching *The Color Purple*: where does the first-person blues discourse of Celie's story position us as readers, and how may that positioning be affected by our own racial and cultural identities?

A Right to Sing the Blues: Identification and Difference

When Billie Holiday sings 'I've Got a Right to Sing the Blues' in that slow, cracked way of hers, we hear not only a song of lost love (as the sleeve notes have it), but her own history of abuses of all kinds and – indeed – that of the history of African Americans generally.[35] The lyrics hark back to the time of slavery, but the river as trope of escape now signifies release of another kind: that of suicide. 'Negroes are the only descendants of people who were not happy to come here', writes LeRoi Jones in *Blues People*.[36] 'The foundation of the blues is working behind a mule way back in slavery time', adds Houston Baker in *Blues, Ideology and Afro-American Literature*, courtesy of bluesman Booker White.[37] And Sally Placksin calls the blues 'America's classical music' in her historical survey *Jazzwomen*.[38] All three are concerned to counter a popular impression that the blues is a twentieth-century phenomenon, arising from the big migrations north in the 1920s and 1930s, and as such a unique expression of American modernity. For Jones, the spirit of the blues originates in the experience of the Middle Passage: 'people who were not happy to come here'. For Baker, the lyrics and musical form of the blues evolved from work songs which not only helped to lighten the load of field labour during slavery but also served to comment on the exploitation of that labour, in a coded, signifying way, as Angela Davis points out.[39] These were the songs that Frederick Douglass wrote about in his *Narrative*, the songs that gave white people the impression of 'happy darkies' – people hear what they want to hear:

> I have often been utterly astonished, since I came to the north, to find persons who could speak of the singing, among slaves, as evidence of their contentment and happiness. It is impossible to conceive of a greater mistake. Slaves sing most when they are most unhappy. The songs of the slave represent the sorrows of his heart; and he is relieved by them, only as an aching heart is relieved by its tears.... The song of a man cast upon a desolate island might be as appropriately considered as evidence of contentment and happiness, as the singing of a slave; the songs of the one and of the other are prompted by the same emotion.[40]

The reception of *The Color Purple*, cross-culturally and interracially, poses a related problem of a possible mishearing or misreading. Not that anyone is likely to interpret Celie's 'song' – her letters – as a happy one; when Shug sings her tribute to Celie in Harpo's bar, we know that what she sings is the blues. Yet there is a danger that we read Celie's narrative as a sad story made good, as if the suffering which has gone before is erased in the airbrushed picture of a happy family, reunited in harmony and wealth at the end. For the moment, I want to put that final idealised snapshot of the family on the porch aside and look at the phenomenon of readers' sense of identification with Celie's gender-based suffering, a suffering which we also find articulated in, say, the blues as sung by Billie Holiday in classics such as 'My Man' or 'Good Morning Heartache' or, pre-eminently, 'I've Got a Right to Sing the Blues'.[41]

Cora Kaplan's essay 'Keeping the Color in *The Color Purple*' raises important questions about reader identification, across the Atlantic and across the divide of racial difference, as a possible instance of (mis)appropriation of black women's historical experience. In that seminal essay, Kaplan argues that her white British students' reading of Walker's best-known novel was disturbingly decontextualised as, simply, 'women's writing'. She advocated a pedagogy in which students are confronted with the work of Walker's male peers and predecessors, to get a sense of the sexual politics of *The Color Purple* as not just feminist but engaged in a very specifically African American debate around the black family, the history and legacy of slavery and also black sexism. For Kaplan, keeping the colour in *The Color Purple* meant work: a lot of historical and intertextual work to remedy cross-cultural ignorance and to counter the 'indulgence' of a too-easy identification which elides the substantial class and racial differences between white women and the Celies and Billies of this world.[42] Although I broadly agree with Kaplan's analysis in the context of teaching white students on a women's writing course, my own experience in the classroom or seminar room shows a slightly different set of problems. I have come across three kinds of responses: a feeling of, at best, exoticism and at worst primitivism ('weird people doing weird things and talking funny', in the words of one student); empathy with Celie's plight and delight in the happy ending; and identification of a highly traumatic kind, with Celie as a victim of sexual abuse and violence. Maya Angelou's *I Know Why the Caged Bird Sings* has provoked the same, profoundly painful recollections, which I would like to think of as therapeutic in the long run. In the short run, however, they call for a sensitive pedagogy.[43] Whilst contextualisation might help, and is indeed intellectually essential in the first of these responses, it does not do much for the latter two reactions except distance students from their deeply felt (and often cathartic) reading experience. Some of my students, for example, when they are asked to read Kaplan's article, often object to having their reading 'prescribed', as they see it, and their identification proscribed or invalidated. Although this can lead to heated and productive arguments around the critic's role in 'policing' the text, and although such distancing is desirable in the educational process, the question arises whether it need also necessarily devalorise the intensity and importance of readers' initial empathic responses, for such responses are not automatically to be dismissed as naive. For me, as for many of my peers, listening to Billie Holiday and other women blues singers prepared the ground for reading, and later taking a critical interest in, Alice Walker's work. Reading *The Color Purple* and getting involved in it is not unlike listening to Billie's cracked voice singing a song of abuse and lost love. But when readers feel they can 'identify with' such songs, or 'relate to' the experiences which they seem to name so poignantly, what exactly is it that they hear in the blueswoman's voice, from so far away, so long ago?

Before addressing that question, it might be useful first to trace the role of the blues in Walker's previous novels. In *The Third Life of Grange Copeland*, when Grange witnesses in New York the desertion of a white woman by her lover and sees her 'icy fortitude', he thinks to himself that no blues can ever come from such determination that her grief should not show.[44] Grange diagnoses, accurately, that such composure, such suppression of pain, is characteristic of an Anglo-European cultural definition of strength, but a strength which leads to sterility and death (as indeed it does, in this instance, because the white woman drowns as a result of refusing Grange's help). *Not* saving face might mean to save life, and creativity, and art; in articulating suffering the blues transcends it as well, and Grange knows this. In *Meridian* Lynne knows it too, albeit almost unconsciously. Lynne sees the people of the South, more particularly Southern blacks, as 'Art':

> This she begged forgiveness for and tried to hide, but it was no use.[. . . .] to her, nestled in a big chair made of white oak strips, under a quilt called The Turkey Walk, from Attapulsa, Georgia, in a little wooden Mississippi sharecropper bungalow that had never known paint, the South – and the black people living there – was Art. The songs, the dances, the food, the speech.
> 'I will pay for this', she often warned herself. 'It is probably a sin to think of a people as Art.' And yet, she would stand perfectly still and the sight of a fat black woman singing to herself in a tattered yellow dress, her voice rich and full of yearning, was always – God forgive her, black folks forgive her – the same weepy miracle that Art always was for her.[45]

On the face of it, Lynne in this passage finds 'Art' in the exotic picture of African American life which she constructs for herself and which is, as she realises, racist. In seeing black people as 'Art', Lynne objectifies them: she looks at her environment as one would look at photographs of 'typical' Southern scenes, which aestheticise the paraphernalia of poverty (the quilt, the rocking chair, the tattered dress, the artless, paintless, wooden house). Lynne is not *of* this world, but observes and admires it from a distance – the distance of class and racial privilege. Yet there is an underlying ambiguity in this passage which is not quite so easily dismissed as simply racist. For what Lynne hears in the black woman's voice, the 'weepy miracle', is an echo and articulation of her own melancholy, her own debased status in Southern society during the Civil Rights era. Lynne, as a white woman from the North, has stepped down from her pedestal only to find that Southern black people have no place for her, no use for her. Discarded by her black husband, mistrusted by her black women peers and rejected by her Northern Jewish family, she has become surplus to requirements. And realising that her position amongst Southern blacks is inevitably, irrevocably compromised, she yearns for the authenticity that she hears in the black woman's voice. Unlike Douglass's Northern whites, Lynne does not mistake the fullness of that voice for contentment or happiness. But, like them, she nevertheless makes a category mistake in romanticising the culture of poverty, and in admiring but also envying the authenticity and beauty of the black woman's cultural expression, without due regard (at least at this moment in the text) for the very different conditions of hardship from which that voice arises. Perhaps readers who think they can 'identify with' Celie's suffering or Billie's blues do something similar to Lynne, because they share a feeling but not the experience which produces its particular articulation. Billie singing 'My Man' undoubtedly expresses sentiments of love betrayed ('he isn't true') and of domestic violence ('he beats me too') that many women recognise. It is a large part of the appeal of the blues, as Ray Pratt writes, that '[I]t speaks to, for, and about unmet needs and represents a catalysation of the desire for a kind of freedom as yet unfulfilled, and perhaps not even fully conceived, yet one that invites participation and experience of its particular *feeling*.'[46]

The Color Purple has the same kind of appeal, invites a similar kind of participation in feeling, both of suffering and of delight in the happy ending. But cross-race, cross-class identification and a certain masochistic investment (if such it is) in women's suffering are problems for any kind of feminist analysis of Alice Walker's novel and women's blues. What am I doing, as an educated, middle-class, European white woman – and a feminist to boot – reading *The Color Purple* as if it were also, somehow, about me? To state such problems is not to resolve them. Who has a right to sing the blues? And who can really read them? A look at two of Alice Walker's short stories and at the history of women blues singers may clarify such difficult questions in the ethics – as well as politics – of cultural reception.

Alice Walker's Blues

The conjunction of Alice Walker and the blues is, of course, no coincidence. Walker has often credited the great women blues singers (Ma Rainey, Bessie Smith, Mamie Smith) in her work, and the short-story collection *You Can't Keep a Good Woman Down* is dedicated to them 'for insisting on the value and beauty of the authentic' as well as deriving its title from a Mamie Smith song ('You Can't Keep a Good Man Down'). The short story 'Nineteen Fifty-five' takes as its subject the misappropriation of a black woman's blues song by a white male singer, Traynor, who looks remarkably like Elvis Presley.[47] When Traynor's manager tries to persuade Gracie Mae Still, the original composer and performer of the song, to sell it to him he unselfconsciously sums up where Elvis/Traynor got his training: 'The boy learned to sing and dance livin' round you people out in the country. Practically cut his teeth on you.'[48] The idea of a white man 'cutting his teeth' on a black woman's music is worthy of Zora Neale Hurston's 'signifying' doublespeak and Gracie Mae Still is aware of the exploitation *and* the bitter irony of having her jook-joint songs packaged and commodified for white people's consumption. At the heart of the story is Traynor's puzzlement concerning the meaning of the song which he goes on to make famous:

> I've sung it and sung it, and I'm making forty thousand dollars a day offa it, and you know what, I don't have the faintest notion what that song means.
> [....] It's just a song, I said. Cagey. When you fool around with a lot of no count mens you sing a bunch of 'em. I shrugged.[49]

Like Lynne, Traynor, who is throughout portrayed as vacuous ('It was like something was sitting there talking to me but not necessarily with a person behind it'), admires and envies Gracie Mae's *living* ('fooling around with a lot of no count mens') for it is the living she's done that has produced the songs – and he knows it.[50] 'Nineteen Fifty-five' thus champions the authenticity and the use value of African American culture. Just as 'Everyday Use', Walker's rather better known short story about an old woman and her quilts, celebrates the black woman's tradition of creative yet useful needlework, so does 'Nineteen Fifty-five' revive black women's blues history; both forms of quotidian cultural production are here recast as art, if purposely not 'Art'.[51] In *The Color Purple* these two strands of African American women's artistic legacy come together as Celie, the seamstress, and Shug, the blues singer, join forces in their mutually healing and nurturing relationship. Shug's significance *as* a blues singer has, perhaps, not been emphasised enough in critics' engagement with *The Color Purple*. For she is not just the one who enables Celie to discover her 'pleasure button' or the colour purple in the fields, just because she happens to be a free-er spirit than Celie is. Shug is, to all intents and purposes, a liberated woman and it is her art which enables her to be so. As LeRoi Jones writes: '[T]he entertainment field [was] a glamorous one for Negro women, providing an independence and importance not available in other areas open to them – the church, domestic work, or prostitution.'[52] For women like Shug, blues singing was a ticket out of the oppressed condition of black women's domestic or sexual or industrial wage labour in the inter-war period. To this economic account of the blues as work, Hortense Spillers adds the dimension of blues singing as also a performance of sexual self-confidence, because the singer

> celebrates, chides, embraces, inquires into, controls her womanhood through the eloquence of form that she both makes use of and brings into being. Black women have learned as much (probably more) that is positive about their sexuality through the practising activity of the singer as they have from the polemicist. Bessie Smith, for instance.[53]

Bessie Smith is indeed a good example, for she (in such songs as 'I'm Wild at That Thing' and 'You've Got to Give Me Some') represents another side of women's blues: a sassy, demanding female sexuality far removed from the victimhood of Billie Holiday's best-known songs.[54]

In *The Color Purple*, then, we can see against this background that the cultural significance of Shug's occupation goes beyond its mere narrative importance, because Shug evokes a whole tradition of women's cultural activity and self-assertion. As a blues singer Shug can teach Celie a lesson in sexual autonomy and desire, which is part of Walker's womanist philosophy for which Shug is the mouthpiece throughout. She also wields the power of economic independence over Albert, which means that he cannot control her as he can Celie. Conversely, though, and much more obliquely Celie, the archetypal victim, also educates Shug in the ethics, if not the aesthetics, of every-day use. For everyday use is what Celie is to Mr____, and also to Shug when they first meet: a doormat, nurse, nanny and cook combined. Shug has to learn to *see* Celie first, and then to value her dignity and integrity over and above her labour – a 'weepy miracle' indeed.

It has been suggested (by Henry Louis Gates, and also by Walker herself in an interview) that feisty, sassy and outrageous Zora Neale Hurston herself was the model for Shug, but there are plenty of other likely originals available in the long line of hard-living, hard-loving women blues singers such as Ma Rainey, Ethel Waters, Bessie Smith, Mamie Smith, Trixie Smith and others, not called Smith.[55] In the autobiography of a good friend of Zora Neale Hurston, Ethel Waters's *His Eye Is on the Sparrow*, we find numerous examples of the kind of blues discourse which inspires Celie's. When Waters writes: 'We are close to this earth and to God.[....] Our greatest eloquence...comes when we lift up our faces and talk to God, person to person', it is almost as if she gives a description of *The Color Purple*, for talking to God 'person to person' is what Celie does in her early letters.[56] And lines such as 'Any God you worship is good if he brings you love. [....] His is almost like an inner voice, soothing and calming' sound like they could have been spoken by Shug.[57] Talking to God does not usually characterise the blues, which is regarded as a secular musical form, unlike the gospel songs discussed in the previous chapter. And indeed, Celie's discourse is secularised as her relationship with Shug develops and she is able to *tell* rather than write. Her development echoes that of Janie in Hurston's *Their Eyes Were Watching God*, who tells her friend Pheoby at the end about the 'Two things everybody's got tuh do fuh theyselves. They got tuh go tuh God, and they got tuh find out about livin' fuh theyselves.'[58] In Waters's autobiography we hear the voices of Shug, Celie and Zora mingled, singing in close harmony. Waters asks: 'if anyone could be so banged around and unloved during childhood days and still come out of it whole, a complete person'.[59] This is a blues question, answered in *The Color Purple* with a resounding 'yes'.

'Banged around and unloved during childhood days' is not just Celie's and Ethel Waters's story, but that of many of Walker's characters (Brownfield Copeland, Meridian, Daughter in 'The Child Who Favored Daughter') and, indeed, of Walker herself. Blues musicians' autobiographies, and African American autobiographies which use the blues discourse as a vernacular articulation of suffering, often begin with such an account of childhood trauma and neglect.[60] The opening lines of *His Eye Is on the Sparrow* could come out of a Walker novel, essay, or short story:

> I never was a child.
> I never was coddled, or liked, or understood by my family.
> I never felt I belonged.
> I was always an outsider.
> I was born out of wedlock, but that had nothing to do with all this.
> To people like mine a thing like that just didn't mean much.
> *Nobody brought me up.* (my emphasis)[61]

In *The Third Life of Grange Copeland*, nobody brings up Brownfield, who turns into a violent man and an abusive husband. Walker herself suffered from childhood violence when she was shot in the eye by her brother with a BB gun and scarred, as she thought, for life, as we saw in Chapter 1. This incident has been endlessly retold in interviews and critical articles as an originary trauma which brought her to writing, and Walker constructs it, mindful of the discourse of 'accidents' in domestic violence, as a prefiguration of gender abuse in adult life: boys will be men. Such physical and psychological abuse of women by men is the stuff that Billie Holiday's blues is made on. But, equally, that stuff includes a critique of gender relations voiced by other, sassier and more self-assertive blueswomen such as Bessie Smith, a critique which counteracts the apparent bleakness and ostensible masochism of women's early blues songs. Michele Russell, therefore, in 'Black Eyed Blues Connections', calls women's blues a 'coded language of resistance'.[62] In another essay she adds:

> Blues, first and last, are a familiar, available idiom for black women, even a staple of life. [....] We all know something about blues. Being about us, life is the only training we get to measure their truth. They talk to us, in our own language. They are the expression of a particular social process by which poor Black women have commented on all the major theoretical, practical, and political questions facing us and have created a mass audience who listens to what we say, *in that form.* (my emphasis)[63]

In that form is important, because for a long time the blues was the only form in which black women's thoughts and feelings could expect to be heard *by the culture at large*. To Russell's list of blues subjects we might add sexuality, including lesbianism, which gives us yet another link into *The Color Purple*. I would call Alice Walker's leitmotif of childhood trauma and physical abuse (something which she extends cross-culturally to clitoridectomy in her later novel, *Possessing the Secret of Joy*) characteristic of her blueswoman's aesthetic. The mourning of a childhood never known is a recurrent theme, and applies as much to slavery (in which a whole race was robbed of a childhood) as it does to Celie and to Walker's own experiences. But it remains vital to realise that the blues as elegy is always counterbalanced by the blues as transcendence. The leap of faith, which occurs so often in the final stanza of blues lyrics, softens or tries to undo the mournful qualities of the blues, and in Walker's happy endings we see the same thing. Such transcendence takes the form of celebration of the black community, of the South's beauty and artistry and of a spiritual belief in social and political change. Most of all, it is achieved in the creative act itself, in the singing of the song or the writing and reading of the text. For, as Ray Pratt reminds us, the blues (and Walker's writing) are not sad, but rather '*a way of laying sadness to rest*' (my emphasis).[64]

So far, I have talked about the blues as musical parallel to the patchwork quilt: made of everyday suffering but giving comfort in the making/performing of it. Walker's womanist blues aesthetic is most famously and clearly expressed in the story 'Everyday Use': like the quilt, which is made from scraps of the past to provide warmth and decoration on the bed, not the museum wall, all art should be used, not framed. But what happens when the blues is taken out of its improvisatory performance context and is committed to paper, frozen and *framed* in a literary form – as Walker/Celie does in *The Color Purple*? June Jordan describes her astonishment at black students' initially negative reaction to Celie's language:

> 'Why she have them talk so funny. It don't sound right.'
> 'You mean the language?'
> Another student lifted his head: 'It don't look right, neither. I couldn't hardly read it.'[65]

This response, on the face of it no different from that of some of my more blinkered white students, shows how unrecognisable the black vernacular becomes *even to those who speak it* when it moves out of its

familiar setting in the blues song or on the street. These students did
not even *want* to identify with Celie, because her language elicited
feelings of shame and embarrassment; the way Celie writes/speaks is
obviously 'incorrect' by the standards of the literary (white) language
that they were used to. Only when Jordan engages her class in trans-
lation of the novel's first sentences into standard English, and the
students find out how difficult that is and how ludicrous the result
('You better not never tell nobody but God. It'd kill your mammy'
becomes 'one should never confide in anybody besides God. Your
secrets could prove devastating to your mother') does it become
clear what Walker is doing in writing down Celie's speech: giving
black English not just a 'voice' (which sounds right) but a literary
legitimacy (which looks right).[66] And this is where awareness of what
Walker does with the epistolary tradition is as important as a recognition of how she uses the blues: the blues discourse functions to 'signify on' standard English and the (white) literary canon.

Identification and the Right to Sing the Blues: Authenticity Revisited

There is a vaudeville version of the blues classic 'My Man' by Ethel
Waters which sounds very different from the painfully plaintive
rendering Billie Holiday gives.[67] Using a classical style of singing,
with a mock French accent and an exaggerated emphasis on 'mon
hoooomme', Waters improvises a whole new song with hardly a trace
of the masochistic investment which the lyrics seem to celebrate.
Waters's version illustrates vividly not just women blues singers'
capacity for (self-) parody but also, in this recording late in her
career, the commodification of the blues and its packaging for a
white audience – as distinct from the black audiences for whom Bessie Smith's records were made in the 1920s, the so-called race
records.[68] In her book *Black Feminist Thought* Patricia Hill Collins
explains how an Ethel Waters gave way to, and gave birth to, an Alice
Walker:

> Commodification of the blues and its transformation into market-
> able crossover music has virtually stripped it of its close ties to the
> African-American oral tradition. Thus the expression of a Black
> women's voice in the oral blues tradition is being supplemented

and may be supplanted by a growing Black women's voice in a third location, the space created by Black women writers.[69]

It would be mistaken, however, to assume that, when Waters sings 'My Man' as crossover music, this is automatically a selling-out of the authenticity of the blues. Waters satirises a notion of Frenchness (foreshadowing the pathos of Edith Piaf) and of a European vocal tradition which she mimics in the way she uses her voice. Her rendering contains an element of critique, which is doubly ironic in face of the fact that 'My Man' was originally a French song, originally a 'Mon Homme'.[70] Only when Waters says at the end of the song 'It's the same in any language' does she contain that critique by in effect universalising the spirit of the blues, extracting sentiment from song and thereby abstracting it from the Southern blues experience: the blues becomes, precisely, sentiment, a 'song of lost love', the same in any language. Obviously, if we take this back to *The Color Purple* we can see what it in turn becomes if we extract from it a story, merely, of sadness with a happy ending with which we can identify. Walker, like Waters, mimics with the epistolary novel a European form *in a different voice* by way of critique. As the blues is 'Europeanised' and 'whitified' and recorded for a mass market, it becomes a commodity, a floating signifier unmoored from its berth in the Southern black experience. But the same has long since happened to African American literature, whether it draws on the oral tradition of the black vernacular or not. Unlike Patricia Hill Collins, I do not think that black women's writing now occupies the place of authenticity vacated by the blues, but rather that the rise of African American women's writing is the product of the same crossover phenomenon that has transformed women's blues. Just as blues improvisation cannot be recorded *as* improvisation, so also is orality not simply transcribable. Instead, it mutates into a different form, as Zora Neale Hurston well knew. Hurston 'framed' African American English in *Their Eyes Were Watching God* and thereby turned it into art; Walker does the same, but in making Celie tell her own story she shows how the art of the oral tradition is also one 'for everyday use'. At the same time, that very act of framing in *The Color Purple* creates a problem for readers, both black and white, because the first-person 'voice' invites identification with Celie on one hand while on the other her language – which is either unknown or all too familiar – makes it uncomfortable, at least initially. In June Jordan's teaching experience black students don't want to identify with Celie's language, whereas in mine whites relate to her pain and 'forget' about cultural, historical and linguistic difference after a while. The text thus positions readers differently, and Walker's legitimation of the black vernacular and critique of the epistolary tradition necessitate a self-reflection and distancing which critics and teachers can mediate in order to bring questions of cultural difference and power *as well as* cross-racial empathy into focus.

The phenomenon of commodification in music is not one which lends itself to nostalgic regret, and neither is *The Color Purple*'s status as a crossover text anything to be suspicious of. Commodification was an inevitable by-product of modernity and a condition for the wide distribution of knowledges and cultural artefacts. In this connection, it is no accident that Celie inserts herself into modernity as an entrepreneur, because this is part of her process of personal transformation and emancipation: instead of being a commodity herself, traded between men, she becomes a producer of consumer goods. While we may regret or critique this capitalist venture as a failure of political vision on Walker's part, it is in keeping with the epistolary tradition and that of the nineteenth-century realist novel that wealth comes, out of the blue, to make the heroine's happiness complete. But it is equally in keeping with Walker's critique of that tradition that capital is increased, not through marriage or colonial exploits, but through the work of a woman's hands. *The Color Purple* articulates, as a distinctly blue note, the passing of the African American oral tradition into writing, print and commodification. In talking to God 'person to person' Celie desperately creates an audience out of nothing, and Walker parodies the European novel of letters to highlight her exclusion whilst at the same time invoking a new, interracial and mass audience for African American writing. The hybrid forms of mass-market recorded blues and African American novel of letters, then, come to represent a kind of 'commodified authenticity' for a black and white market. But this 'commodified authenticity' of *The Color Purple* seems far removed from the aesthetic of everyday use that Walker espoused in the short story of that title, and in the blues story 'Nineteen Fifty-five'. What has happened? I think that both the passage about Lynne in *Meridian* and the ending of *The Color Purple* represent a shift in Walker's slightly naive defence of authentic folk art in 'Everyday Use'. In that story, the mother's poverty, along with her artistry, are in effect extolled over the daughter's educational and economic progress. But it is clear that when Lynne thinks of Southern black people as Art, we are not supposed to concur with that view: she romanticises poverty in a way that only one who does not have to live it can. Poverty is not romantic, and in *The Color Purple* Celie's progress is therefore marked as much materially as it is spiritually and sexually. Modernity and commodification complicate Walker's earlier championing of folk authenticity. And this is where the problem with white women's reception of the blues and of Celie's fate in *The Color Purple* lies. Like Lynne, and like Traynor, they respond to, and yearn for, an authenticity and experience that not only is not *of* them but which is also not *for* them (the only 'authentic' audience, strictly speaking, is that of the black community), and yet the commodity form makes that ersatz experience of the black woman's voice readily available. As Paul Gilroy demonstrates in *The Black Atlantic*, authenticity in music – and I would add in writing – is a complex thing:

> The discourse of authenticity has been a notable presence in the mass marketing of successive black folk-cultural forms to white audiences. [. . . .] [I]t is not enough to point out that representing authenticity always involves artifice. This may be true, but it is not helpful when trying to evaluate or compare cultural forms let alone in trying to make sense of their mutation. More important, this response also misses the opportunity to use music as a model that can break the deadlock between the two unsatisfactory positions that have dominated recent discussion of black cultural politics.[71]

These two unsatisfactory positions are black (cultural) nationalism, which absolutises difference, and a wholesale pluralism, which deconstructs the notion of authenticity altogether. Yet the first of these, cultural absolutism, is not unique to black nationalists. Whenever I speak to (white) blues buffs about the genius of Billie Holiday, for example, I am met with scorn: the 'real blues' is not that, the 'real blues' is always elsewhere: lesser known, farther away, longer ago, more 'authentic'. There is a danger, in teaching *The Color Purple* to white students, that we replicate that dismissive response, by saying 'this is not your experience, you cannot possibly identify with it' or, conversely, by pointing to the text's inevitable artifice in representation, its self-conscious use of the history of the novel, and so on. Contextualising *The Color Purple* in the history of the blues *and* that of the white European novel helps to identify Walker's epistolary blues discourse *as* a critical, hybrid discourse and focuses the attention on letters as opposed to life, in a too-ready identification with Celie's suffering. Even so, readers' Lynne-like experience of having something of themselves articulated in the novel is also valid and need not be delegitimised by this intellectual work; in my experience, white students emerge from their study of *The Color Purple* with both a better understanding of racial difference *and* a sense of solidarity/ empathy with an experience not their own, but not entirely alien either. And, as June Jordan's essay about teaching *The Color Purple* showed, neither are black students simply suffering from a false 'whitewashed' consciousness if they object to Celie's language; instead, study of the politics of Walker's signifying use of the vernacular enables awareness of the institutional and social pressures which posit standard English (and what is that?) as the only norm of correctness, adequacy or creativity.

Who has a right to sing the blues, and who can really read them? The blues, and black women's writing are now part of the crossover repertoire: crossing over, and crossing back. It is the role of teachers and critics to make readers aware of both movements, and to provide them with the necessary knowledge to track them back and forth. In *In Search of Our Mothers' Gardens* Walker has written of the need for writers and readers to partake of both African American and white literary traditions, and not to be satisfied with a segregated canon (see Chapter 1).[72] For Walker, as for me, it is essential to recognise that writing and reading do not take place in a vacuum, but are always already informed by a multiplicity of national, racial and gendered traditions. Paul Gilroy remarks that 'The relationship of the listener to the text is changed by the proliferation of different versions. Which one is the original? How does the memory of one version transform the way in which subsequent versions are heard and understood?'[73] This question is pertinent to our discussion, too. For 'versions' we can also read 'readings' or 'interpretations', and it will be clear that I have improvised my blues reading of *The Color Purple* in part from the different versions I have read elsewhere. In my view, *The Color Purple* is a cultural hybrid which combines epistolary features with the vernacular of the blues tradition. Walker both critiques the history of white women's writing because of its class assumptions and heterosexual matrix, and yet invokes it in her privileging of the domestic sphere and the theme of sexual

abuse. She also, as Missy Dehn Kubitschek has shown, takes issue
with male writers who have treated such abuse (rape) in literature
primarily for its symbolic significance. Even if they don't leave it at
that, '[T]he rape victim', writes Kubitschek, 'remains simply a victim'
in the Euro-American tradition, whereas in African American
women's writing 'she is a complex woman who has survived the
indignity of rape'.[74] Ultimately, *The Color Purple* is a monument, not
just to Bessie Smith and Zora Neale Hurston, but to the black victims
and survivors of sexual abuse who historically have been silenced in
white (and in black male) literature, but who have expressed their
pain in the black vernacular of the blues. It is also, crucially, a monument in which the black English of the oral tradition is forever
carved in stone. June Jordan explains how important it is that linguistic diversity be affirmed rather than displaced by a spurious
notion of standard English:

> Black English is not exactly a linguistic buffalo; as children, most of
> the thirty-five million Afro-Americans living here depend on this
> language for our discovery of the world. But then we approach
> our maturity in a larger social body that will not support our
> efforts to become anything other than the clones of those who are
> neither our mothers nor our fathers. We begin to grow up in a
> house where every true mirror shows us the face of somebody who
> does not belong there, whose walk and whose talk will never look
> or sound 'right', because that house was meant to shelter a family
> that is alien and hostile to us.[75]

In *The Color Purple* Alice Walker shows black and white readers a
mirror which reflects them back in a house of fiction where they
belong. Celie's letters were indeed written, says critic Valerie Babb,
'to undo what writing has done'.[76]

5

The Temple of My Familiar

'Last night I dreamed I was showing you my temple', Miss Lissie
said. [....] 'Anyway, my familiar – what you might these days,
unfortunately, call a "pet" – was a small, incredibly beautiful creature that was part bird, for it was feathered, part fish, for it could
swim and had a somewhat fish/bird shape, and part reptile, for it
scooted about like geckoes do, and it was all over the place while I
talked to you. Its movements were graceful and clever, its expression mischievous and full of humor. It was *alive*! You, by the way,
Suwelo were a white man, apparently, in that life, very polite, very
well-to-do, and seemingly very interested in our ways' (138).[1]

This is how Miss Lissie begins her parable of the temple of my familiar, a parable which explains not just the title of Walker's fourth and
most voluminous novel, but also its message and overarching theme.
The setting of this scene is near the beginning of the book, when
Suwelo, an African American man who has come to Baltimore from
San Francisco in order to take care of his recently deceased uncle's
estate, is getting acquainted with Uncle Rafe's close friends, Miss Lissie and Mr Hal. Recognising that Suwelo is in something of an emotional and spiritual crisis because his marriage as well as his career as
a history teacher are obviously in trouble, the old – and decidedly
odd – couple proceed to enlighten him by telling him their personal
histories. In Miss Lissie's case, this history is long and varied, since
she can remember former lives stretching back to a time before
humanity even existed. In the passage above she is remembering a

121

spell as a priestess in – we assume – Africa, visited by Suwelo in his previous incarnation as a white explorer 'seemingly interested in our ways'. The fact that Suwelo in this story is a white man is significant, because at that point in the framing narrative of the novel he is likewise still 'a white man' by education and inclination, trying to hold on to his wife Fanny, and unable to teach history as anything other than that which is on the record, that is, written in white men's books. What we see in this scene, then, is a confrontation between African and Western cultures and modes of knowledge, a confrontation which leads to the escape of Miss Lissie's familiar – in both senses of that word. For, in order not be distracted from her conversation with the explorer, the priestess tries to contain the familiar by imprisoning it in ever more drastic ways, until in the end it breaks out and flies away. The lesson Miss Lissie learns from this is that the urge to curb another's freedom always rebounds on you, or as the epigraph to Part Two of the novel has it: 'Helped are those who learn that the deliberate invocation of suffering is as much a boomerang as the deliberate invocation of joy' (164).

But there is another lesson too: Suwelo's imposition of his white discourse on Miss Lissie causes her familiar – here in the sense of women's ancient wisdom and cultural lore – to escape. Alienated from his African American past as an academic historian, Suwelo has lost sight of his African heritage as well as his female side and this wilful blindness makes for his increasing emotional and intellectual confusion. Miss Lissie's parable of the familiar serves to reconnect him (and us, as readers) with an unrecorded history; it is her personal *memory* which explains the epistemological break caused by colonialism, a break which discredited African tradition and orality and replaced it with Western rationality and written discourse. Therefore, the loss of the familiar is not only lamented because of its beauty or its status as faithful companion or 'pet', nor is the familiar simply a symbol for discredited knowledge. It has multiple associations. In the context of the novel as a whole, the combination of its birdlike, fishlike and reptilian features make it into a hybrid creature, much like the human characters whom we get to meet and who are all of mixed ancestry, even if they do not know it yet. As we shall see, part of the narrative's trajectory is the tracing of this ancestry back to a common source, which is that of humankind's unity with the natural world. When that unity was severed – first because of men's domination of women, and then again because of colonialism

– humans were set adrift, divided from each other along racial and gender lines and divided within themselves, their spirits broken. Suwelo's and Carlotta's situation at the beginning of the novel is of this kind, but both recover their wholeness in the course of their search for regeneration. The extent to which others can help them in this search is signalled by their connection with the natural world. Snakes, fish, lions and monkeys populate Miss Lissie's memories as well as her paintings. Zedé and Arveyda are the feathered creatures, both of Indian ancestry. They have the red parrot as their familiar (146), whilst Fanny's earliest memory is also of a red bird (175) – an early indication of her spiritual kinship with Arveyda. The peacock feathers from which Zedé makes her capes are echoed in the name of the great-great-aunt of the white American woman who rescues her, Eleandra Burnham-Peacock, a cross-cultural traveller like Zedé herself. As the (his- 'n her-) stories of these characters gradually become more intertwined, their identities and distinctive features begin to merge into one interracial and multicultural family, a hybrid organism like the familiar. Just as the novel fuses history with memory, booklearning with spirituality and humanity with the natural world, the familiar's beauty, composed of the talents and traits of various species, thus metaphorises and synthesises the multiplicity of stories and characters that we find in *The Temple of My Familiar*.

That said, making sense of the narrative is nevertheless a challenge for readers and critics alike. All the usual expectations of a novel have to be suspended, and for this reason Lillie P. Howard calls it a 'maddening' book:

> *The Temple* is about everyone and everything...almost since the beginning of time, including this time. Its movement flings one back and forth across millennia, continents, physical and spiritual wastelands sometimes inhabited by people bereft of themselves, unaware of and afraid of their essence. The result is mental and physical disorientation [....] The work defies full explanation because it is meant to be experienced, without judgement, rather than explained or rendered anew.[2]

If Howard is right, then the critic's job becomes almost impossible, yet I think it is important to at least try to guide the reader through this epic story across centuries and continents, and to explain what Walker's purpose in deliberately disorienting the reader might be.

In what follows I shall suggest three possible approaches, not mutually exclusive, which might give some shape to the ostensible chaos
which is *The Temple of My Familiar*. They are, in order of appearance:
the increasing influence of Jungian psychology on Walker's writing,
to be continued in the next chapter; the family saga as a generic
model with a long ancestry in Southern fiction; and the concept of
diaspora literature as it is currently being developed in post-colonial
literatures and theories. These three approaches are all centrally
concerned with the interplay of history and memory, as my concluding remarks will make clear. In this chapter, then, I shall try and
make *The Temple* familiar by forging a hybrid criticism of my own.

Spirituality and the Creative Process

At the end of *The Color Purple* Alice Walker thanks 'everybody in this
book for coming' and signs off as 'A.W., author and medium'.
Walker explains what she meant by that intriguing statement in the
essay 'Writing *The Color Purple*'. There she describes how Celie, Shug
and the other characters first were trying to contact her by speaking
through her and then, having forced their author out of New York
and San Francisco, came to 'visit' her in the northern California
countryside in order to tell their stories. Less than a year after she
had started to write it *The Color Purple* was finished and, says Walker,
it was as if she had lost everybody she loved at once.[3]

What are we to make of this? Was Alice Walker suffering from
delusions? Or did she, on the contrary, express here some ancient
African understanding of the spiritual world which white Western
thinking is wont to regard as superstition? *Or* was she merely trying
to explain the intractable forces which compel an artist to create
something which she cannot necessarily predict or plan in advance?
On the face of it, Walker's schizophrenic account of characters who
talk not only through, but also *at* their author in the process of
creation, combines two contradictory notions of what writers do
when they write. On one hand, the author constructs and controls
the characters like a puppeteer, scattering them across the globe and
giving them a hard time only to reunite them, happily ever after, at
the end. On the other hand, the medium records what the characters tell her of their own lives, and acts simply as a conduit for their
stories and their voices. The medium, in other words, is unable to

control the characters' independent existence; she becomes their instrument and mouthpiece. In designating herself 'author and medium' Walker thus is *both* puppet (her string pulled by her characters) and puppeteer: she claims and disavows responsibility for the creative process at one and the same time. But perhaps we should not be too quick to assume that this paradox reflects an impossible combination of Western and African conceptions of artistic production. After all, Walker's experience of her characters as real people who talk to her accords with that of many creative writers. Gloria Anzaldúa, for example, describes it thus:

> When I create stories in my head, that is, allow the voices and scenes to be projected in the inner screen of my mind, I 'trance'. I used to think I was going crazy or that I was having hallucinations. But now I realize it is my job, my calling, to traffic in images.[4]

Alice Walker's description of a sense of loss upon finishing the novel is equally commonplace and not at all surprising if we imagine, first, a writer's seclusion with those voices and scenes and then, once the process of externalisation is completed, the void left behind. In the context of *The Temple of My Familiar*, Walker's self-designation as 'author and medium' more importantly concords with a Jungian conception of subjectivity in which each of us, whether we acknowledge it or not, is always already two: a conscious and an unconscious being. 'It is by no means a pathological symptom;' writes Jung,

> it is a normal fact that can be observed at any time and everywhere. It is not merely the neurotic whose right hand does not know what the left hand is doing. This predicament is a symptom of a general unconsciousness that is the undeniable common inheritance of all mankind.[5]

In his therapeutic practice Jung developed this idea, as Anthony Storr explains, to the extent that he encouraged his patients to personify, or anthropomorphise, different aspects of their own and his personality, even to the point of giving them names and having dialogues with them. Jung himself conducted conversations with a figure who appeared in his dreams, and whom he named Philemon, for example. 'The language he uses about such figures suggests that, *as mediums believe*, he thought of them existing in an "imperishable world" and manifesting themselves from time to time through the psyche of an individual', writes Storr (my emphasis).[6] Alice Walker is thus not alone in her delusion, if such it is, that Celie and Shug exist in some other sphere beyond that of what we commonly perceive as reality. But neither do we have to believe that she is uniquely gifted as a medium, blessed with second sight, because of the fact that she does perceive them. Jung believed as well that all of us have that capacity if only we would use it, and far from driving us mad it would actually enhance our well-being and make us more sane, because

> Modern man does not understand how much his 'rationalism' (which has destroyed his capacity to respond to numinous symbols and ideas) has put him at the mercy of the psychic 'underworld'. He has freed himself from 'superstition' (or so he believes), but in the process he has lost his spiritual values to a positively dangerous degree. His moral and spiritual tradition has disintegrated, and he is now paying the price for this break-up in world-wide disorientation and dissociation.[7]

We can hear the voice of Miss Lissie here, harmonising with Jung's. Alice Walker's signature as 'author and medium', then, derives from a Jungian conception, not just of the creative process, but of subject-ivity and psychic health itself.[8] In such a conception of psychic health the conscious activity of writing is happily joined with an uncon-scious receptivity to the spirits, and in *The Temple of My Familiar*, as in *Possessing the Secret of Joy* where he appears in human form, Jung's spirit is pervasive.

'A Sorry Sack of Silliness': Spirituality, the Western Tradition and the Critics

It doesn't take much more than a superficial reading of *The Temple of My Familiar* to see that Walker is concerned, there, with the 'world-wide disorientation and dissociation' that Jung diagnoses, and with the rehabilitation of 'superstition' in order to heal human-kind and put the world back together again. It is obvious, in the journey that Suwelo makes, for example, that rationalism is not the *episteme* of choice in this novel, just as it is clear that his initial con-ception of a book-learnable, linear history which can be taught and swallowed whole will not hold in Walker's larger scheme of things. Carlotta, who discovers this before Suwelo does, believes that academic teaching is now obsolete, because it does not teach people what they 'need to know' (417). Why should that be so? The implication in *The Temple of My Familiar* as a consciousness-raising novel for the new age is that that new age demands more than book-learning, but there is a political dimension to this wider and more 'organic' conception of education too. The African writer Ngũgĩ wa Thiong'o writes in his seminal essay *Decolonising the Mind* that the education he received in Kenya, modelled on the British university system, did not empower people but made them feel diminished as Africans:

> Education, far from giving people the confidence in their ability and capacities to overcome obstacles or to become masters of the laws governing external nature as human beings, tends to make them feel their inadequacies, their weaknesses and their incapacities in the face of reality; and their inability to do something about the conditions governing their lives. They become more and more alienated from themselves and from their natural and social environment. Education as a process of alienation produces a gallery of active stars and an undifferentiated mass of grateful admirers.[9]

In the African context Ngũgĩ sees university education, taught in English, as inextricably bound up with colonialism and Eurocentrism and thus, by definition, unable to equip people with the tools they need to resist the imperialism of the West. For Walker, the issue is obviously a different one since she is writing in the United States – in Ngũgĩ's terms, now the prime perpetrator of economic imperialism in Africa – but there is a kinship between the two. The revised model of education which Walker presents in *The Temple of My Familiar* is remarkably similar to the one Ngũgĩ puts forward. For both, the oral tradition and the cultural memories embedded in everyday practices such as storytelling, music and dance are central to the project of educating or re-educating black people, whether they be Africans or African Americans. As far as Walker is concerned, anybody who is willing to question the hegemonic Western tradition which produced slavery and colonialism as well as rationality and scientific progress must subject him- or herself to such a process of re-education. And this is what *The Temple of My Familiar* is all about, as Lissie Lyles's epigraph to the novel testifies: 'If they have lied about Me/ they have lied about everything'. It is important to understand this, because critics, reviewers and many so-called ordinary readers have not taken kindly to *The Temple of My Familiar*. What they see as Walker's increasingly mystical tendency to foster belief in spirits, to hear voices and to consort with creatures encountered in former lives, as Miss Lissie does, is in fact a misrecognition of the serious questioning of the Western *episteme* that goes on here or – indeed – indicative of a refusal to engage with it in the first place. It betrays also, of course, an ignorance of the Jungian dimension of this questioning, and whatever one may think of that, at least it should be noted before the proverbial child is thrown out with the psychoanalytic bathwater. In 'A Turning of the Critical Tide?' Carol Iannone is hopeful that with *The Temple of My Familiar* Walker fans will finally see the error of their ways. She notes that reviews have been highly critical of Walker's generalisations, 'smugness' and inaccurate uses of history; that her inability to 'create plot and structure effectively' is now evident for all to see, and that the attraction of ever happier endings is beginning to pale. *The Temple of My Familiar*, Iannone concludes, is 'a sorry sack of silliness' and the sooner we recognise that the better it will be for us and for literature at large.[10] Obviously, from a critic who states first off that she is against 'infusion of politics into literature' and who dismisses the positive reception of *The Color Purple* as 'literary affirmative action', we cannot expect a serious engagement with Alice Walker's work. I cite Iannone's argument, nevertheless, because it is one which better-informed and well-meaning readers have advanced as well. Walker's move to faddish, frivolous San Francisco has done her work no good, some say, and her womanism has lost its roots in Southern blackness and is worshipping a Californian goddess of the good life instead. Indicative of such a shift from a concern with political and social issues in the earlier novels to the realm of the spiritual in this one, might be Walker's explanation, in *The Temple of My Familiar*, of how the Americas' original inhabitants came to be named 'Indians'. Whereas received wisdom has it that European travellers mistook the native peoples of the Americas for those of India, the next continent along (and thus misnamed them, as colonisers have a habit of doing), Carlotta discovers that 'an Italian explorer considered them, on first take, to be *indios*, "in God"' (19). Carlotta/Alice Walker borrows this idea from the

Native American activist Russell Means, who argues that it is, therefore, quite acceptable to call Native Americans 'Indians'.[11] On this
account, Columbus, the Italian explorer, unwittingly got it right,
and colonial misprision is redefined as respectful recognition of a
superior spirituality: 'Indian' is now not an improper, but a proper
name for the native peoples of the Americas. Walker, following
Means, thus appropriates the colonised's name and turns it into an
honorific. What matters here is not so much whether the received or
the new wisdom about how the Indians got their name is historically
correct, but the way in which each functions as shorthand for our
conception of the colonial enterprise. In renaming Indians as beings
'in God', the colonial record of (mis)appropriation of lands and peoples (in which the Indian 'Manhattan' becomes 'New Amsterdam',
and then 'New York', for example) is erased. Carlotta's discovery
then absolves the colonists of their historical guilt, and a negative is
turned into a positive. In the Jungian scheme, such a use of the past
in order to serve present needs is known as *zurückphantasieren*, or
retrospective fantasy.[12] In his 1929 lecture 'Some Aspects of Modern
Psychotherapy' Jung advocates retrospection not so much as a
means of 'discovering' childhood trauma to explain the cause of present ills, but as a way of unlocking the collective unconscious: '[the
patient] will enter first into the treasure-house of collective ideas and
then into creativity. In this way he will discover his identity with the
whole of humanity, as it ever was, and ever shall be.'[13] Jung clarifies
this in terms reminiscent of cultural relativism in another lecture
from 1929, 'The Aims of Psychotherapy', where he says that it is a
mistake for the missionary to pronounce the strange gods of the colonised to be 'mere illusion ... as though our so-called reality were not
equally full of illusion. In psychic life, as everywhere in our experience, *all things that work are reality*, regardless of the names men
choose to bestow on them' (my emphasis).[14] If this is so, then obviously the distinction between use and abuse of historiography, and
that between therapeutic and ideological purposes of retrospective
fantasy, are easily blurred and highly problematic, for historians and
literary scholars alike. The critics of Walker's revisioning of history
in *The Temple of My Familiar* thus have a point, as do those who see in
it a San Franciscan influence of new age thinking. It is true that in
this novel Walker's earlier concern with Southern racism, with poverty and the resulting oppression of women and children by means
of domestic violence and emotional abuse, has disappeared and is

replaced with an exploration of new modes of consciousness amongst the affluent middle class. It is no longer the poor Southern family, or the mixed-up, messed-up young black woman who takes up centre stage, but the artist him/herself. Towards the end of the narrative Arveyda, the musician, thinks of himself, Fanny, Carlotta, Suwelo, Carlotta's mother Zedé and all their children as a 'new age clan' (446). And this is exactly how they appear by that stage: unburdened by material worries they can be a loving, creative, extended family which is diverse in plumage and without a care in the world – other than that of the survival of the Planet. Global, spiritual and ecological concerns have replaced the local, political and domestic ones of the earlier novels (although, of course, Walker would equate the two: the local is now the global, ecology is political and the spiritual is – precisely – the domestic and familiar). Again we are reminded here of the end of *The Color Purple*, where Celie addresses her last letter to 'Dear God. Dear stars, dear trees, dear sky, dear peoples. Dear everything. Dear god' and ends it with the happiness that has given her a new lease of life: 'Matter of fact, I think this is the youngest us ever felt.'[15] This is very much in the spirit of *The Temple of My Familiar*, which also ends in universal bliss and harmony. Walker's critical revision of history and of the Western *episteme* thus entails a vision of personal and communal wholeness along Jungian lines, a microcosmic representation of 'worldwide orientation and association' in which 'superstition' is revalued as knowledge and moral and spiritual traditions are reintegrated in a collective consciousness. Celie, Shug, Tashi and Olivia all make their reappearance here to live out their new age, which paradoxically – but in a way that Jung would understand – means remembering their old, pre-historic ages as well.

San Francisco understands it too, and this may be why Ursula LeGuin, the critic of the *San Francisco Book Review*, is rather more receptive to Walker's time travel in this novel than is J. M. Coetzee in the *New York Times Book Review*. More than this being simply a matter of the difference between East- and West-Coast sensibilities, it is possible that Ursula K. LeGuin understands the imaginative, magic realist qualities of Walker's work as a science-fiction writer would, and is therefore more inclined to accept what others merely see as the indulgence of an absurd kind of fantasy. Coetzee objects that '[W]hatever new worlds and new histories we invent must carry conviction: they must be possible worlds, possible histories, not untethered fantasies; and they must be born of creative energy, not dreamy fads.'[16] Whereas LeGuin notes that

> So many women are writing such imaginations now that it is surely a communal undertaking responding to a communal need. Those whose minds are locked in the conservatism of 'growth', and even 'higher' technology based on unlimited exploitation, see these tribal societies (real and imagined) only as escapist regressions; they cannot understand that women are studying such societies in a radical and subversive effort to think back to before things went wrong.[17]

It is not that Coetzee does not recognise the critical edge which Walker gives to her reinvention of history – he does – but more that, as a (white) African writer of historical fiction, he has difficulty with a notion of history as storytelling, whether that story is told by authoritative white males (in their own image and interest) or by counter-hegemonic black women who remember previous lives (in *their* own image and interest). In this case, the reviewers' own position as creative writers thus clearly forces their evaluation of *The Temple of My Familiar* in opposite directions, and it may be as well to remember the polarising effect that this novel tends to have on readers, depending on their political and epistemological orientations. I shall return to the question of history and storytelling in due course, but first we must look more closely at the narrative itself and its extensive cast of characters. The genre of the family saga might provide us with a more conventional map of reading than the Jungian approach of retrospective fantasy does but, as we shall see, the two are intimately connected.

Familiar Stories: Rewriting the Family Saga

Alice Walker's interest in the family saga was already apparent in *The Third Life of Grange Copeland* and in *The Color Purple*. Both are novels set in the South, and both of them tell the story of a dysfunctional family across generations, a family which is made whole again by the action of enlightened individuals. In *The Family Saga in the South* Robert O. Stephens surveys the long pedigree this genre has in Southern literature. He lists the major conventions of the family saga as follows:

continuity of the consanguine family through multiple generations; identity established at the time of removal to a new homeland; preservation of the family's special attribute; the lingering
influence of patriarchal–matriarchal conflicts; displacement of the
inheritance; decline in later generations when compared with the
strength or nobility of the earlier; work of a historian–narrator to
collect and evaluate evidence of the family past; correlation of
family history with public history; puzzlement about actions and
motivations of the ancestors; recognition of type scenes; awareness
of the significance of talismanic objects, places or actions; and
achievement of moments of vision.[18]

This is a fairly full description of what the genre – in popular as well
as 'literary' writing – entails, and some of the traits that Stephens
identifies are readily recognisable in Walker's work. And yet, rarely
will the white bias of a literary genre (or of the definition of it) have
been so clear as it is here. Although Stephens does discuss the black
family saga in his book as well, it is obvious in the description above
that the African American family saga is rather unlikely to have displaced inheritances as a major part of the plot, nor is identity likely to
be 'established at the time of removal to a new homeland', with the
family mansion serving as the Faulkneresque architectural expression of a dynasty's rise and fall. The plantation saga is where
Stephens's summary finds its full expression, and African American
family sagas can but be poor and deviant relations of this model.
Nevertheless, Stephens's schema for the family saga in the South is
useful because it sets us on the trail of Walker's revision of it, first in
The Third Life of Grange Copeland, where few of the features survive
other than in bitterly ironised form ('lingering patriarchal–matriarchal conflicts', for example), then in *The Color Purple* (where there
is a 'displaced inheritance' and a historian–narrator who achieves
moments of vision), and here in *The Temple of My Familiar*, where all
the conventions apply in metaphorised or reversed incarnations.
For a start, Walker redefines consanguinity, in the story which
brings Carlotta's and Suwelo's respective clans together, as spiritual
kinship – as I have already indicated – but a kinship also of the
African American and the Amerindian. And not for the first time:
remember Meridian's great-grandmother Feather Mae, and the
quotation from Black Elk in *The Color Purple*. Here Ola is writing a
play about Elvis as an Indian (213); Corinne's mother's turns out to

have been a Cherokee (172) and we are encouraged to read, as Fanny does, William Loren Katz's book *Black Indians*. Walker's theory about American hybridity is expressed, as so often, by Ola in this novel, who explains that

> in [Elvis] white Americans found a reason to express their longing and appreciation for the repressed Native American and black parts of themselves. Those non-European qualities they have within them and all around them, constantly, but which they have been trained from birth to deny. [*sic*] (214)

The message could not be stated more clearly. The second characteristic of the family saga on Stephens's list, identity, is therefore established here not as a unitary thing but as a recognition of hybridity, and it is done not through settlement but through migration and return. And if we follow the list further, other revisions of the convention also come into focus: 'decline in later generations' here and elsewhere becomes progress in later generations, and the family's 'special attribute' is, if anything, abuse and conflict – notably 'matriarchal/patriarchal conflict' writ large – which are not to be preserved, but resolved. In *The Third Life of Grange Copeland* the theme was the perpetuation of abuse against women and children, across generations, and how to change it. Grange's migration to the North, the political education he receives there and the love he finds, upon his return, for his granddaughter Ruth are the three factors which enable him to redeem himself, the South and a future for Ruth. Migration then – here in the shape of the Great Migration which drew so many Southern blacks in the early part of the century to the Northern industrial cities – is a key element in this early family saga, but equally important is the trope of return to the homeland of the South. Migration enables enlightenment, but it is the return which makes reconciliation and redemption possible. It is probably no coincidence that, as Hazel Carby points out, this same trope of educational journey and a return which then enables the sharing of insights gained, is also evident in one of Walker's favourite novels, Zora Neale Hurston's *Their Eyes Were Watching God*: 'Janie, as intellectual, has travelled outside of the community and defines herself as "a delegate to de big 'ssociation of life"; her journey is the means by which knowledge can be brought into the community', Carby argues.[19] Something similar occurs in *The Color Purple*, if we can see

Nettie's journey to Africa as having a role to play in Celie's education, and Shug's multiple departures and returns as part of her
experiences of the wider world which in turn benefit Celie. She,
unlike Grange and Janie, does not have the opportunity to explore
that world directly but Celie's and Nettie's correspondence and
Shug's blues singing are – not just instrumental in, but actually con-
stitutive of, Celie's own journey from victim to heroine, without her
ever having to leave home. *The Color Purple* as a family saga therefore
takes the themes of repetitive abuse and migration/return further
than *The Third Life of Grange Copeland*. It begins, in the mould of the
earlier novel, as a figuration of the break-up of the African American
family reminiscent of slavery, with family members bought and sold
and gender relations in the black family mimicking those of the master and slave on the plantation. We might also note that *The Color
Purple* even has a Middle Passage in reverse, when Nettie travels to
Africa as a missionary. This journey severs her, albeit unwittingly,
from her sister in America through the intervention of Mr___ in the
role of Celie's 'Master' and owner, just as the slaves were cut off from
their African families when being brought from Africa to America.
The novel ends, however, with an integration of the acculturated
'African' and American branches of this fragmented family, when
Nettie returns with Celie's now Africanised children Adam and Olivia, the latter of whom reappears in *The Temple of My Familiar*. Adam's
African wife Tashi, moreover, becomes the protagonist of Walker's
fifth novel, *Possessing the Secret of Joy*, thus making a trilogy of the
adventures of Celie's ever-growing family tree. At the same time, of
course, these three novels become a family saga in themselves in that
they are books which continue each other in the most literal sense:
they form a textual family.

The role of Stephens's narrator–historian is most visible in *The
Temple of My Familiar*, although Nettie's efforts to piece her and
Celie's histories together *and* to put them in context and connect
them with the public history of colonialism and Southern racism
deserve mention here as well. In a sense, the role of historian–
narrator is duly divided in that novel between the sisters, with Nettie
as the historian, writing in a public discourse, and Celie as the vernacular narrator. Narrative perspective in *The Temple of My Familiar*,
which is third-person but shifts from section to section, does not
allow for the conventional younger family member to try and puzzle
out her history by reading diaries, hearing stories and leafing

through photo albums. Instead, *The Temple of My Familiar* has multiple historians and narrators, some of whom conform to the model very closely (Mary Jane Briden, Suwelo), whereas others – notably Miss Lissie – act primarily as sources, and others, again, are detectives who intrepidly go out in search of clues and follow them through. Fanny is a good example of the latter, and it is not so very startling, given her postmodern condition of psychic fragmentation and feminist frustration, that her clues lead her eventually to the therapist's consulting room. This, we may say, is a very strange family saga indeed, but then that is Walker's point: our true family cannot be found in the home, but first in familiarisation with the self and then in connection with like-spirited others, and finally with the universe.

As will be clear from what I have said so far, it is difficult, even impossible, to describe the plot of *The Temple of My Familiar* in anything but the broadest *or* the most detailed terms. As a family saga, or rather: as yet another revision of the conventional family story with its generational continuities and structural linearity, it is the story of how two families come together at the end through multiple migrations of mind and body. Beginning with Zedé and Carlotta's flight from Central America to California, where Carlotta meets and marries Arveyda in San Francisco, the story then moves to Suwelo's recent journey from San Francisco to Baltimore, where he meets Mr Hal and Miss Lissie, the 'elders' who become his guiding spirits in a process of re-education which takes him from straight and rational thinking into the convoluted (oral) histories of the people of the African diaspora. Suwelo's wife Fanny takes her own journey to Africa in order to grow and to shed her hatred of whites. If we concentrate just on this set of main characters, we see how at the end the two opposing couples (Arveyda and Carlotta, Fanny and Suwelo) cross over and mix into an extended family or 'tribe', epitomised by Fanny's recognition of Arveyda as her spirit, and Arveyda's of Fanny as his flesh (449).

But a lot of water has to flow under the bridge before they get there. Their stories are criss-crossed by others, picked up and dropped in a seemingly haphazard way. *The Temple of My Familiar* is packed with stories and sub-stories; its structure – insofar as one is discernible – resembling nothing so much as a Russian doll-type sequence of embedded narratives. Looked at more closely, it becomes clear that all these mini-stories have something to contribute to the larger frame of Arveyda and Carlotta, Suwelo and Fanny.

The story about ancient traditions of worship of the Mexican goddess, which Zedé uncovers in Central America when she goes there
with Arveyda, for example, is later echoed by Miss Lissie's memory of
goddess worship in an African context. When Fanny goes to Africa
she, in turn, finds out about the kinship between cults around
Medusa, Isis and Athena – yet another group of goddesses later
replaced by male idols. Every element, however seemingly anecdotal, is echoed by another, usually one from a different cultural
context. Or take the story Arveyda hears in his home town, Terre
Haute, from the Jewish greengrocer Mr Isaac. He, having left Palestine for America, one day decides to go back to Israel because he
misses hearing the sound of the Arab language with which he grew
up: 'For Arabs had lived all around him in Palestine, just as colored
people lived all around him in Terre Haute' (26). Mr Isaac, then, is
another migrant who learns something on his travels, even if it is
something he actually already knew.

Perhaps the best characterisation I can give of *The Temple of My
Familiar* is that it is a 'talking book', a book of stories. Divided into five
parts and dozens of chapters, again we see Walker's preference for
the short form, albeit in a novel of epic proportions. But then storytelling is another Southern convention, as Eudora Welty recalls:

> As it happens, we in the South have grown up being narrators. We
> have lived in a place … where storytelling is a way of life. [… .] We
> heard stories told by relatives and friends. A great many of them
> were family tales. … If we weren't around when something hap-
> pened, way back, at least we think we know what it was like simply
> because we've heard it so long.[20]

The Temple of My Familiar is a storytelling book not because, in Welty's
sense, people are rooted in place and community and therefore
exchange familiar tales, but precisely because they *lack* such a sense
of place and connection: storytelling is a way to achieve it. The narrative frame therefore surrounds representation of a variety of cultural practices in which people pass on their knowledge and
experiences. Little actually 'happens' in it, but what action there is is
conveyed through exchanges of stories: Miss Lissie reminisces in
person and on audiotape, in letters and in the paintings that she
leaves Suwelo. Mary Jane/Ann Briden discovers her great aunt's Victorian diary in a library in England, and we read extracts from that

diary. Suwelo sorts through Uncle Rafe's belongings and finds among them Miss Lissie's muddied white high-heeled shoes, a material reminder of her life in the South in the 1950s. Fanny goes into therapy and recounts her story and her feelings about being a black woman in America to her therapist – a Chicana woman, and therefore of mixed ancestry like herself. Arveyda learns from his trip with Zedé; Suwelo learns from Lissie's time travelling, Fanny from her analyst and her African father and sister, and Mary Jane/Ann from her own family history. The formal and thematic revision of the Southern family saga which Walker undertakes in this and previous novels thus neatly fits in with the storytelling tradition of her native South, as it does with the process of re-education that the characters, and we as readers, undergo in engaging with *The Temple of My Familiar*. We might even say that ultimately we are the ones who have to undertake the task of the historian–narrator ourselves in joining up the disparate strands presented in the novel. The family saga, then, provides one possible trace, whereas hybridity and the African diaspora represent another, as we shall see.

Continents Lost and Gained: Hybridity and the Black Diaspora

Walker's textual family has its members increasingly scattered across the globe. *Possessing the Secret of Joy* is set predominantly in Africa but also in Europe and the United States, and *The Temple of My Familiar* moves backwards and forwards between the United States, Africa, Central America and Europe. Following on from *The Color Purple*'s final reunion of Celie's and Nettie's families, its main focus is on Africa and the United States, but the cultural formation and 'place-ment' of African Americans is here made more complex by the tracing of connections with Indians and Europeans as well. Hybridity is the key in all these migrations. The trip that Fanny, Olivia's daughter (and Celie's granddaughter), takes to Africa, for example, may at first seem indicative of a search for her African roots. Fanny writes that upon meeting Nzingha Anne, her African half-sister, she felt that she was looking into a mirror which reflected only the African (279). Fanny, it appears, has found some kind of racial essence or truth about herself in her sister, but on closer inspection it is not quite as simple as that. For what Fanny discovers is a reconnection with *part* of herself, a part (call it blackness or – more accurately – a different,

non-Western and non-oppressive mode of being) which has been denied expression in white-dominated America. What looks like a reflection of an essence is in fact, as the critic Terry Dehay puts it, a
revelation of something deeper and rather less narcissistic:

> Fanny's discovery of her African self, and also of the truth of the
> socio-political nature of Africa, helps her to integrate the separate
> parts of herself and to reconstruct the nature of her relationship
> with the culture in which she lives. [....] She confronts her anger
> with white society by returning to the African country that repre-
> sents *half* of her cultural heritage, where she learns that her anger
> is real but that in directing it at white people, she is missing the real
> target: any society that represses the enemy, regardless of color
> [my emphasis].[21]

Dehay's final phrase recalls the parable of the imprisoned familiar
which escapes, but with a variation: any society that represses anything (including its friends, which it cannot recognise as such) is the
enemy. In Africa, after all, Fanny finds that governments and ruling
elites oppress minority peoples and suppress dissident opinions –
like those of her father, the playwright Ola – in ways that are not so
dissimilar from Western societies, and this is what Dehay means by
Fanny's discovery of 'the socio-political nature of Africa'. Africa is
thus not represented here as the homeland that Fanny as an African
American can 'return to' in order to find her 'true self', for her true
self is more dynamic and variegated than that. Fanny is indeed a
woman of many parts, of which Africa and America are but two.
Dehay also draws attention to the fact that Fanny's journey to Africa
is one of two journeys to a real or imagined 'home' in this novel. Zedé
travels to Central America after she and Arveyda (her son-in-law)
have fallen in love. For Zedé, born and bred there,

> [I]t is a true return from exile to the Central American country
> that was her home and to herself as a member of that cultural real-
> ity. Her return and remembering of herself also enables her
> daughter, Carlotta, to incorporate this remembered identity into
> her own sense of self as a Latina living in the United States.[22]

Not Zedé's and Fanny's journeys are paralleled here so much as
the tasks that both Fanny and Carlotta face as hybrid citizens of the

United States, *their* homeland, in integrating the different parts of their parents' histories and cultural heritages. And it is no accident that both Fanny and Carlotta live in San Francisco, where the mix of races and ethnicities is particularly apparent. Early on in the novel Arveyda, the rock star from Terre Haute, Indiana, sees himself 'mirrored' in Carlotta's Indian looks. Carlotta, likewise, feels a kinship with the Hmong people in the Bay area: 'who seemed particularly intense and ancient to her, as they carried their tiny babies on their backs in bright multicolored clothing covered with mirrors, bells, shells and beads' (19). Such bells and shells are Carlotta's instruments towards the end of the novel, when she has reconciled herself with Arveyda and become a musician herself. Fanny, Carlotta and Arveyda, then, are all of mixed ancestry, and their enlightenment consists in coming to terms with that fact, not in a negative or resigned way but by learning from the diverse cultures and histories which have gone into their making. In various ways, this is true of all the main characters: either literally or metaphorically, they are of mixed ancestry and have to learn to integrate – first with themselves and then also with each other. It is true even of Miss Lissie, because she – who has lived *and remembers* many previous lives – in the end also has to face up to the fact that she was a white man in at least one of them (and one in which s/he kills the familiar, rather than merely letting it escape). Among the more ordinary mortals Mr Hal, who describes to Suwelo his childhood on the islands off the coast of Baltimore as blissful, because removed from white people, goes through his own process of enlightenment and reconciliation when he makes friends with Mr Pete, a Southern white 'cracker' in the nursing home where he ends up after Lissie's death.

If we think of migration, re-education and integration as major themes, then, it no longer seems so bewildering (or so bad) that *The Temple of My Familiar* is a book to get lost in. Eva Lennox Birch says in *Black American Women's Writing* that '[It] demands a high level of reader sophistication to handle the diversity of characters, and their interrelationships, as well as shifts in time and location.'[23] This is true, if you are looking to restore a conventional narrative order, but this may not be the point. Another way of understanding the novel is to see that Walker does here what Toni Morrison said of *Beloved*, that it 'yanked' the reader – through sheer disorientation and confusion – into the world of the slaves, or, more particularly, into a similarly disrupted subjectivity to that of those who experienced the Middle

Passage and its subsequent physical and cultural violations.[24] *The Temple of My Familiar* does not, of course, reproduce the violence of slavery but rather the complexity and geographical, familial and cultural negotiations of the history of the black diaspora, that which Paul Gilroy has called – in his book of that title – the black Atlantic. For Gilroy, the paradigm of absolute cultural difference between black and white, Eurocentric and African traditions, is not only worn out by now, but was probably always a misrepresentation of the actuality of interchange and cultural mixing in the traffic between not two, but at least three, continents: Africa, the Americas and Europe. Gilroy writes:

> Regardless of their affiliation to the right, left or centre, groups have fallen back on the idea of cultural nationalism, on the over-integrated conceptions of culture which present immutable, ethnic differences as an absolute break in the histories of 'black' and 'white' people. Against this choice stands another, more difficult option: the theorisation of creolisation, métissage, mestizaje, and hybridity.[25]

Gilroy then proceeds to offer just such a theorisation of hybridity, in an effort to make us think more productively and more accurately about the interconnections, as well as the differences, between Western culture and that of Africa and its diaspora. And he is not the only one whose intellectual energy is, in the context of postmodernity and globalisation, devoted to a reconceptualisation of black/white oppositions and their attendant cultural simplifications. In his seminal work *In My Father's House* the philosopher Kwame Anthony Appiah attempts just such a project, beginning with his own experience of a diasporic family, which it is worth quoting at length:

> This book is dedicated to nine children – a boy born in Botswana, of Norwegian and Anglo-Ghanaian parents; his brothers, born in Norway and in Ghana; their four cousins, three boys in Lagos, born of Nigerian and Anglo-Ghanaian parents, and a girl in Ghana; and two girls, born in New Haven, Connecticut, of an African-American father and a 'white' American mother. These children, my nephews and my godchildren, range in appearance from the color and hair of my father's Asante kinsmen to the

Viking ancestors of my Norwegian brother-in-law; they have names from Yorubaland, from Asante, from America, from Norway, from England. And watching them playing together and speaking to each other in their various accents, I, at least, feel a certain hope for the human future.[26]

It is not just the last sentence which echoes Alice Walker's sentiments in *The Temple of My Familiar*, delighting in this rainbow coalition of familial ties. It is also the fact that it would be as complicated to describe the two 'clans' which merge into one in that novel as it is for Appiah to enumerate the members of his family of various ethnic and national descents. Walker's families, deriving from South America, the United States and Africa, and the rest of her cast of characters, which incorporates Europe as well, are no fanciful anomalies or merely the fruits of wishful multicultural thinking; they exist in the real world in ever-increasing numbers. Nor is it the case that Appiah's diasporic family, or Arveyda's multifarious new age clan, are simply produced by class mobility (Appiah is a member of the Asante royal family in Ghana), educational privilege (which got him to England and later America), or by the cosmopolitanism that success affords. Migration, for poor peoples as well as rich individuals, is a feature of the postmodern world, as is the mixing and matching of races, ethnicities and cultures that goes along with increasing globalisation of the economy and the media. For this reason alone theorists like Gilroy or Appiah feel impelled to look again at our concepts of racial and cultural difference, and to critique the histories of Western nationalism as well as those of Pan-Africanism and black cultural nationalism in the United States, since these concepts and histories are no longer viable today. This is, however, the only thing they have in common with Walker's project in *The Temple of My Familiar*, for Walker is – as noted earlier – more concerned with spiritual lessons to be learned from diasporic cultures than she is interested in their historical development or theoretical validity. As a novelist rather than a theorist, Walker sees her task as an imaginative project of revaluation and revisioning, in which the word 'vision' is crucial: what is present in the past can be uncovered, and can be mobilised in order to make for a brighter future. But there is more to be said about Appiah's hope for humans when he looks at the children of the diaspora playing together. Wolfgang Karrer writes of Walker's characters that they may travel to South America or Africa or even Baltimore, but their true home is their common history, the history of humanity embodied in the goddess Lissie. [. . . .] Walker makes them citizens of a multicultural and interethnnic world where going home means going forward into new relationships.[27]

Karrer's observation about 'home' as the 'history of humanity' and Appiah's hope for a multi-ethnic future remind us of what Alice Walker writes in the essay 'Saving the Life that Is Your Own' about the future of literature as 'an immense story coming from a multitude of different perspectives' (see Chapter 1).[28] It is possible that Walker meant to explain that black and white writing complement each other, and that together they make up the multicoloured quilt that is 'this immense story' of world literature. But it is also possible to read this statement differently, in the light of Walker's concerns in *The Temple of My Familiar*, for here she seems to pack the 'multitude of different perspectives' into one novel, which includes the stories of white Europeans as well as those of Native Americans, African Americans, Jews and Africans, men and women. As we have seen, this is not just a matter of content. Walker draws on a 'white' Southern genre like the family saga, but also on South American magic realism, on the oral, storytelling traditions of Africa and African America, on an historical fantasy like Virginia Woolf's *Orlando* and on Jungian psychoanalysis.

Writing Diaspora

These various genres and forms are, moreover, used in their appropriate contexts. Suwelo and Fanny are principally involved in the family saga, while Miss Lissie performs the role of the African *griot* (or village storyteller) and keeper of ancient wisdom. The features of magic realism are especially evident at the beginning, fittingly, in the story of Zedé and Carlotta's existence in an unspecified Central American country:

Life was so peaceful that Zedé did not realize they were poor. She found this out when her father, a worker on the banana plantation they could also see from their house, became ill. At the same time, by

coincidence, the traditional festivals of the village were forbidden.
By whom they were forbidden, or 'outlawed' as her father said,
Zedé was not sure. The priests, especially, were left with nothing to
do. [. . . .] Her father, a small, tired, brownskin man with graying
black hair died while she was an earnest scholarship student at the
university, far away in the noisy capital. Her mother now made
her living selling her incredibly beautiful feather goods to the cold
little gringa blonde who had a boutique on the ground floor of an
enormous new hotel that sprung up near their village, seemingly
overnight. (12)

The style of this passage, with its juxtaposition of rural idyll with
approaching modernity and political unrest without concrete reference to a particular time and place, is reminiscent of Latin American
fiction. It raises more questions and mystery than it actually answers,
in order to keep us guessing but also to posit an alternative reality
and sense of time and place to that which the conventional realist
novel offers. Later Zedé becomes a schoolteacher and ends up in
prison, from which she is rescued by Mary Ann Haverstock (later
Mary Jane Briden), then still a young American woman with radical
inclinations and family money to burn, who brings Carlotta and
Zedé to America in her aptly named yacht *Recuerdo* (memory). Such
happenings, as well as the narrative of Carlotta's father Jesús and his
role in the jungle as keeper of the (holy) stones, 'something not
understood by norte americanos; this I know' (88), Zedé says, would
not be out of place in any Isabel Allende novel or a story by Gabriel
García Márquez. The use of magic realism is more obvious as pastiche (as it is when Miss Lissie is described, later on, as having been
born without a hymen (104)) than the ways in which Walker draws
on Woolf's *Orlando* and Jungian psychoanalysis in *The Temple of My
Familiar*. The opening paragraph of *Orlando* is cited at the beginning
of Part Four, in which Fanny writes her letters to Suwelo from Africa,
where she is discovering her heritage. That heritage includes a
family history of women warriors, but Fanny's letters also incorporate
her critique of African gender relations and they tell Suwelo of her
father Ola's new play, in which he belatedly atones for his abandonment of his first ('bush') wife. All this makes sense as a counter-nar-
rative to Woolf's historical fantasy *Orlando*, whose beginning reads:
'He – for there could be no doubt of his sex, although the fashion of
the time did something to disguise it – was in the act of slicing at the

head of a Moor which swung from the rafters' (262). *Orlando* is now
chiefly known as the novel in which Woolf put her androgynous theory of writing into practice, but it is also the artistic biography of a
poet who lives from the seventeenth through to the twentieth century. Its often ironic tone with regard to gender and official historiography tends to obscure the colonialist assumptions it makes about
English identity, right from this first sentence. In *The Temple of My
Familiar* Walker creates just such historical fantasy with an even
broader time span than *Orlando*, in which gender roles become mut-
able not through a change of body (Orlando undergoes a sex-
change) but a change of mind. In Fanny's letters, the empire 'writes
back' to *Orlando* to remind us of Africa's history before colonialism
and women's role within it (like that of Nzingha, the Angolan war-
rior-queen). Part of Walker's polemical engagement with *Orlando*
also is the fact that the artist takes centre stage here not as a
noble(wo-)man poet, but as a creative practitioner for everyday use;
Carlotta, for example, becomes a musician and Fanny a playwright.
They do so not through the usual route prescribed by artists' biographies, charting their sensitive childhood years and showing their
early (and initially misrecognised) predisposition towards artistic
genius. Instead, both pick up their creativity along the way, not as
some exceptional talent which they discover but rather as a new
interest, a mode of co-operative work inspired by other people – the
professional artists like Ola and Arveyda. The conception of the artist here is thus very different from the traditional one in that Zedé's
craft with her feathers, Arveyda's music, Ola's plays and also Fanny's
massage skills are shown as all on a continuum of creative *work*, involving the body as much as the mind and spirit. M'Sukta, Mr Hal and
Miss Lissie's painting are part of this continuum as well: M'Sukta is a
hut painter, not one who is engaged in fine art in the Western sense,
yet the painting school which Mary Jane establishes in her honour
builds on this indigenous tradition in order to foster the development of African art. We might look to Jung again for some background to this kind of creativity. Describing how difficult it is in
therapy to reshape the conscious ego of troubled adults who have
already found a role in the world (even if they are not happy with it),
Jung advocates creative expression as a means of access to the collective unconscious, and therefore of connection with the primeval
past and with the universal archetypal images. Of this type of patient
he says:

Social usefulness is no longer an aim for him, although he does not deny its desirability. Fully aware as he is of the social unimportance of his creative activity, he feels it more as a way of working at himself to his own benefit. Increasingly, too, this activity frees him from morbid dependence, and he thus acquires an inner stability and a new trust in himself.[29]

This valuation of creativity *as* therapy or self-fulfilment characterises Suwelo and Fanny, Carlotta and Arveyda at the end; they are less artists than craftspeople, and less craftspeople than *amateurs* in the true sense of that word: people who do what they do for the love of it. It is tempting to interpret Walker's continuum of artistic production as a comment on the state of the modern novel, and to read it as a loss of faith in writing as still important in the postmodern world. Her forays into film-making (with Steven Spielberg on *The Color Purple* and with Pratibha Parmar on *Warrior Marks*) might support such a view, if we believe that they signal Walker's recognition of the fact that we now live in a media-dominated, post-literate culture. But I do not think any great enthusiasm for visual media or the new information technologies is evident in the novel. The arts and crafts that Walker's characters turn to in *The Temple of My Familiar* are, if anything, of a pre-modern, more organic kind: massage rather than video performance, and live percussion rather than electronic music. The distinction that the critic Susan Willis makes between mass and popular culture might be useful here. Willis writes:

[P]opular culture defines a cultural community where the producers of culture are also its consumers. [....] This community of production/consumption is cancelled out by mass culture, which is synonymous with capitalist culture, and the commodity form, whose primary feature is the distinct separation between those who control and produce the cultural commodity and those who buy it. Mass culture limits participation to consumption.[30]

In Willis's terms, *The Temple of My Familiar* foregrounds the kinds of cultural practices which belong to popular culture *as a mode of resistance* to mass culture's incursions into subjectivity and daily life. In the light of this novel's message that the future for humankind lies in a reconnection with the earth, the spirit and most of all with the other (first and foremost the other within ourselves), we might read its form as an experimental one which attempts to reconnect literary representation with more 'organic', collaborative modes of imagining which reunite the realms of production and consumption. And we can come at this formal experimentation from an intertextual angle, too. Besides Virginia Woolf, the African novelist Bessie Head also plays a part in *The Temple of My Familiar*. Head expressed her faith in the future of writing in her autobiographical essay 'Notes on Novels' thus:

> I have found that the novel form is like a large rag-bag into which one can stuff anything – all of one's philosophical, social and romantic speculations. I have always reserved a special category for myself, as a writer – that of a pioneer blazing a new trail into the future. It would seem as though Africa rises at a point in history when world trends are more hopefully against exploitation, slavery and oppression – all of which has been synonymous with the name, Africa. I have recorded whatever hopeful trend was presented to me in an attempt to shape the future, which I hope will be one of dignity and compassion.[31]

The novel as 'rag-bag' and the writer blazing a new trail into the future accurately describe what Walker in *The Temple of My Familiar* is doing, and it is surely no coincidence that Head relates this new form explicitly to the history and current status of Africa as a continent of exploitation and the African novel as a counteracting force. Ngũgĩ wa Thiong'o, whom I cited earlier, says something very similar in 'The Language of African Fiction':

> Not so long ago the novel, like God, was declared dead, at least in its eighteenth and nineteenth century forms. There was even a movement in search of a *nouveau roman* but I am not sure whether there was also a movement in search of a new God or, for that matter, whether the search was fruitful. What's clear is that something answering to the name 'novel' has been showing significant signs of life somewhere in Africa and Latin America. The death of the novel was not therefore one of my problems.[32]

Like Bessie Head – like Alice Walker also, I think – Ngũgĩ expresses here a confidence in the future of the novel which is closely allied to post-colonial and to political writing, as a mode of resistance to the

Western *episteme* of realism, rationalism and individualism. The fact that he mentions the search for new gods in this extract as well is fortuitous, because it enables me to draw a further analogy between Walker's choice of form in *The Temple of My Familiar*, her emphasis on hybridity and migration and new conceptions of the artist, on one hand, and the search for the goddess on the other.

J. M. Coetzee, in the review mentioned earlier in this chapter, says that '*The Temple of My Familiar* is a novel only in a loose sense. Rather, it is a mixture of mythic fantasy, revisionary history, exemplary biography and sermon. It is short on narrative tension, long on inspirational message.'[33] Coetzee is clearly critical of the mixture of fantasy and history, and he is surely right in his judgement that the novel lacks narrative tension. That, however, may not matter so much in light of the fact that Coetzee overlooks the role of gender and Walker's polemical engagement with the Western (male-dominated) literary tradition here. We should now be able to see how the author/ medium, in a novel which tries to write the black diaspora and documents the search for the forgotten goddess, abandons the authority of the author as god and puts the goddess (or, in Eva Lennox Birch's words, 'a prophetess') in its place.[34] What does this mean? Ngũgĩ parallelled the search for a new novel form with the search for a new god, and we might say that in *The Temple of My Familiar* we have such a new form and a new she-god. For those who accept the validity in Western culture of binary oppositions such as nature/culture, mind/ body and male/female, the analogy might run something like this: whereas the nineteenth-century novel was concerned with empire, with the plight of the bourgeois male, with progress – the latter conceived as linear and mirrored in the novel's structure – and was narrated from the perspective of an omniscient author-as-god, the new age novel has the goddess as 'author' (or perhaps 'medium') and is therefore its opposite. Like female-centred religions, this novel works along maternal lines, aligns herself with nature and the body, with Africa and Central America, and with supposedly female qualities such as nurturing and healing. It has a cyclical rather than a linear structure, no plot to speak of – for it is not interested in the destination but in the journey – and its narration is conducted through multiple and speculative voices rather than just one authoritative one. You do not have to believe that binary oppositions operate in an essentialist and unchangeable way to see how they nevertheless function hierarchically in Western culture, and how

Walker's critique of the novel form and of the role of the author serve to highlight that hierarchy by upsetting it. The novel as 'ragbag' is thus a hybrid form which reflects its concern with diaspora and the hybridity of peoples and cultures; as a matrilinear text it borrows from Bessie Head and Virginia Woolf, and Miss Lissie's multiple lives represent the multiple – and silenced – voices of black women's history, including that of the ancient goddesses of Africa and Central America.

Remembering the Goddess: Challenging History Through Memory

Merlin Stone writes in *When God Was a Woman*:

> The theory that most societies were originally matrilineal, matriarchal and even polyandrous (one woman with several husbands) was the subject of several extensive studies in the late nineteenth and early twentieth centuries. Scholars such as Johann Bachofen, Robert Briffault and Edward Hartland accepted the idea of ancient matriarchy and polyandry, substantiating their theories with a great deal of evidence, but they regarded these systems as a specific stage in evolutionary development. They suggested that all societies had to pass through a matriarchal stage before becoming patriarchal and monogamous, which they appear to have regarded as a superior stage of civilization.[35]

Stone reminds us here of two things: that the study of ancient female-centred religion is not some recent invention or a crackpot radical feminist idea, *and* that scholarship is not necessarily true and objective knowledge production, but rather a cultural practice invested with particular ideological interests. In the nineteenth century – the age of scientific racism and of Darwinism, after all – those interests often concerned a validation of the status quo: of empire, patriarchy and of progress through the exploitation of the natural world. Clearly, Alice Walker wants to reverse this notion of evolutionary superiority, and she employs the character of Miss Lissie to do so. Miss Lissie is polyandrous (she has two 'husbands', Mr Hal and Uncle Rafe), and she has been a goddess as well as a witch in her times. She describes in a letter to Suwelo how – and why – her life as a witch ended:

'The first witches to die at the stake were the daughters of the Moors.' *Moors?* he mused skeptically. 'It was they (or, rather, we) who thought the Christian religion that flourished in Spain would let the Goddess of Africa "pass" into the modern world as the "Black Madonna"'. After all, this is how the gods and goddesses moved from era to era before, though Islam, our official religion for quite a long time by now, would have nothing to do with this notion; instead, whole families in Africa who worshipped the Goddess were routinely killed, sold into slavery, or converted to Islam at the point of the sword.

'Yes', and here Suwelo imagined a long, hesitant breath, 'I was one of those "pagan" heretics they burned at the stake.' (222)

Miss Lissie writes this letter in invisible ink, emphasising the invisibility of this largely forgotten history. However, her supposed 'memory' of being 'one of those "pagan" heretics who burned at the stake' does not enhance the credibility of this history; Lissie, as some critics have noted, is more a narrative device than a character in the conventional, realist sense – Ursula LeGuin calls her 'a whole cast of characters by herself'.[36] And yet, Miss Lissie's submerged history of the displacement of the Goddess by patriarchy is not something she, or Alice Walker, has simply made up. A body of scholarship now exists in feminist theology as well as mainstream archaeology which attests to the widespread existence in prehistory of goddess worship and of the violent means which were deployed (by Christians, Muslims and Levites) to eradicate it. Besides, in this extract Miss Lissie interestingly links up racism ('They burned us first – well, we were so visible') with the witch-hunts in Europe. Next, she describes how Christianity retained some of the ancient goddess worship from Africa, by combining the iconography of the Virgin Mary with that of black African goddesses like the Egyptian Isis or Nut/Neith or Hathor. This has a basis in fact: the Black Madonna is worshipped in places like northern Spain to this day. Third, she puts the blame on Christianity and Islam for eradicating the ancient female-centred religions by force, relating in the process how slavery was not just perpetrated by whites but was in fact already an indigenous practice of conquest in northern Africa. Merlin Stone advances a very similar argument in her book, except that she dates the northern invasion around 2400 BC, much earlier than the mediaeval times we tend to associate with witch hunts. Stone argues:

As the invaders gained more territories and continued to grow more powerful... this synthesized religion [the northern religion superimposed upon the native one] often juxtaposed the female and male deities not as equals but with the male as the dominant husband or even as Her murderer. Yet myths, statues and documentary evidence reveal the continual presence of the Goddess and the survival of the customs and rituals connected to the religion, despite the efforts of the conquerors to destroy or belittle the ancient worship.[37]

Miss Lissie thus in one short paragraph describes a potted (but not necessarily potty) version of a highly complex historical process. Unlike Miss Lissie, or a feminist writer like Merlin Stone, the historian Martin Bernal is not interested in gender specifically, but his famous two-volume study *Black Athena* also traces connections between goddess worship and iconographies of Greek and Egyptian figures. Strong similarities such as those between Athena and Neith, and Isis and Demeter, confirm Merlin Stone's and Miss Lissie's analyses of the mixture – the hybridity – of ancient religions during periods of cultural and political transition.[38] The need for a revised understanding of ancient history is pressed home when Bernal asserts that: 'it will be necessary not only to rethink the fundamental bases of "Western Civilization" but also to recognize the penetration of racism and "continental chauvinism" into all our historiography, or philosophy of writing history'.[39] This issue leads us back to the beginning of this chapter, to the status of *The Temple of My Familiar* as such a rethinking of Western civilisation as well as a recognition, not only of racism and Eurocentrism (Bernal's 'continental chauvinism'), but also of sexism in the writing of history. It also leads us back to Jung's notion of retrospective fantasy, and the material that can be found in ancient civilisations as expression of the collective unconscious and archetypal images.

As we have seen, fact and fantasy are almost inextricable from each other in Walker's novel, and this is one important reason why readers and critics have such trouble with it. On one hand, it may be more productive to go with the flow of narrative association than it is to try and distinguish which is which. On the other hand, some detective work can throw up intriguing possible sources and cross-cultural connections, which otherwise would remain invisible or inexplicable. One story which haunts the novel for me, for example,

is that of M'Sukta, the African woman who lives in the Natural
History Museum in London, where the aunt of Mary Jane Briden's
great aunt, Eleandra Burnham-Peacock, 'discovers' her as a live
exhibit. It seems incredible now that an African woman should have
been put on display in a European museum as some kind of natural
specimen. And yet: a South African woman called Saartjie Baartman
was paraded around Western Europe in the nineteenth century as a
natural specimen because of the size of her behind and her genitals –
she was billed as 'the Hottentot Venus'.[40] Furthermore, at the beginning of this century, Ishi, the last of the Californian Yahi Indians,
ended up on display in a museum at the behest of the anthropologist
Alfred Kroeber (who, interestingly, was Ursula LeGuin's grandfather, which might explain why LeGuin is sympathetic to *The Temple
of My Familiar*). The museum where Ishi 'lived' is what is now the
Phoebe Hearst Museum of Anthropology in Berkeley, not far from
Alice Walker's home. M. Steven Shackley, Assistant Research Archaeologist at the Phoebe Hearst Museum, begins his leaflet accompany-
ing the 1994 exhibition about Ishi thus: 'Ishi was not only one of
the last Native Americans to live the aboriginal lifeway, he was also
one of the last Native American stone tool makers. This display
exhibits the cores, debitage and arrowpoints produced by Ishi *while
he lived at the museum*' (my emphasis).[41] Ishi's fate, in other words, was
a likely model for M'Sukta. But there is more: Phoebe Hearst was a
philanthropist and heir to the Hearst newspaper empire, like Patricia Hearst, the 1960s rebel who caused a scandal by joining the
Symbionese Liberation Army after she had been kidnapped by them.
Patricia Hearst is in turn a possible model for Mary Ann Haverstock
– later Mary Jane Briden – in *The Temple of My Familiar*. Walker
makes her own comments on sources and inspiration in 'Turquoise
and Coral: The Writing of *The Temple of My Familiar*', and does not
mention any of the parallels I am tracing here.[42] Yet they are suggestive: the stories of both Hearst and Haverstock involve captivity
by American radicals and a subsequent crossing-over, in which they
shed their bourgeois aspirations and take up the radicals' cause
instead. M'Sukta and Ishi likewise, of course, are captives confronted
by a culture and ideology alien to their own. If we follow this trail
of associations and connections, we find another family history (that
of the Hearsts) and we discover another literary tradition: that of
the captivity narrative, which has a long ancestry in American literature.[43] We also see that Walker weaves an intricate web of hidden

references – or rather, allusions – which, once excavated, reveal new layers of significance. I would be tempted to call this allusive method again (as in Chapter 3) 'deep historiography': a revisioning which combines fact and fantasy, and which weaves together the methods of the (counter-)historiographer and of Jungian analysis.

The Temple of My Familiar interrogates official historiography in several ways. The first, and most obvious, is through storytelling as a means of passing on submerged or discredited forms of knowledge. At its most informal, Miss Lissie and Mr Hal do this by reminiscing with Suwelo about their lives on the island off the coast of Baltimore, but then, of course, Miss Lissie's memories take a different turn and become more mythical as she goes further back into her previous lives. At the same time, the ways in which her memories are recorded become increasingly formal: she writes, she uses audiotapes, and her paintings and old photographs become another material source for Suwelo to draw upon in his re-education. Arveyda also uses his art – his music – to communicate what he has learned, and Ola's plays and his meetings with Fanny tell her what she needs to know about her history. Fanny in turn passes this knowledge on to Suwelo in her letters. Unlike Suwelo, Fanny and Arveyda (who are in effect students and teachers of an oral and informal history) Mary Ann Haverstock, as a white woman, apparently has no such recourse to a living history. Her great-aunt Eleonora Burnham, whom she visits in a nursing home, is already a relic of the past – a confused old lady, and a racist to boot. Like a 'proper', scholarly historian, therefore, Mary Ann is left with the moth-eaten archive of her great-aunt's aunt, Eleandra Burnham-Peacock, only to discover that she, too, has precursors in the Victorian women travellers who went to Africa – and who were culture-crossers like herself.[44] The gaps in Eleandra's diary, as well as Suwelo's refusal to read the (academic) books that Fanny recommends to him, highlight the incompleteness and inaccessibility of the official, written record of what counts as knowledge in the Western world. Suwelo's practice had been that of what Carlotta calls a 'guerilla historian' (418):

> He wanted American history ... to forever be the centre of everyone's attention. What a few white men wanted, thought, and did. For he liked the way he could sneak in some black men's faces in later on down the line. And then trace those backward until they appeared even before Columbus. [....] But now to have to

consider African women writers and Kalahari bushmen! It was too much. (203)

Clearly, such revisionist history is no longer satisfactory for Suwelo. His plan, later on, to write an oral history of Miss Lissie and Mr Hal similarly comes to nothing, for it would be 'one of those unofficial-looking books, full of "he said" and "she said", that he'd always despised' (217). Just as Fanny decides to abandon books and to 'read trees instead', thereby going back to source as it were, Suwelo takes up carpentry in the end and abandons academia altogether. Both of them accept Miss Lissie's conviction that 'The time of writing is so different from the so much longer time of no writing. The time of living separate from the earth is so much different from the much longer time of living with it, as if being on your mother's breast' (401–2). The equation of literacy *per se* with separation from the earth is not one that the novel as a whole endorses, however – or else Walker would be rendering her own *métier* obsolete. Alongside the validation of orality there are also passages in the novel which emphasise the value of writing – academic as well as creative – because writing is also a way of preserving memory. The attentive reader comes away with an extensive bibliography of alternative or 'minority' literature and historiography, ranging from William Loren Katz to *Two Thousand Seasons* by Ayi Kwei Armah and – most notably – *Maru* and *A Question of Power* by Bessie Head. The reference to Head is particularly important, for *A Question of Power* is just as visionary a novel as *The Temple of My Familiar* wants to be, and has as its protagonist a woman who, like Miss Lissie, has two lovers and an extraordinarily rich psychic life. It is tempting, even, to see Head's character as the model for Miss Lissie, and to interpret the latter's name as an amalgam of Alice and Bessie. For Fanny Bessie Head's work is more important as a source of knowledge 'of a way of life that flowed for thousands of years [in Africa], which would otherwise be missing from the human record' than a whole library of history books (203). African scholars would dispute Fanny's notion that a twentieth-century writer can give us knowledge going back 'thousands of years' – in effect, such a belief deprives Africa of any history at all. The knowledge we can have about pre-literate societies from oral sources is different from that based on written transmission. Kwame Anthony Appiah, for example, argues that orality enables the 'image of knowledge as unchanging lore, handed down from the ancestors', but he also makes it clear that such an image is illusory, because it obscures the possibility of changes which have taken place and of inconsistent interpretations in the handing down of such oral traditions.[45] Yet Fanny's point still stands: novelists can illuminate parts of experience that historians simply cannot reach, even if such parts are ultimately conjectural and speculative – which is precisely their strength. But this is hardly news. What matters more here is the recognition that what looked like 'mythic fantasy' in *The Temple of My Familiar* to Coetzee, or new age home-grown philosophy to me at the beginning of this chapter, is actually shared ground between novelists, historians and post-colonial theorists. In other words: between all those who are interested in the gaps in official historiography and who think that memory and orality might be enlisted in writing new histories, histories this time not written exclusively from the point of view of the winners.

The Temple of My Familiar: Sites of Memory

Toni Morrison is another novelist interested in writing new histories aided by memory and imagination, as is evident in *Beloved*. She in turn draws on the work of other African American women writers before her:

> Zora Neale Hurston said: 'Like the dead-seeming cold rocks, I have memories within that came out of the material that went to make me.' These 'memories within' are the subsoil of my work. But memories and recollections won't give me total access to the unwritten interior life of these people. Only the act of imagination can help me.[46]

Morrison writes this in an essay called 'The Site of Memory', a title which she derives from the work of the French historian Pierre Nora; in *Beloved* she draws on Nora's ideas for her concept of 'rememory'. Nora's *lieux de mémoire* (sites of memory) are landmarks of the past invested by an individual or a group with 'symbolic and political significance', as Géneviève Fabre and Robert O'Meally's explain in *History & Memory in African-American Culture*. A site of memory, in this rather general definition, can therefore be a monument, a photograph, a story, a book, an historical figure, – indeed almost anything which generates 'processes of imaginative recollection and the historical consciousness.'[47] This is not an easy concept to grasp, since sites of memory as (usually material) repositories of the past are not mere archives, as Nora himself points out, and neither are they simply a source of alternative knowledges or of memories which have not found their way into official historiography. For Nora, sites of memory lie somewhere *between* living memory and history: 'We speak so much of memory because there is so little of it left.'[48] In the absence, or ever-accelerating rupture, of traditional ways of life, of ancient custom and of ritual under the postmodern condition of globalisation and the hybridisation of cultures, the past can no longer be preserved in what Nora calls 'spontaneous memory', but passes into history which 'is the reconstruction, always problematic and incomplete, of what is no longer'.[49] We might parallel Nora's insight with the passing of orality into literacy, where a similar movement from living and dynamic memory into a fixed and inevitably incomplete 'record' can be perceived. The study of material culture, of music (such as the blues), of vernacular language or – indeed – of religious practices can therefore lead us, as sites of memory, into a forgotten, suppressed or even an unconscious past, but only if such sites are invested by a group or by an individual with symbolic significance and with the *intention* to remember. Both Walker and Morrison, in *The Temple of My Familiar* and in *Beloved*, are interested in such in-between spaces of remembering where memory can be brought to life through the imagination, but whereas Walker creates Miss Lissie as an incarnation of age-old spontaneous memory who leaves various sites of memory behind after her death, the ghostly presence of Beloved serves a very different function. The contrast is worth drawing out, because it goes to the heart of Walker's and Morrison's quite different projects in rewriting African American history: for Morrison, as for Walker, sites of memory have a role to play in coming to terms with a traumatic past, but unlike Walker, Morrison's imaginative work in reconstructing the experience of slavery cannot *redeem* the trauma of that experience. For Morrison, mourning remains necessary, and Beloved's story is therefore 'not a story to pass on', even if, paradoxically, it *is* passed on in the novel. *Beloved's* ambivalent ending, in which something is resolved but something – an irreducible core of grief – is also left over, has led critics to psychoanalytic readings in which Freud's notion of *Nachträglichkeit*, or retrospective action, provides a way of articulating a tension between the present and the past which Morrison deliberately leaves in place.[50] What Walker does in *The Temple of My Familiar*, and which I have explained with reference to the Jungian idea of *zurückphantasieren* or retrospective fantasy, is to *dissolve* such traumatic tension by creating a past to serve present needs.[51]

If we take Nora's ideas to *The Temple of My Familiar*, then, we can identify Miss Lissie as a fantasy figure in whom the *desire* for spontaneous memory going back for thousands of years is personified. All by herself she represents both ancient and more recent pasts, but even she is not immortal. After her death she leaves various sites of memory behind: all the forms of cultural transmission which I listed above (letters, tapes, diaries, photographs, conversations, paintings, music) are repositories of the past invested by Suwelo with the 'symbolic and political significance' that Fabre and O'Meally, following Nora, talked about. Suwelo uses the 'archive' of Miss Lissie's legacy to educate himself and those around him; he constructs from it an alternative history for African Americans which has a redemptive force, unlike the history of slavery which Morrison reimagines in *Beloved*.

Other sites of memory of the black diaspora enable Walker in this novel to make cross-cultural connections which otherwise would remain invisible or seem too tenuous to hold. The most disturbing of these, in my view, is the story of M'Sukta, as noted previously. M'Sukta's degraded condition, living as 'The Savage in the Stacks', as the Victorian newspaper headline has it, a simulacrum of an 'authentic African' but also the last of her tribe to survive, echoes that of the young woman in a glass cage whom Suwelo sees in a peepshow (270–1). That image in turn recalls an episode where Miss Lissie holds up a mirror to caged lions in the zoo. What is the implication of these parallels? M'Sukta, the stripper, the lions: all are live exhibits, objects of fascination, pleasure, exoticism, fantasy – but they are also historically and culturally specific. M'Sukta's plight is clearly objectionable and shocking to us, whereas that of the lions and the stripper are much more familiar, if not entirely acceptable, perhaps. The imagery which links them links them also with the imprisoned familiar and makes visible that what is 'normal' in one era becomes grotesque in another. One day the familiar will escape and we may find it unbelievable that once upon a time civilised people were in the habit of putting naked women and wild animals on display for fun. On the face of it, what is grotesque about M'Sukta *as a site of memory* is the accrued significance of the normality of scientific racism in the nineteenth century.

But this, it turns out, is only one side of the coin. M'Sukta's story, as Mary Ann Briden discovers it in her great-great-aunt's diaries, is not unambiguously and simply a tale of racist objectification. For, through her frequent visits to the museum Lady Burnham-Peacock learns a great deal about M'Sukta and her culture and it inspires her to go to Africa herself. M'Sukta is thus not only a site of memory for the crimes of colonialism, but also for an ancient philosophy and a way of life, as Ishi, the last Californian Indian, was also. Moreover, the anthropologist Sir Henley Rowanbotham, who 'rescued' M'Sukta, may not be the villain, but in fact the hero of the piece because he is the one who ensures that she can live in the museum and therefore pass on her tribe's way of life when there is no one else left to do so. Neither is there anyone left who understands her language, which is why 'Rowanbotham had dubbed her "the African Rosetta stone"' (258).

It is difficult to know what to make of this, other than to remind ourselves of the story of how the Indians came to be named, which I recounted at the beginning of this chapter. There, also, Walker inverted the colonial narrative (of misnaming) by giving it a positive twist (in Dios = in God), which is what happens here. M'Sukta may be dehumanised and reduced to object-status, but *as* a site of memory she can nevertheless be a source of knowledge and a transmitter of culture. As Nora writes:

> Contrary to historical objects . . . *lieux de mémoire* have no referent in reality; or rather, they are their own referent: pure, exclusively self-referential signs. This is not to say that they are without content, physical presence, or history; it is to suggest that what makes them *lieux de mémoire* is precisely that by which they escape from history. In this sense, the *lieu de mémoire* is double: a site of excess closed upon itself, concentrated in its own name, *but also forever open to the full range of its possible significations*. (my emphasis)[52]

M'Sukta is, like the Rosetta stone and like Nora's self-referential sign, *both* indecipherable and enigmatic *and* is in the end 'readable' by those who are willing and able to understand her in and on her own terms. M'Sukta as a site of memory with at least two ostensibly opposed meanings (as colonial object *and* historical subject) helps us to see how Walker writes not simply a counter-history to the domin-ant one, but a different *kind of* history which does not try to suppress or eliminate memory but actively incorporates it and infuses it with imagination. The historian Howard Zinn has described the domin-ant account of American history thus:

> The treatment of heroes (Columbus) and their victims (the Arawaks) – the quiet acceptance of conquest and murder in the name of progress – is only one aspect of a certain approach to his-tory, in which the past is told from the point of view of govern-ments, conquerors, diplomats, leaders. [. . . .] The pretense is that there really is such a thing as 'the United States', subject to occa-sional conflicts and quarrels, but fundamentally a community of people with common interests. [. . . .] My viewpoint, in telling the history of the United States, is different: that we must not accept the memory of states as our own. Nations are not communities and never have been.[53]

Zinn's *A People's History of the United States* replaces the memory of states with the memory of a diverse people. I think that Walker's *The Temple of My Familiar* rewrites the memory of the United States as the memory of the black diaspora, which is always already suffused with that of Europe, South America and native America. What unites Jungian psychoanalysis, the family saga, diaspora writing and the desire for an imaginative rewriting of history is an interest in sites of memory, where the familiar can finally be rediscovered and restored to its ancient and multifarious splendour.

6

Possessing the Secret of Joy

Tashi, the young African woman who appears briefly in *The Color Purple* as Adam's wife and Celie's daughter-in-law, gets a novel of her own in *Possessing the Secret of Joy*. Her story traces individual and cultural motivations for female circumcision in Africa and systematically charts the deleterious effects of that practice upon women and children and, ultimately, society as a whole. Told through the multiple voices of Tashi and members of her family, as well as those of the anthropologist Pierre and the psychotherapists Jung/Mzee and Raye, the story begins with her African childhood and ends with Tashi's execution at the hands of the post-colonial government in her country of birth, punishment for her crime of murdering M'Lissa, the woman who circumcised her.

After the happy endings of *The Color Purple* and *The Temple of My Familiar*, it is a shock to be confronted in the third part of Celie's family saga with this harrowing story of physical and psychological torture, and a surprise to have it presented in such a taut form. Eva Lennox Birch shows that style and content of *Possessing the Secret of Joy* serve each other well:

> The enormity of the 'cleaning out' of the female genitals . . . is not left to reader imagination. And yet, although the subject-matter is painful, the manner and style of the narrative is not. This novel is less discursive, more economic and concentrated than any of [Walker's] previous novels, in its focus upon one issue and the consequences it had for a woman and her close family.[1]

In her afterword 'To the Reader' Walker states that this is not a sequel to either *The Color Purple* or *The Temple of My Familiar* and that she has used poetic licence to deviate from the earlier novels in order to tell Tashi's story as she saw fit, selecting only what she needed to write about female genital mutilation (266).[2] Be that as it may, I believe that *Possessing the Secret of Joy* does continue the family saga, because it crucially explores yet another aspect of African American diasporic relations – which are figured, again, as family relations – through the single issue of female circumcision. Diasporic migration to America and back has shaped both the profound cultural differences that exist between Africa and the United States and a particular sense of kinship between black Americans and Africans. Hence Walker writes in the same afterword that 'I have created Olinka as my village and the Olinkans as one of my ancient, ancestral, tribal peoples. Certainly I recognize Tashi as my sister' (268). In stressing such sisterhood, Walker, at the same time, as Kadiatu Kanneh points out,

> insists on a collective female experience, possible through empathy...[which] is proposed to exist within the identical and extra-cultural frame of the sentient female body, through which sexual identities and psychologies are assumed to subsist in a (spiritually) communal space of transparent femininity, beyond the artificial barriers of medical and familial cultures.[3]

Kanneh thus highlights the biological essentialism underlying Walker's protest against female genital mutilation, because it is only by virtue of such essentialism that a cross-cultural sisterly empathy can be invoked, and this will be the central problem I want to address in this chapter. It is, as I noted above, because of the taut form in which Tashi's suffering is represented, that that suffering is readable at all *as* a call for female solidarity. Yet we may wonder why Walker chose such a distressing topic for a novel which is beguilingly entitled *Possessing the Secret of Joy*. Is it only because, as Walker says, 'Tashi...refused to leave my mind' through the writing of *The Color Purple* and *The Temple of My Familiar*? (267). Before we explore the problem of essentialism and female solidarity further, I think we need to look into the history of Walker's preoccupation with female genital mutilation, because this history goes back further than *The Color Purple*. The fact that the spectre of the mutilated African woman preceded the character who comes to embody it, might explain why this single issue indeed overshadows the novel in more ways than one and demands that the reader take up a position against it.

'*One* Child of One's Own': White Feminism and the Black Woman's Body

In her 1979 essay '*One* Child of One's Own' Alice Walker writes about a black woman without a vagina. Describing a visit to the artist Judy Chicago's feminist exhibition *The Dinner Party*, in which the great figures of women's history each had their own dinner plates represented as 'creatively imagined vaginas', Walker notes that the plate representing Sojourner Truth is the only one without a vagina, but with a face painted on it instead. Or rather three faces: one weeping, one screaming and one smiling, to signify the African woman's oppression, heroism and 'authentic' joy respectively – the latter as if, Walker writes archly, 'the African woman, pre-American slavery, or even today, had no woes'. She then extends her critique of Judy Chicago's exhibition to white feminism's general lack of imagination when it comes to confronting black women's sexuality: white women cannot imagine black women as women, that is, with vaginas, or perhaps 'if they can, where imagination leads them is too far to go'.[4]

The essay is a tribute to the poet Muriel Rukeyser, Alice Walker's teacher and mentor whilst she was a student at Sarah Lawrence. It opens with a grateful acknowledgement of Rukeyser's life-lesson which 'brought the fundamentally important, joyous reality of The Child into the classroom'.[5] Rukeyser's affirmation of the centrality of the child – of children, but more crucially of the child within one's self – is for Walker 'political in the deepest sense'.[6]

This insight, and the three clichéd faces of the African woman on the Sojourner Truth plate, form the chrysalis of what was to become Walker's most overtly political novel to date. For anyone who has read *Possessing the Secret of Joy* the importance of The Child, and the scathing suggestion that white women cannot bear to think of African women's woes, let alone of their sexuality, will have a peculiar resonance. As if in answer to the questions she had raised in '*One* Child of One's Own' about the taboo subject of black women's bodies in white feminism, Walker's imagination leads us to consider the situation of Tashi, whose external genital organs have been removed and who has been deeply traumatised by this event. In confronting the question of female genital mutilation head-on, Walker therefore makes an African woman's woes the subject of *Possessing the Secret of Joy*. Discussing Tashi's plight in these terms, however, immediately brings us up against the problem of a politically charged terminology to describe what Tashi and Dura have undergone. Whether one calls what they have suffered 'female genital mutilation', 'initiation', 'female circumcision' or 'clitoridectomy' makes a difference, both clinically ('clitoridectomy' does not involve the wholesale removal of the inner and outer labia and the scraping of the vagina; 'circumcision' usually refers to the removal of the clitoral hood, somewhat analogous to male circumcision in which the foreskin is removed) and ideologically: 'initiation' puts it purely in a cultural frame, whereas 'female genital mutilation' signals a political analysis which implies condemnation of the practice. It is difficult to solve the problem of terminology here without prejudicing the discussion which follows later in the chapter about cultural relativism and cultural imperialism; as an uneasy compromise – an attempt at neutrality through diversity – I shall use these terms interchangeably for the time being, and define them more closely and more contextually later.

Like Queen Nzingha and Ola's 'bush-wife', the warriors who appeared in *The Temple of My Familiar* as reminders of women's active role in African history, and indeed like Sojourner Truth herself in American history, Tashi emerges as a woman/warrior who uses her own suffering to help eliminate that of others. Walker explains the connection between suffering and activism in *Warrior Marks*, the documentary film and book of the same title that she made about female genital mutilation with the British director Pratibha Parmar. She recounts the story of her brother shooting her in the eye with a BB gun when they were children, and of the resulting scar tissue which much later had to be surgically removed, and says

> It is true that I am marked forever, like the woman who is robbed of her clitoris, but it is not, as it once was, the mark of a victim. What the woman warrior learns if she is injured as a child, before she can even comprehend that there is a war going on against her, is that you can fight back, even after you are injured. Your wound itself can be your guide.[7]

The autobiographical fact of having been shot in the eye, which she terms a 'patriarchal wound' , thus motivates Walker's personal sense of sisterhood with sexually mutilated women. By supplementing the text of *Possessing the Secret of Joy* with a film and a book, which contains the screenplay of the film as well as other documentation concerning the campaign against female genital mutilation, she in effect makes the novel part of her crusade against a practice that she calls – significantly in the subtitle of *Warrior Marks* – 'the sexual *blinding* of women'. This is meant quite literally. Not only does Walker use this phrase to highlight the continuum of pain between her own injury and that of women who have undergone female circumcision, but she also says in the film and writes in both books that the light has gone out of the eyes of mutilated children.[8] Equally, in this formulation, sexuality is seen as a *sense* akin to seeing: without the ability to experience sexual pleasure a girl/woman loses a way of seeing, of feeling and of knowing. It is this sexual sense, this sense of wholeness that Walker feels *The Dinner Party* exhibition denied Sojourner Truth, who was a mother as well as a preacher and a fighter for the freedom of women (black and white) and slaves (men, women and children). White feminists, she felt, did not understand the complex problems that black women in Africa and America have to deal with; instead, they romanticised Sojourner Truth as a heroic figure *of the past* who embodied both the strength and the suffering of black women and could serve (I use the word advisedly) as a role model for whites. It will be clear that in *Possessing the Secret of Joy* Walker returns to this old ground and denies the (white, Western) reader any such romanticisation of the 'strong black woman' in raising awareness of Tashi's woes, but without reducing her to a mere victim.

There are, then, intricate connections to be made between '*One Child of One's Own*' and this novel, connections which are as problematic as they are also enlightening.

Tashi is introduced to the reader as a child, crying, uncomprehending, over the death of her sister Dura. When she later decides to be circumcised herself, as an act of allegiance to her tribe, she does so in defiance of colonial rule and missionary teaching, but also because she cannot bear to remember, or to understand, what caused her sister's death. The narrative which ensues, in which Tashi eventually kills the old woman M'Lissa who circumcised her sister and herself, is as much an acting out of grief for the loss of her own sexuality as it is one of vengeance for what was done to Dura. Unlike in '*One* Child of

One's Own', the issue in *Possessing the Secret of Joy* is not whether white women can bear to think of the black woman's body with a vagina, but whether anyone can bear to imagine this African woman's pain of being effectively without. To think of Tashi as a black *woman*, traumatised, without sexual organs but with her dignity and agency intact, is possible because Walker has made it so through her art. The novel tries to preserve a delicate balance between representing the sexually mutilated woman as a victim on one hand, and as a survivor who decides to act in her own cause on the other. That balance is achieved in the narrative through Tashi's psychotherapeutic experience, which traces her transformation from madwoman to warrior and, in this sense, the novel resembles a psychoanalytic case study. In America, Tashi (then known as Evelyn) is prone to fits of murderous rage necessitating psychiatric treatment in mental hospitals which fail to cure her. Only when she visits the psychoanalyst Carl Jung in Switzerland can she begin to remember her African childhood and access the trauma from which her cure will evolve, but such cultural distance from Africa is posited as necessary for the process of cure to be set in train.

Jung's approach enables Tashi to confront the memory of what it was like to be whole, able – and willing – to experience sexual pleasure. This is how she can come to think of herself *as* a black woman who is incomplete and whose life has been ruined, rather than as 'Completely woman. Completely African. Completely Olinka', which is how she had rationalised the experience of circumcision before she went into therapy (61). Tashi, in short, is represented as having been in possession of the secret of joy before she lost it. Because she has known sexual pleasure and is encouraged to remember it in the safe environment of the Swiss consulting room, she can also confront the reality of pain and take action, an action which culminates after her death in the emerging resistance movement of other African women against the indigenous tradition of female circumcision. In positing this collective solution at the end the novel goes beyond the psychoanalytic case study, whose successful conclusion normally consists in the individual's reintegration of self. This happens here too, but over and above that Tashi's healing process is only properly completed when other women take up the cause of protest, a completion which paradoxically coincides with her death.

'*One* Child' is ostensibly about racism in the women's movement, about the way in which white women, just like black and white men, cannot conceive of black women as *both* black *and* women, used as they are to appropriating the category of (universal) womanhood for themselves. Walker chides white feminists – like Judy Chicago and the literary critic Patricia Meyer Spacks (see also Chapter 1) – for excluding black women from their canons of female artists, because for the true feminist, she argues, racism is impossible.[9] This does not mean that the true feminist is necessarily black, however, for Walker also berates those black women who see their struggle as first and foremost a racial one; those who believe they must support black men at any price are blind to the feminist cause as *their own* cause.[10] Women of colour have important work to do in the rest of the world as well as locally: '*From the stopping of clitoridectomy and "female circumcision" in large parts of Arabia and Africa*' to taking action against urban poverty and the blights of the ghetto (my emphasis).[11]

I find it interesting that this mention of female circumcision (already in ironic quotation marks) should occur in the context of a discussion of writing and motherhood. '*One* Child' begins with the question whether writers should have children and ends, via the byways of Chicago's *The Dinner Party* and Spacks's *The Female Imagination*, with a rejection of white women writers as role models and an affirmation of black motherhood instead. Just as white feminists can't imagine black women as women, it seems, they also can't conceive of themselves as both writers and mothers (Austen, the Brontës, George Eliot, Woolf and, finally, Plath). But in the process of exploring the theme of writing and motherhood the essay also addresses what Walker calls 'female folly': the kind of wisdom handed down from mother to daughter which says that she should have more than one child, and that pain of childbirth is no excuse, because – and here she quotes her own mother – the more pain a mother suffers in childbirth, the more she will love her child.[12] Mrs Walker's counsel that the mother–child bond is enhanced by the experience of pain is echoed in Tashi's initial belief that the pain of circumcision will tie her more closely to her people; true femininity equals self-sacrifice. Both are examples of female folly perpetuated by cultural sanction, and in this sense also '*One* Child' prepares the ground for *Possessing the Secret of Joy*. In this novel the relationship between mothers and daughters and the matter of female folly are quite literally put on trial. Orality, which is the means by which this folly is transmitted from generation to generation, is put on trial too, albeit in a much more understated way which deserves some close analysis.

A Child's Big Letters: Orality, Literacy and Female Genital Mutilation

In Olinka culture, mothers tell their daughters that they should comply with tradition, that to be 'bathed' – as the euphemism goes – will make them more valuable to their families, their future husbands and their people. The much vaunted African oral tradition, in other words, is not in this case the medium for the passing on of a valuable cultural heritage, but the ideological instrument of torture. Walker here breaks with two tenets of Afrocentric feminist thought at one stroke: first, that the oral tradition is a source of alternative knowledge which is to be revered and, second, that mothers always have their daughters' best interests at heart.[13] *This* female wisdom (that circumcision is necessary, or even desirable), Walker implies, is indeed female folly; the fact that it is passed on orally in a tribal context lends it a cultural authority against the ideological incursions of the West, but it also means that that authority cannot be questioned from within African culture, for to question it equals betrayal of the heritage.

Because the source of this 'wisdom' *is* oral, no-one can cite chapter and verse as to where the custom of female circumcision originated and why. There is no written law or religious tract which can be repealed or reinterpreted; there is only time-honoured tribal tradition consisting in word of mouth. As the theorist Walter Ong explains in *Orality and Literacy*, oral cultures by their very nature tend to be traditionalist or conservative:

> Since in a primary oral culture conceptualized knowledge that is not repeated aloud soon vanishes, oral societies must invest great energy in repeating over and over what has been learned arduously over the ages. [. . . .] By storing knowledge outside the mind, writing and, even more, print downgrade the figures of the old wise man and the wise old woman, repeaters of the past, in favour of younger discoverers of something new.[14]

In the court case which culminates in Tashi's death sentence there is no reference to a legal requirement for female circumcision; instead, the trial revolves around the murder of M'Lissa, with the circumciser as a symbolic figurehead of post-colonial national identity. 'They do not want to hear what their children suffer', Adam observes,

'They've made the telling of suffering itself taboo' (155). Tashi, the mutilated woman, significantly defends herself and the integrity of the female body by countering the traditionalist and nationalist authority of orality in writing, but her writing is in a sense also mutilated. Preparing to go on trial for the murder of M'Lissa, Tashi sits down to make a sign of protest: 'Scribbling my big letters as if I were a child. It had occurred to me on the plane that never would I be able to write a book about my life, nor even a pamphlet, but that write *something* I could and would' (103). Her sign says 'If you lie about your own pain, you will be killed by those who will claim you enjoy it' (102). The irony, of course, is that Tashi gets killed by those, her former countrymen, who cannot abide the fact that she did not 'enjoy' it; Tashi may be on trial for murder but she is convicted, equally, for betraying the nationalist cause by speaking out about her pain. She writes like a child would, in big letters, making sure that unlike the tears she cried when she was little, this time her protest and grief will not be ignored. Although in narrative terms Tashi's action makes sense, when we consider the wider implications of her childlike writing the issue is less straightforward and rather more contradictory. On the face of it, Walker uses this episode in the novel to highlight African women's agency; Tashi's is the central voice in the novel and she writes her own protest. But at the same time, in writing and publishing *Possessing the Secret of Joy* Alice Walker wields her power as a well known African American novelist to take up Tashi's/African women's cause, thus implying that they cannot speak for themselves. Is Tashi's childlike writing, then, a case of arrested development? Is she mutilated as a writer because she is a mutilated woman?

From the beginning it is clear that Tashi has a writer's imagination: she is introduced to us as a storyteller on the very first page ('I did not realize for a long time that I was dead. And that reminds me of a story: there was once a beautiful young panther' (3)). But this storytelling habit, it turns out, is perhaps less a saving grace than a mere mode of escape; a form of lying to herself, even. When she is in therapy with Raye, the African American analyst, Tashi makes a connection between her pain and her storytelling:

I mean, if I find myself way off into an improbable tale, imagining it or telling it, then I can guess something horrible has happened to me and that I can't bear to think about it. Wait a minute, I said, considering it for the first time, do you think this is how

storytelling came into being? That the story is only the mask for
the truth? (124)

Tashi's creativity is here represented as primarily a defence, or
indeed, in psychoanalytic terms, a *symptom* of resistance. A symptom,
nevertheless, is a clue for an underlying cause, and although her
therapist 'looks sceptical' when Tashi advances this theory of what
storytelling is for, we as readers are here invited to consider Walker's
agenda for the novel: *this* 'way off improbable tale' is merely a mask
of multiple stories told by multiple voices *for the truth*. That truth concerns women in Africa who are mutilated by their mothers, grandmothers and aunts in the name of female wisdom, cultural tradition,
hygiene or marriageability.

Yet African women writers have addressed this issue in their work
too. The Egyptian Nawal El Sadaawi, for example, gives a harrowing
description of her own circumcision and her mother's betrayal in *The
Hidden Face of Eve*:

> I did not know what they had cut off from my body, and I did not
> try to find out. I just wept, and called out to my mother for help.
> But the worst shock of all was when I looked around and found
> her standing by my side. Yes, it was her, I could not be mistaken,
> in flesh and blood, right in the midst of these strangers, talking to
> them and smiling at them as though they had not participated in
> slaughtering her daughter just a few moments ago.[15]

And Ama Ata Aidoo begins her article 'Ghana: To Be a Woman' thus:
'I had sensed vaguely as a child living among adult females that
everything which had to do exclusively with being a woman was
regarded as dirty. At definite traditional landmarks in a woman's
life-cycle, she was regarded literally as untouchable.'[16] Aidoo does
not mention genital mutilation in her essay, but she does describe
her trials as an African woman writer who, because of her critique of
Ghanaian patriarchy, can expect to be read and respected in the
West more than in her own country, as 'an internal wound' and 'a
ceaseless emotional haemorrhage'.[17] She therefore makes, in her
imagery, the same connection between writing and the body that
Tashi represents and that Walker articulates in '*One* Child': a
woman's sexuality is integral to her art; both are forms of creativity
which feed, and feed off, each other. But if African women writers

have eloquently expressed this truth in their work as part of their critiques of particular patriarchal cultures and practices, was it really necessary for Walker to 'mask' it in Tashi's story? In the critical debate that *Possessing the Secret of Joy* has provoked this is a very real question. Are sexually mutilated African women like Sadaawi, also mutilated writers like Tashi? Can African women speak for themselves or does Walker have to do it for them? Obviously these questions pertain to the novelist's – any novelist's – right to write about what she pleases; fiction, after all, should be a space for the creative exploration of where the imagination leads us, even if, or especially if where it leads us is 'too far to go'. And yet, the paradox we are presented with in *Possessing the Secret of Joy* makes such a view of fiction as a safe and free space untenable, for on one hand the novel masquerades as story, whilst on the other it stakes a claim for truth. It does so not only in the thematic treatment of Tashi's mutilated creativity, but also in its form and authorial frame.

In her afterword 'To the Reader', Walker gives statistics and a bibliography on female genital mutilation as practised historically and today. Separated from the narrative by only a blank page – a blank page like the many blank pages which signal the gaps in Tashi's discontinuous narrative – the afterword occupies an ambiguous place in the text as both coda and separate entity. As part of and yet distinct from the fictional discourse, 'To the reader' makes explicit the novel's claim to truth- rather than simply storytelling, and in so doing goes beyond the imperative of imagination to the imperative for education and action. As in her afterword to *The Color Purple* Walker explains here how *Possessing the Secret of Joy* came to be written: Tashi's image stayed in her mind and seeing the young Kenyan actress who played Tashi in Steven Spielberg's film of *The Color Purple* it was as if that image was personified. The actress's presence reminded her of the fact that female circumcision was still being practised in Kenya and that children were dying from it (267). Tashi, however, is not a Kenyan woman but a fictional Olinkan – member of an invented African tribe with an invented African language. In *Possessing the Secret of Joy*, therefore, Walker goes much further in her political critique than African women writers like Nawal El Sadaawi or Ama Ata Aidoo have done, in that she takes on, not a specific practice or culture which she knows from the inside or about which specific data are available concerning female genital mutilation, but a homogenised 'African' culture and an unspecified, but clearly painful

and dangerous form of 'genital mutilation'. Walker adopts the plight
of 'the' African woman as her own, and because of this appropriation
she has been criticised for making an intervention, as an outsider
from the West with a Western feminist agenda, into what some see as
African internal affairs. All kinds of politically thorny issues come to
the fore here, of which the justification for female 'circumcision' is
but one, and possibly not the most important. More crucial in the
critical debate that *Possessing the Secret of Joy*, and the film and book
Warrior Marks, have generated, is the question of who has the right
and the authority to speak out about female circumcision, and to
whom. Arguably Walker herself, by representing Tashi as a mutilated
writer and by appending the afterword in which she restates the
novel's claim to truth, has provoked this debate for the purpose of
educating her readership. I shall return to this debate at the end of
the chapter, because it requires some more groundwork first. Once
we understand how aesthetic qualities are manipulated in the novel
so as to give the illusion of a convergence of Tashi's story with 'the
truth' about 'African women', we are in a better position to weigh up
the arguments that critics have levelled against *Possessing the Secret of
Joy*.

Secrets of Joy: Sexual Pleasure, Blackness and Resistance

As well as a revenge narrative, a psychoanalytic case history and an
ethnographic fiction, *Possessing the Secret of Joy* also resembles a
detective story. As in so many murder mysteries, the question is not
who committed the crime but *why*, and this pertains both to the death
of a child (Dura) and to the murder of an old woman (M'Lissa). We
discover that the crime which has caused both deaths is not premed-
itated murder, but female genital mutilation; every aspect of the plot
in this novel points to that single issue over and over again. Yet the
central mystery for the reader, who is told about the evils of female
circumcision fairly early on, lies elsewhere: in novel's title. What is
the secret of joy and who can possess it?

'RESISTANCE is the secret of joy' says the banner the women
hold up defiantly at the end, when Tashi is executed, but of course
there is more to it than this. Women's sexual pleasure and self-pos-
session are also secrets of joy, well-kept secrets in Olinka culture
because – unlike Tashi – most women never have the chance to

experience it. But if African women, who are circumcised at the normal pre-pubertal age, cannot possess this secret of joy, why is blackness later on in the novel posited as essential to such possession? Mbati, Tashi's pretend-daughter, reads in a book written by a white colonialist woman that 'Black people are natural . . . they possess the secret of joy, which is why they can survive the suffering and humiliation inflicted upon them' (255). This statement comes from Mirella Ricciardi's *African Saga*, where it serves to justify colonial exploitation of black people, who are perceived as the 'happy darkies' of racist stereotype.[18] As in *The Temple of My Familiar* Walker inverts the racist meaning of this quotation and appropriates it for her own uses: her title, and Tashi's story of physical death but spiritual triumph – an 'African saga' of suffering and survival, after all. But it is also an American saga, for it is this pain which in turn connects her with her adopted country, as Tashi explains: 'Americans . . . rarely resembled each other and yet resembled each other deeply in their hidden histories of fled-from pain. [. . . .] an American looks like a wounded person whose wound is hidden from others, and sometimes from herself. An American looks like me' (200). She says this in response to M'Lissa's question 'What does an American look like?' This searching for the traits of a national identity echoes St John de Crèvecoeur in the eighteenth century, who famously asked in one of his *Letters from an American Farmer*, 'What is an American?' Both Tashi and her (French colonial) predecessor come up with the answer that Americans are refugees, but whereas for Crèvecoeur finding *refuge* is the operative term, Tashi emphasises the pain that the immigrants have fled *from*. America, in her definition, is not the place of proverbial freedom as compared to Africa, but merely a vantage point of cultural difference from which her originary trauma can be examined. In her answer to M'Lissa, who can only conceive of a racially homogeneous nation-state and who thinks of America as the country of 'ghostly whites', Tashi claims the American part of her identity on the grounds of a shared history of oppression and hybridity. So, although her definition of America may look like the hegemonic land of the brave and the free, Tashi suggests that such freedom is not automatically granted by law and democracy, but is a matter of individual integrity: 'wounded persons' are not free as long as they hide their pain from others or again – and most of all – from themselves. As in Walker's previous works, it is in the confrontation with and working-through of trauma, which necessitates Tashi's return to

Africa, that liberation lies and in liberating herself Tashi can also, by
example, free other women.

Through the associative chain which links pain with storytelling,
Americanness with 'fled-from pain' and blackness with joy, joy with
resistance and women's sexual pleasure, Walker sets up a virtuous
circle in which women's sexuality and black American writing are
constituted as acts of resistance – a sexual/textual politics – against a
culture which, in M'Lissa's words, produces 'torturers of children' in
the service of forging a post-colonial national identity (210). This is a
strong message indeed. The detective work required to retrace one
woman's trauma leads to indictment of a whole culture, or even a
continent, and it is of course no accident that the circumciser herself
is made to speak these words and to incriminate herself, unlikely as
this seems, because that way the recognition of the 'crime' of female
genital mutilation comes not just from outside but also from within
'African' culture. No one can be surprised, least of all Walker herself,
that this indictment has provoked virulent criticism. One such critic,
Margaret Kent Bass, accuses Walker of 'cultural condescension', not
because she disagrees with Walker's call for an end to female genital
mutilation, but because she objects to the way that she sees that call
presented in the novel – as an argument for Western values, as if the
West can occupy the moral high ground in teaching Africa how to
treat its children. As regards the formal organisation of the novel,
Bass points out that

> Walker certainly anticipates the criticism that she *could* receive
> from many readers of *Possessing the Secret of Joy*, and she includes
> all arguments against her position and attitude in the narrative. In
> other words, she uses Tashi to offer arguments for tribal custom
> and uses the enlightened American, Evelyn, as her own voice in
> the novel.[19]

Bass is right that Walker dramatises the debate over female circumcision by structuring the novel as an intricate dance of argument and
counter-argument. But she is wrong to assume that Evelyn moves on
Walker's behalf – this dance has no such obvious lead performers.
Evelyn and Tashi do represent a double consciousness – 'two unre-
conciled strivings; two warring ideals in one dark body', as W. E. B.
DuBois famously put it in *The Souls of Black Folk* – but not in the sense
that Bass perceives it.[20] The character whom, so far, I have referred

to as Tashi, is named variously as Evelyn, Evelyn-Tashi, Tashi-Evelyn and Tashi-Evelyn-Mrs Johnson respectively, culminating in the unhyphenated Tashi Evelyn Johnson Soul of the final chapter. These different names signal different modes of consciousness, different narrators in an important sense, because some are more trustworthy than others. For example, 'Evelyn' does not at first want to believe the white American woman Amy Maxwell, who tells her that she has experienced clitoridectomy too, not in Africa but in the United States, because to believe that would destroy her ('Evelyn's) idealised image of America (177). 'Evelyn', therefore, is depicted in this chapter as clearly misguided about America's benevolent attitude to women. By the time she tells M'Lissa that 'an American looks like me', meaning like a 'wounded person', she is less naive about this and is therefore named Evelyn-Tashi, because her African memory now informs her consciousness of American reality (200). Conversely, she becomes Tashi-Evelyn once she knows of the African indigenous tradition of goddess worship and the sacred doll Nyanda, which represents women's sexual pleasure (256). Repossessing that secret of joy gives primacy to her African name, which is now merely supplemented by the American Evelyn. What looks at first like an idiosyncratic sequence of naming, therefore, in fact has a logic to it: the different names suggest that the African and American parts of this woman's identity, posed in opposition to each other at first, gradually integrate to form a harmonious whole in which 'Tashi' evolves into Tashi Evelyn Johnson Soul: an African, American, wife and mother, spiritually alive at last.

Triangulation: Form, Image and Argument

The dance of argument and counter-argument which structures *Possessing the Secret of Joy*, then, is enacted through the multiplicity of narrative voices. Everyone – even the circumciser M'Lissa – gets a voice in this novel, and they all have an angle on Tashi's predicament which in some way serves themselves as much as it benefits her, even the psychoanalyst Mzee. Just as M'Lissa gets to recognise in Tashi her own history of pain and alienation from the child that she used to be and forgot (206), Mzee writes to his niece Lisette that he is finding himself in Tashi and Adam as 'ancient kin' from whom he can learn (81). Mzee and M'Lissa, the old woman and the Old Man, form one of various contrasting pairs and threesomes of characters who dance the argument that Walker has choreographed for them. M'lissa has caused Tashi's trauma and Mzee is the one who makes the first advances in curing her, but Raye's support and insight accompany her the rest of the way. Raye synthesises the opposing qualities of Mzee/Carl Jung, the white analyst, and M'lissa, the African witch-doctor in a way which is similar to Adam and Lisette's son Pierre, the 'blended' person, who embodies the America of his father and the Europe of his mother. This dialectical model in which opposites fuse to form a new, positive hybrid is also represented geographically in the traffic between Africa, Europe and America: this, again, is a tale of three continents.

Imagery contributes to this sense of strict formal symmetry. Tashi's habit of escaping in storytelling literalises a familiar expression: she takes off on 'flights of imagination'. Tashi is consistently associated with flying, from the bird in her first story which steals the penny that her mother had given her to buy bread (6), to the crow that she likens herself to when she is in America and watches Adam pack for Paris (208), and the dragonfly that she imagines herself to be in the courtroom (149). Most startling of all, of course, is the painting of the cock which rekindles her memory and initiates her recovery, the cock which gobbles up her sister's genitals after the operation (and which is obviously not that distant a cousin of the bird who 'steals the penny'). Pierre, as the offspring of Adam and Lisette's adulterous union, becomes the focus for Tashi's rage while she is in America. Throughout, her rage and pain are imaged as boulders or rocks; Pierre's name, of course, means 'little stone', and when he arrives at Adam and Lisette's house in California Tashi pelts him with stones in a fit of uncontrollable anger.

The novel's circular frame is yet another example of formal control. The first and last pages mirror each other, since the tale of the female panther Lara, who embraces death contentedly when she kisses her own reflection in the water and holds it 'all the way to the bottom of the stream' (5) is echoed by Tashi's last words: 'There is a roar as if the world cracked open and I flew inside. I am no more. And satisfied' (264). The panther story looks like an African version of the Greek myth of Narcissus, so in love with his own image that he drowns in it. Lara's fate prefigures Tashi's own, but not in every detail. Unlike Narcissus, it is not Lara's vanity which condemns her to death, but the envy of her husband Baba and co-wife Lala, whose fighting over her she cannot endure. For Tashi and Lara, narcissism – their newly found self-love – is a saving grace and polygamy is not condemned in the novel but condoned, if it is practised without envy. Since Adam cannot achieve pleasurable sexual relations with his wife, because of her mutilation, he cannot, the novel implies, be blamed for seeking fulfilment elsewhere. As in every Walker novel so far, this triangular relationship between Adam, Tashi and the French woman Lisette, is central. Brownfield Copeland, Truman Held in *Meridian*, Mr____ in *The Color Purple* and Suwelo in *The Temple of My Familiar* were all involved with two women, and in every case the man was displaced from his position of power once the women forged a relationship (whether love or friendship) of their own (in *The Temple of My Familiar* on the other hand, the relationship between Miss Lissie, Mr Hal and Uncle Rafe is harmonious through-out, as if with a woman at the centre such power struggles would not occur). Here, such an alliance between the women is impossible: although Tashi is certainly jealous of Lisette's and Adam's union, it is clear throughout that her rage stems from the trauma of mutilation. What Lisette has that Tashi lacks is not Adam's devotion (Tashi does have that), but physical integrity and the ability to experience sexual pleasure – even whilst giving birth. Petit Pierre, Adam and Lisette's son, 'practically slid into the world' (95), in sharp contrast to Tashi and Adam's son Benny, who is born brain-damaged.

These contrasts between Lisette and Tashi, Pierre and Benny are rendered very starkly and explicitly. Lisette is a white European woman, physically whole, independent and with a feminist bent – the exact opposite of the damaged Tashi. With Benny and Pierre, likewise, not just the manner of their birth is sharply opposed but also their later development: whilst Benny suffers from mental retardation which means that his memory is impaired, Pierre goes to Harvard and trains as an anthropologist. He is the one who finally enlightens Tashi and her supporters about a cultural myth that has served since time immemorial to disguise – and justify – the reason why female genital mutilation is considered necessary; as an ethno-graphic helper he is as instrumental in effecting Tashi's cure as the psychoanalyst Raye is in uncovering her cultural memory. At the heart of this myth about the clitoris, figured as a termite hill, lies the belief that men and women should be clearly distinguished from each other: '[W]hen the clitoris rose... God thought it looked mas-culine. Since it was "masculine" for a clitoris to rise, God could be excused for cutting it down' (218). Pierre, the bringer of this news, who is of mixed race and bisexual, is the living embodiment of the falsehood of this belief in absolute sexual difference. He epitomises the virtues of hybridity in that he uses his European upbringing by a French feminist, his American education and his bisexual nature to illuminate his and Tashi's African roots, so as to unmask the brutal patriarchal 'truth' of the oral tradition. Again it may seem that Walker here assumes the authority of Western knowledge over the wisdom (she might call it 'cultural folly') of indigenous cosmology, but again the dance of the argument is more complicated than that. Pierre, the Harvard scholar, does not simply occupy the privileged position of Western enlightenment. The source of his knowledge about the myth of the termite hill is a book by a French anthropologist, Marcel Griaule's *Conversations with Ogotemmêli*. Griaule's informant in turn was Ogotemmêli, one of the elders of the Dogon tribe and their self-appointed spokesman. Pierre's detective work to find the original cultural motivation for female genital mutilation thus leads him via his Harvard education in anthropology and a French book right back to the source, which is Africa. We now come to another turn in the argument, for just as the American Amy Maxwell's clitoridectomy was 'copied' from the African practice as 'read' by American doctors on the bodies of enslaved, circumcised women, so also is Pierre's knowledge predicated upon a Western reading of African culture. Female oppression on one hand, and the understanding necessary to critique and counteract it on the other, are thus narratively produced by diasporic relations between Africa, Europe and America. As in *The Temple of My Familiar*, Walker counterposes the criminal diasporic movement of the Middle Passage with the critical, but potentially liberating movement of return. It is not in America that Tashi finds her freedom or enacts her revenge, but in Africa as *both* the scene of the crime *and* the place of redress. Tashi, the African woman, is liberated in the end with the help of the hybrids Jung/ Mzee, Raye and Pierre, and the triangular relationship between Tashi, Adam and Lisette represents the triangular dynamic of the African diaspora in both its historically oppressive and its potentially redeeming aspects in the future.

I hope this exposé of structural parallels and formal symmetries demonstrates just how carefully thought out this novel is *as an argument* in which various sides of the question why female genital mutilation is practised are explored. Systematically, the reasons *for* that practice are given (resistance to colonialism, hygiene, marriage-ability, tradition) and dismantled: Tashi's 'circumcision' does not make her a better resistance fighter and it alienates her from, rather than binds her to, her people; the operation is dangerous and spreads HIV; Tashi and Adam cannot have proper marital relations; childbirth is well-nigh intolerable for the mother and damages the child. Finally, but by no means least, the vaunted 'tradition' of female genital mutilation turns out to originate in a patently patriarchal story of creation which displaced another tradition, that of goddess worship and the valorisation of women's sexual pleasure and bodily integrity, which persists only in the now secret and underground cult of the doll Nyanda.

Convincing as this seems in a highly emotive *narrative*, there are many problems with it as a novelistic *argument*. The first may be the question of intended readership: whom does Walker want to convince, and to what end? On the face of it, only the most hard-hearted and stony-faced of readers can come away from *Possessing the Secret of Joy* without being deeply affected by its representation of female genital mutilation. Yet to say this is to assume that readers are not already aware of the practice, and that they will automatically share in the novel's condemnation of it because the narrative, through its rhetorical–argumentative strategies, leads them there. It is assuming, in other words, a reader who is fairly ignorant not just of female genital mutilation, but of cultural difference generally. What is perhaps the most disturbing about this assumption is that such a reader may even believe that s/he has gained some knowledge of 'African culture' in the process of reading *Possessing the Secret of Joy*. But this, as a look at Walker's anthropological and psychoanalytic sources will show, is emphatically not the case. Neither our knowledge of how and where female genital mutilation is practised in the world (that is: not just in Africa or sporadically in America), nor our knowledge of 'African culture' are advanced by reading this novel. To believe that it is, is to fall for storytelling as truth – it is to escape, as Tashi does, from reality by taking flight in imagination. Without denying Walker the right to tell her fictional truth as she sees it, and without ignoring the impact this novel has had in raising awareness of female genital mutilation and stimulating political and cultural debate, it is nevertheless important not to confuse Walker's fictional orchestration of the case against female genital mutilation with the reality of 'African' cultural practices. This is a confusion which Walker's afterword

'To the reader', as we saw earlier, encourages and which is enhanced by the film and book *Warrior Marks*, in spite, or perhaps because of, all the documentary evidence that Walker and Parmar present there. Neither Walker nor Parmar is naive about the controversial nature of their work. Asked what kind of responses she has had to her writing about a 'taboo subject', Walker answers:

> There are people who think that to speak about this is to stick your nose in somebody else's affairs, somebody else's culture. But there is a difference between culture and torture. I maintain that culture is not child abuse, it is not battering. People customarily do these things just as they customarily enslaved people, but slavery is not culture, nor is mutilation.[21]

The rhetorical statement that torture is not culture serves to justify Walker's campaign against female circumcision on humanitarian grounds, and to forge bonds of female solidarity between women in the West and those in Africa. Difficult as it is to resist such an appeal – for who would want to defend 'torture'? – it is nevertheless easy enough to counter the logic of it. The mere fact of physical pain, even when purposely inflicted upon another person, does not necessarily constitute 'torture'. We only have to think of amputations as a medical procedure in the treatment for cancer, for example, or of minor self-inflicted forms of pain such as tattoos or body piercings to make this point. Even if pain is suffered under duress, to call it 'torture' is already to interpret the fact of pain as an experience, but of course pain can be experienced and interpreted in all kinds of ways, of which pleasure or endurance for the sake of some higher ideal (childbirth being a prime example) are but two. Female circumcision, in other words, is not necessarily experienced as a form of 'torture' or even 'mutilation'. Of course the *material* reality of having parts of your body removed transcends cultural difference, and therefore may seem to lend itself to transcultural empathy. But such empathy is an act of interpretation; as a practice and as an experience circumcision is meaningless outside the context of culture, since it is culture which constitutes it as a meaningful experience at all, whether positive or negative. When Walker states, also in *Warrior Marks*, that

> We can also tell you that mutilation of any part of the body is unnecessary and causes suffering almost beyond imagining. We can tell

you that the body you are born into is sacred and whole, like the earth that produced it, and there is nothing that needs to be subtracted from it[22]

she is speaking from her own experience of having been blinded in one eye, but she generalises this trauma to the point of absurdity. A belief in the right to bodily integrity, part of the West's Enlightenment heritage, or indeed a belief in the sacredness of the 'natural' body, is as culturally determined as the idea that women's genitals are unclean and therefore have to be removed. Beyond the materiality of the body, there are no universals here, only value judgements, and values – such as those which invoke 'nature' against 'torture' – are always already culturally inscribed. While it is true that the body speaks, it is not always clear what it says: perhaps we can only ever understand it in the language of our own culture, unless we learn to translate it into that of another.

The Novel as Ethnography: Walker and the Predicament of 'African Culture'

In his opening chapter to *The Predicament of Culture: Twentieth Century Ethnography, Literature and Art* James Clifford makes a strong argument for an historical vision which has hybridity at its centre. 'I argue that identity, considered ethnographically, must always be mixed, relational, and inventive', he writes. 'Intervening in an interconnected world, one is always, to varying degrees, "inauthentic": caught between cultures, implicated in others.'[23]

Walker's intervention in 'African culture' can be read benevolently in the spirit of Clifford's insight that in an (increasingly) interconnected world we are always already implicated in other cultures and other histories, because they intertwine with our own. In her afterword 'To the Reader' Alice Walker explains why she feels that she has a right to such cultural intervention as *Possessing the Secret of Joy* in effect represents: because of slavery 'I do not know from what part of Africa my African ancestors came, and so I claim the continent' (267–8). The same reasoning underlies her decision to invent an African language and she says, with a Jungian twist, that her invented Olinka words (like 'tsunga' – for circumciser) are 'from an African language I used to know, now tossed up by my unconscious' (267). Any obvious criticism of Walker's inventing a language rather than taking the trouble of learning an existing one, and of inventing an amalgamated continent rather than locating her story in a specific place, culture and political system, is thus averted by the author who puts her own history of dislocation and dispossession in the frame here. It is because her ancestors, who might have come to America with mutilated bodies, were cut off at a stroke from their cultural, historical and linguistic contexts in Africa so she cannot now claim a specific heritage but has to make one up. The link between herself and the 'other' culture in other words is that of slave women's mutilated bodies. Again, I would not want to dispute Walker's right as a novelist to imaginatively trace this connection back and to restore those mutilated bodies to personhood and womanhood, by endowing Tashi as their representative with subjectivity and agency as a kind of retrospective justice. But it does seem highly problematic that the issue of female genital mutilation in fictional Olinka comes to stand for the oppression of women in *both* traditional cultures *and* post-colonial societies in 'Africa' as a whole, regardless of the continent's internal diversity. In representing only the most complete form of female genital mutilation Walker distorts the reality of diverse African practices to suit her polemical purpose. Nawal El Sadaawi explains that female genital mutilation means different things in different places:

> In Egypt it is only the clitoris which is amputated, and usually not completely. But in the Sudan, the operation consists in the complete removal of all the external genital organs. They cut off the clitoris, the two major outer lips (*labia majora*) and the two minor inner lips (*labia minora*).[24]

The wound is then repaired and the outer opening of the vagina narrowed with stitches, which have to be opened on the wedding night. Yet another version is described in Awa Thiam's book *Black Sisters, Speak Out*. In the case that Thiam quotes from, the outer lips are left intact but the vagina is scraped and then closed up very tightly by sewing the labia minora together with thorns – this is known as infibulation.[25] Whether part of the clitoris is left intact, whether excision (of the clitoris and lips) takes place and whether infibulation is also involved makes a big difference, not just as regards the effects of the operation but also in terms of its cultural meanings and motivations.[26] In some cases, sensation may not be completely lost, and where only the clitoris is affected, childbirth and first intercourse are no more difficult than they are for women who have not undergone some form of genital initiation. None of this is to say, of course, that these less extreme forms of mutilation are therefore experienced as 'less painful', nor is it to say that Walker exaggerates in how she represents Tashi's operation – according to Thiam, excision and infibulation are practised in 'Ivory Coast, Burkina Faso, Mali, Guinea, Niger, Senegal, Somalia, Sudan, among the Afar and Issas, in Saudi Arabia, Egypt, Ethiopia, Yemen, Iraq, Jordan, Syria, Southern Algeria and Benin'.[27] This is not 'Africa' generally, but it is a large part of it – mostly but not exclusively the Islamic countries. To question Walker's invented 'Africa', then, and to highlight varying degrees of female circumcision, is to say that the novel in an important sense dramatises its protest against female genital mutilation in a vacuum: it ignores any kind of regional variation as well as the diversity of meanings with which different versions are invested. Thiam's list does not include Kenya, which is the one country mentioned by name, twice, in *Possessing the Secret of Joy*. Jomo Kenyatta, the first president of Kenya, is indicted in the text as one of those leaders who endorsed circumcision during the struggle for independence as a tribal custom to be retained against the influence of Europeanisation (114). And in the afterword Walker mentions Kenya, where in 1982 fourteen children died from the effects of female genital mutilation (267). We can therefore with reason look at the case of Kenya to see how it compares with Walker's invented 'Africa'.

In Kenyatta's own *Facing Mount Kenya: the Tribal Life of the Gikuyu* some of Walker's contentions, such as that it is taboo for men to marry uncircumcised women and that it is feared that if the practice were abolished the whole social fabric would disintegrate, are confirmed. He even admits that one of the reasons why circumcision is considered necessary is to stop girls from masturbating, which is 'considered wrong'.[28] Interestingly, however, he writes of the circumcision of *both* boys and girls, and he insists on the procedure's importance as a mode of initiation into the tribe's laws, customs and traditions – an educational experience, in other words. Fulminating against the missionaries who in his view have exaggerated the detrimental effects of circumcision, in their own interest, of course, as a means of fostering Christianity and furthering colonial interests, Kenyatta argues that 'The real anthropological study, therefore, is to show that clitoridectomy, like Jewish circumcision, is a mere bodily mutilation which, however, is regarded as the *conditio sine qua non* of the whole teaching of tribal law, religion and morality.'[29] Note how Kenyatta on one hand does not hesitate to call the procedure 'mutilation', yet on the other defends it on the grounds of cultural integrity – people in the West do not question the civilised nature of Jewish circumcision, he intimates, so why interfere with Africans and call them 'barbaric'? In his detailed account of the initiation rite among the Gikuyu, furthermore, a great deal of attention is paid to the (indigenous) medical care with which the initiates are surrounded, and – likening the circumciser to 'a Harley Street surgeon' – he explains that only the tip of the girl's clitoris is cut off.[30] He also mentions in his Preface that he knows about the procedure as it is performed upon girls because 'the young initiates of both sexes talk freely to each other afterwards'; there is no great secret about it.[31]

I cite Kenyatta in such detail not by way of juxtaposing his 'truth' with Walker's fiction – his patriarchal investment is as clear as one might expect from a political leader writing in 1938 – but to highlight the context in which in traditional societies circumcision was practised. John Mbiti, in *African Religions and Philosophy*, also provides such context when he explains how the pain both boys and girls suffer in initiation is meant to prepare them for adulthood, and how the blood that is shed symbolises a rebirth, sometimes accompanied by a new name.[32] Mbiti (who is a Christian) gives many of the same reasons for the practice of clitoridectomy as Kenyatta does and emphasises that in the African world-view generally the physical and the spiritual are 'but two dimensions of one and the same universe', even if the manifestations of that union differ in their particulars in different regions and cultures.[33] By looking at such African studies of indigenous cultures Walker's project comes into focus. We now see even more clearly how her novel counters defences of traditional society, such as those that Kenyatta and Mbiti put forward, by making Tashi an anomaly and placing her *outside* her Olinka cultural context. Not circumcised while she was little (and the country still under colonial rule), she opts for the initiation voluntarily during and *as part of* the struggle for independence. In the passage where she explains this decision to Raye, an explicit parallel is set up between her devotion to Our Leader (leaders like Kenyatta and Nelson Mandela) and religious devotion: Our Leader is frequently likened to Christ, martyrdom included (108–9). Tashi also intimates that this devotion had an erotic component, that she could not love Adam because she was in love 'like every Olinka maiden' with Our Leader (114). Cultural nationalism and the Leader's exemplary martyrdom against colonialism and Christianity (remember Clifford's 'interconnected worlds') thus 'made her do it', but, equally, the sense of betrayal that Tashi experiences once she has gone through with her circumcision – alone in the rebels' camp, without the surrounding rituals and honours normally bestowed on newly initiated girls – parallels, or is mapped on to, the general betrayal of the post-colonial state. In other words, Tashi was never a part of the community of women ready for adulthood that the initiation is supposed to bring into being, she does not get any of the benefits and surrounding care of such a community and ritual, and in that sense also her experience is abnormal. As a woman she is screwed by her Leader's advocacy of traditional rites and then screwed over again by the post-independence government, after the Leader's death. In this scenario, the social fabric does not disintegrate because women are not circumcised; it has already disintegrated due to the influence of the missionaries (and Tashi's contact with Adam and Olivia, the missionaries' children, taints her and isolates her from the community) and the in-fighting among the rebels themselves, some of whom are believed to have murdered the Leader. The way Walker represents Tashi, then, as an outsider from beginning to end, aids her argument but does not necessarily reflect the situation of African women today who undergo circumcision, whether they do so voluntarily or involuntarily.

Apart from the mention of Kenya and Kenyatta, the only other piece of concrete information that we get in *Possessing the Secret of Joy* as regards a particular culture, rather than a generalised and homogenised 'African'/Olinkan one, is the explicit reference to Marcel Griaule's *Conversations with Ogotemmêli* (164). This ethnographic study concerns the Dogon in Mali, whose tribal customs and religious beliefs were scrutinised and documented by a team of anthropologists in the 1920s and 1930s. Much is made in the novel of the significance of the Dogon creation story and the termite hill, which Pierre interprets in a fashion true to the anthropological tradition. By making various structural analogies between the phallic shape of the termite hill and the tower of Tashi's dream, he arrives at the conclusion that both are clitoral representations of female sexual power. Tashi then discovers that, according to the Dogon myth, 'The dual soul is a danger; a man should be male, and a woman female. Circumcision and excision are . . . the remedy' (167). Sexual difference and spiritual difference are thus accomplished, by force, in one stroke of the knife, according to Tashi's reading of Griaule's book, which in turn is Griaule's reading of Ogotemmêli's reading of his own culture. This is presented as ethnographic authority, a final uncovering of the true reason for female circumcision in 'Africa'.

Ethnography, however, as James Clifford usefully reminds us, cannot be invested with such authority.[34] Not only is the ethnographic study a textual production like the novel, in which many voices speak, but the ethnographer is also like the literary interpreter, or rather the traditional critic 'who sees the task at hand as locating the unruly meanings of a text in a single coherent intention'.[35] This is also Tashi's and Pierre's – and by extension Walker's – dubious enterprise: it makes no sense to think of the Dogon creation story as having a 'single coherent intention', nor can one legitimately take the part (the Dogon story) to stand for the whole (as a mythological 'explanation' of female genital mutilation in Africa). Griaule, Clifford points out, did have a native informant in Ogotemmêli but he had no female sources, and the process of gathering his tales and collating them into a cohesive *oeuvre* was a highly complex one. Clifford therefore calls the work of Griaule and his collaborators 'elaborate inventions authored by a variety of subjects, European and African'. He calls them inventions because of the anthropologists' inflated claim that the book was an accurate rendering of the way the Dogon think (or even of the way 'the Negro' thinks, as Griaule was to assert later on in his career).[36] To say that they are inventions, however, Clifford warns, is not to dismiss them, but to 'take them seriously as textual constructions'.[37] The similarity between Griaule's ethnographic text and Walker's novelistic one as both inventions with totalising claims to representing 'African culture', authored – or in the novel's case narrated – by an amalgam of different voices with different cultural interests, will be obvious by now. They should be taken seriously as textual constructions, but not as claims to some ultimate truth. What is more striking than this less than blinding insight, however, is the Jungian resonance in the passage about the 'dual soul' that Tashi reads from Griaule's book. Carl Gustav Jung was, after all, convinced of the duality of the human soul, of the animus in woman and the anima in man, and we know of Walker's interest in Jungian psychology.[38] As in *The Temple of My Familiar*, we have to therefore return to Jung; if *Possessing the Secret of Joy* draws on but ultimately cannot claim the authority of an ethnographic text, because it interprets Tashi's body and psyche and via that body misreads, like Griaule did, 'African culture', it might yet be read more successfully as a Jungian case history, which is what we shall turn to next.

The Novel as Case History: Jung's Fifth Tavistock Lecture

'Negro women', the doctor says into my silence, 'can never be analyzed effectively because they can never bring themselves to blame their mothers.' [....] It is quite a new thought. And, surprisingly, sets off a kind of explosion in the soft, dense cotton wool of my mind. But I do not say anything. Those bark-hard, ashen heels trudge before me on the path. [....] African women like my mother give harsh meaning to the expression 'furrowed brow'. (17–18)

This is the beginning of Tashi's painful process of remembering her childhood. When Jung mentions black women's difficulty in blaming their mothers, the 'explosion' leads her straight to the traumatic memory of walking behind Catherine after Dura's death, the 'furrowed brow' not just an image of her mother's toil but also associatively linked to the furrow between her legs, and Tashi's own. Carl Jung, in this early chapter, is still referred to as 'the doctor' or even 'this stranger', not yet the 'Old Man' or the honorary African 'Mzee' that he is to become later, as his magic begins to work on Tashi to confront her with her dreams and her archetypal images. And his therapeutic magic does work: Tashi relates her dream of the tower, which is so important as a clue to her repressed sexuality, first to him, and his showing of a documentary film made in Africa sparks her frenzied painting of the giant cock, which in turn enables her to remember the trauma of actually witnessing Dura's murder. Near the end of her therapy, Jung writes to Lisette that Tashi/Evelyn's case has made him discover a 'truly universal self' through the kinship he feels with her and Adam's suffering:

They ... are bringing me home to something in myself. I am finding myself in them. A self I have often felt was only halfway at

home on the European continent. In my European skin. An
ancient self that thirsts for knowledge of the experiences of its
ancient kin. [....] A self that is horrified at what was done to Evelyn, but recognizes it as something that is also done to me. (81)

This 'recognition' on Jung's part of the other as kin through the
therapeutic experience is a clear case of what analysts term counter-
transference, when the analyst is affected by the emotions of the
patient and comes to experience them as part of him- or herself. In
Jung's fifth Tavistock lecture of 1935, whose subject is transference
and counter-transference, he relates the case of 'an elderly woman of
about fifty-eight... from the United States' who comes to him in
Switzerland 'half-crazy' after having been in analysis in America.[39]
He discovers that his approach to analysis, one in which the doctor is
not an objective observer but an active participant who shows his
own emotions, is so different from the woman's American experience of treatment that it produces the desired therapeutic effect in
itself: the mutually affective analytical relationship is what constitutes the healing. If this is reminiscent of the relationship which
Tashi forges with Jung, there are several other elements in this
lecture which link it to *Possessing the Secret of Joy*. Jung relates in this
lecture another case history concerning an American woman 'and I
can safely tell you of this case because she is dead', who 'was totally
unconscious of herself as a woman; she was just a man's mind with
wings underneath'.[40] Jung describes this woman as 'a bird', which in
the original German does not necessarily have a metaphorical con-
notation, but is suggestive of Tashi's birdlike imagery in the novel.
The woman comes to Jung because she is involved in a dysfunctional
relationship with a married man. Both, writes Jung, are unconscious
of themselves, 'and a woman never becomes conscious of herself as
long as she cannot accept the fact of her feelings'. He then relates this
woman's lack of self-awareness to the fact that she is American, and
he likens the more authentic self, that she has yet to confront, to
Africa:

We often discover with Americans that they are tremendously
unconscious of themselves. Sometimes they suddenly grow aware
of themselves, and then you get these interesting stories of decent
young girls eloping with Chinamen or with Negroes, because in
the American that primitive layer, which with us is a bit difficult,

with them is disagreeable, as it is much lower down. It is the same phenomenon as 'going black', or 'going native' in Africa.[41]

Generally speaking Jung's observation is unsurprising, since the idea of Africa as associated with 'the primitive' or the 'lower down' (that is: with sexuality, particularly female sexuality), and of Americans as pragmatic rather than self-reflexive, are favoured stereotypes of Eurocentric thought in the mid-twentieth century; Freud, after all, designated female sexuality 'the dark continent'.[42] In the light of Walker's novel, however, the resonance of this passage with Tashi's case is loud and clear, the more so as Jung's lecture then relates how this American woman's cure is effected through analysis of her dreams, culminating in a dramatic climax, 'a sudden explosion'.[43] Tashi, like this woman, has to rediscover and accept the African in her – however traumatic – before she can become whole. When she first meets Jung, he calls her simply a 'Negro', which angers her because she thinks of herself as an African woman, not a 'Negro', meaning an African American. Yet in his mis-recognition of her Jung in fact turns out to be right, because when she first comes to him she is indeed unconscious of herself, her African self, in the American way. Later on in the lecture Jung discusses other themes which we also find in Tashi's case history, such as painting as a diagnostic aid, the distinction between 'active imagination' which provides therapeutic clues (such as Tashi's compulsion to make up stories) and mere wishful fantasy, and the phenomenon of what he calls the 'Saviour complex'. The latter is a manifestation, an archetypal image, of the collective unconscious which becomes activated at times of historical change, and refers to the need for people to invest an individual with exalted qualities of leadership.[44] Not only are analysts in danger of having the Saviour complex thrust upon them, but political leaders are as well, and more dangerously so. For Jung, historical events (such as, in the novel, the shift from colonialism to independence, under Our Leader/Saviour) are not brought about by conscious activism but by movements in the collective unconscious.[45] Fanaticism, moreover, religious, analytical (cultural or political, we might add), 'is always a sign of repressed doubt' (just as Tashi's insistence on having her Olinka initiation is motivated by unacknowledged doubt, as her discussion with Olivia makes clear).[46] In the conclusion of this lecture Jung emphasises again that individuals should not look for happiness in events, or circumstances, or saviours outside themselves, but should realise that 'everything depends on whether [the individual] holds the treasure or not. If the *possession of that gold* is realized, then the centre of gravity is *in* the individual and no longer in an object on which he depends' (my emphasis).[47] That 'gold', of course, is the secret of joy which Tashi discovers in herself and in women's resistance at the end of the novel.

It would probably be an exaggeration, and a simplification, to say that *Possessing the Secret of Joy* merely dramatises such psychoanalytic concepts as Jung presents, in condensed form, in the fifth Tavistock lecture, but the multiple parallels between them are more than just suggestive: they make it possible to read the novel as a case history whose salient features derive from Jungian thought.

But we do need to note, again, that Walker revises Jung as she revises the anthropological record: Tashi's cure comes about not just through the individual solution of psychoanalytic treatment, but is completed only in collective political action against the mutilation of women. The African American therapist Raye's role is critical in this respect, since it is she who shows Tashi the broader picture of women's oppression in America as well as Africa. Raye disabuses Tashi of the illusion that flight (whether into the imagination, or to America) can relieve the suffering in itself, and Raye makes it possible for Tashi to make cross-cultural connections. Unlike Jung's argument in the lecture, the novel does not construct political action as a mere manifestation of unconscious and unacknowledged motives, but as necessary for individual and collective well-being. With this proviso, we may still conclude that it makes more sense to read *Possessing the Secret of Joy* as a Jungian case history than as an ethnographic text about 'African culture', or even an unambiguously Western feminist protest against female genital mutilation. Not only does Walker draw on Jung's African experiences (in Kenya, again) and anthropological interests in order to critique, implicitly, the white bias of classical Freudianism, but she also uses the transcultural frame of Jungian psychoanalysis to question the current popularity of a romanticised Afrocentrism in the United States, which serves as cultural nationalist philosophy to bolster an 'authentic' African American identity. This critical stance vis-à-vis Afrocentric thought is part of the debate which has developed around Walker's intervention on female genital mutilation in Africa, a debate which is more about discursive power relations than about female genital mutilation *per se*, let alone the novel's literary merits, as we shall see.

Cultural Relativism Versus Cultural Imperialism: Who Speaks? Who Listens?

Positive reactions to *Possessing the Secret of Joy* celebrate it as a radical political statement on global sisterhood, and tend to uncritically adopt Alice Walker's humanist agenda and the essentialist analysis of female genital mutilation that goes along with it. Some, like Charles Larson in *The Washington Post Book World*, manage to evade the feminist issue altogether and read the novel as 'about' the suffering of children, whereas Eva Lennox Birch admires Walker's courage in 'daring' to write about clitoridectomy, not because it is a contentious issue but because of the sheer horror of the procedure as she sees it.[48] More problematically, other admirers value the novel because they believe it to be breaking new ground. Kimberley Joyce Pollock, for example, says that because of *Possessing the Secret of Joy* 'women are able to speak the unspeakable' and she applauds Walker for showing 'the universality of the act of genital mutilation' by including Amy Maxwell's story. Reviewer Tina McElroy Ansa calls the novel a 'stunning beginning' of a much needed political debate.[49] Praise in these terms betrays not just an ignorance among Western readers of the practice of female genital mutilation, but also of the sizeable literature on the subject produced by campaigners who are mostly African women or women of African descent. As Margaret Bass indicates in the article I cited earlier, African women's resistance against female genital mutilation has a much longer track record than reading Walker's work would lead us to believe, even if Walker cites some of that movement's literature in her postscript. Bass charges Walker with sensationalism and 'cultural condescension': 'African women are not creatures enshrouded in helpless, hopeless ignorance and misery – longing for rescue by the West and Alice Walker', she concludes, and 'we' (in the West) should therefore 'leave them [African women] alone'.[50] Bass's call for a hands-off policy where African women's interests are concerned seems hardly satisfactory for those of 'us' who want to maintain a constructive dialogue between Western and African women's activism, but at least she recognises that an assumed and unproblematic solidarity across cultural difference is unlikely and perhaps undesirable. 'Cultural condescension' is only the mildest term used by critics who are opposed to Walker's novel. 'Cultural imperialism' is more often used, and it is a phrase which, if accurate, makes Walker complicit in the very history of Western exploitation of Africa that she so strongly criticised in *The Temple of My Familiar*. The question of whether that charge is justified is important, because it focuses the debate on the real issue, which is not whether female genital mutilation is a good or a bad thing, but whether a Western feminist/womanist has the right, and the authority, to say that it is not.

> 'Female circumcision' has become almost a dangerous trope in Western feminisms for the muting and mutilation of women – physically, sexually and psychologically – and for these women's *need for* Western feminism. Circumcision, clitoridectomy, infibulation become one visible marker of outrageous primitivism, sexism, and *the* Third World woman[51]

writes the critic Kadiatu Kanneh in 'Feminism and the Colonial Body'. Kanneh highlights here the connection between Western feminism's interest in female circumcision and a presumed neocolonial representational dependency of 'the' Third World woman on Western feminists to speak in her behalf.[52] In this analysis, the circumcised African woman becomes the fetishised object of the Western gaze, which is no less imperialist in its effects for all its supposed sisterly empathy. The question we are faced with, then, is whether Walker's novel is complicit with, and draws its readers into, such an imperialist discourse which homogenises 'the' Third World woman's plight and reduces her to a stereotype of ultimate victimisation once more.

Certainly Gay Wilentz seems to think so, since she argues that 'There is an aspect of voyeurism in Walker's approach; [which]... puts her in the company of other Western writers before her for whom 'Africa' merely represented the exotic or the grotesque'.[53] Wilentz thus accuses Walker of stereotyping, whereas for Angeletta K. M. Gourdine the problem lies with Walker's personal investment: 'Walker excavates Tashi's history and in the process discovers her own connection to Tashi, blackwoman to blackwoman. In so doing, Walker categorically castigates African women's histories and possesses their bodies in a bizarre struggle to free her own.'[54]

Gourdine's sense that Walker's autobiographical investment in *Possessing the Secret of Joy* does the novel no good relates to other critics' questioning of the discursive political relations between Western feminism and African women. By putting herself in the frame, as

Walker does in the afterword and in *Warrior Marks*, she may – perhaps unwittingly – obscure the image of the African woman and hinder rather than help their cause. Since the publication of *Possessing the Secret of Joy* and *Warrior Marks*, it is as if the campaign against female genital mutilation has Alice Walker's name on it, and there is a danger that in the controversy surrounding it African women's voices may be lost. Pratibha Parmar, with whom Walker made *Warrior Marks*, seems to have foreseen this danger, and the likelihood that Walker would be accused of patronising African women by imposing her feminist discourse upon them. In an interview with *Black Film Bulletin* in 1994 she says:

> I had seen quite a few documentary films on this subject in the past and some had sensationalised the issue and some had approached it as Western outsiders. I often asked where were the African women's voices. In my research I found that African women had been fighting against this traditional practice for many years so, I was very keen to ensure that a wide variety of African women's voices would be in there in the film.[55]

It is true that African women figure prominently in the film *Warrior Marks*, but there is less of a 'variety' than Parmar would have us believe because, as one would expect in a campaigning film, most of the African women who speak are already involved in activism against female circumcision and the ones who are not, or who approve of it (like the elderly circumciser), respond to the leading questions of Walker as interviewer with hostility or silence. The voices which are heard are the voices which Walker and Parmar wanted to be heard, whereas others who disagree are represented as misguided in the film.

What, then, to conclude from this brief survey of critical responses? There is no doubt that *Warrior Marks* and *Possessing the Secret of Joy* have raised consciousness and continue to generate an important discussion, not just about female genital mutilation but also about readers' and viewers' cultural values and the possibility of global sisterhood across cultural difference. One voice that has not been heard in that discussion, however, is that of the woman who values her circumcised body and who sees circumcision itself as part and parcel of her feminism, her right to decide. That voice I found, typically by accident, scribbled in the margins of a library copy of Asma El Dareer's study *Woman, Why Do You Weep? Circumcision and Its Consequences*, where an anonymous woman made it heard. In annotation after annotation, amounting to a running commentary on Dareer's text, this woman voiced her dissent.[56] Where Dareer explains the procedure of infibulation, in clinical terms, which nevertheless do not leave much to the imagination, the anonymous woman's voice adds '(= total purity)'. Where Dareer reports that she witnessed a circumcision in which the girl's relatives ululated loudly to drown out the child's cries, the notes in the margin say 'family honor; mothers suffered painful operations but enjoyed the long-term benefits'. And when Dareer describes her meeting with a gynaecologist, who is opposed to the practice and punishes midwives who perform it, this is interpreted in the margin as 'patriarchal authority opposing noble female rites'. Finally, the voice exclaims in exasperation: 'why can't male politicians and medics accept that we *enjoy* circumcision and like the beauty and chastity it gives us?'

This voice, literally marginalised in a library book and metaphorically so in Walker's work, is ignored in the wider debate as well. But however misguided or incomprehensible this woman's experience of female circumcision might seem to an outsider, her voice is worth listening to, because if we do it is just possible that we can learn from it that one person's 'torture' is – indeed – another's culture. To learn this is not to be flippant about feminist consciousness and political responsibility. It is, rather, to agree with Gina Dent in her thoughtful discussion of Walker's novel in 'Black Pleasure, Black Joy' that

> [T]his 'choice' – between modern, feminist, US-based black culture and traditional African culture – is the paradigm we must learn to unread. [....] To deconstruct the paradox of Tashi's choice between Africa and America, between culture and gender, between woman's acceptability and woman's pleasure is not merely to state that within the context of western rationalism she can exert no agency. It is to go even further than complicating the means by which we determine an action, and more significantly here, a cultural text, to be progressive or conservative, positive or negative. It is to begin dismantling our understanding of the very means by which we are able to know, to decide, and to act.[57]

7

A Writer's Activism: Alice Walker, Her Critics, and 'the' Tradition

A footnote to 'Recording the Seasons', an essay about leaving Mississippi written in 1976, states that whenever Walker was called an 'activist' or 'veteran' of the Civil Rights movement, she 'cringed' at the inappropriateness of these epithets. For the true activists and veterans, she says, were the young people in SNCC or women like Fannie Lou Hamer and men like Dr Martin Luther King Jr, people who risked their lives for freedom.[1] Although Walker had been writing since the early 1960s, leaving Mississippi did mark the start of her writing career and her withdrawal from activism as defined by the Civil Rights movement: putting your body on the line, campaigning under dangerous conditions, living at the grass roots without the possibility of retreat. Activism and writing, both of which require one's full concentration and commitment, are usually seen as antithetical; Tillie Olsen, one of Walker's models, has written about their incompatibility.[2] Like the 'author' and the 'medium', the activist and the writer seem mutually exclusive identities, temperamentally and practically opposed to one another. And yet, as I mentioned in Chapter 1, Alice Walker has sought to maintain both throughout her career. More than twenty years after 'Recording the Seasons' was written, she subtitles *Anything We Love Can Be Saved*, her latest collection of articles, autobiographical writings and essays, *A Writer's Activism*, and explains what she means by that:

193

My activism – cultural, political, spiritual – is rooted in my love of nature and my delight in human beings. [. . . .] I have been an activist all my adult life, though I have sometimes felt embarrassed to call myself one. In the Sixties, many of us were plagued by the notion that, given the magnitude of the task before us – the dismantling of American apartheid – our individual acts were puny. [. . . .] The most 'revolutionary' often ended up severely beaten, in prison, or dead.[3]

In recalling the previous sense of 'embarrassment' Walker here both reclaims the activist identity she had disavowed in the footnote to her earlier essay and redefines it: activism can be 'cultural and spiritual' as well as political, it consists in rewritings of history and of the literary tradition as much as it does in campaigning on behalf of Native American land rights or protesting outside the prison where Dessie Woods is held. Neither form of activism can stand in for the other, but they are complementary: activists who put their bodies at risk often lack time for self-reflection, whilst the words of those who have it will be hollow if they are not heard and acted upon.

In Walker's definition, sometimes merely staying alive can be a form of activist defiance of the powers that be. She acknowledges her great-great-great-great-grandmother May Poole, an American slave, for fostering her belief in activism because May Poole's 'attitude and courage . . . made it possible for her to attend the funerals of almost everyone who'd ever owned her'.[4] In May Poole's well-nigh mythical case (reputedly she lived to be 125 years old) 'activism' evidently consisted in surviving the ravages of Southern history. Marjorie Pryse gives an interesting intertextual dimension to May Poole's incredible age and the connection Walker feels she has with this ancestor, when she notes the similarity between Walker's reference to this same grandmother in *In Search of Our Mothers' Gardens* and Susie King Taylor's *Reminiscences* of 1902, which records Taylor's knowledge of a great-great grandmother of 120 years old who was from Virginia and half-Indian. Pryse notes that this knowledge and conscious use of heritage contradicts the standard account of African American discontinuities in family history, and that it might point to 'a women's tradition, handed down along female lines'.[5] There is, of course, a good deal of hyperbole in Walker's invocation of this ancestor which implies, through the fact that others recognise Walker in a photograph of the old woman, that May Poole's attitude and courage have been passed on to her. As in her search for Zora Neale Hurston (see Chapter 1), it seems that the survival of Walker's work and of her person cannot be taken for granted. In both her introductions to the complete poems and the complete short stories, published in the 1990s, Walker expresses surprise at the fact that she is still alive ('I assumed I would be a suicide by the age of thirty' and 'I have outlived the telling of these tales! I don't believe I ever thought I would'), as if the conditions of living in the late twentieth century as a confused and depressed young black woman writer, and those of May Poole's life as a slave were somehow analogous.[6] But then, as Libby Brooks writes in a recent interview with Walker, '[Her] particular activism reflects a lyrical worldview which relies on individual voices rather than intellectual rigour. Her belief in telling your own tale is firmly rooted in her own story.'[7]

Her Critics

This is true, but such 'rootedness' does not mean that the significance of Walker's work should be collapsed into the significance – or not – of such autobiographical hyperbole (see Chapter 1). Some of the most simplistic – and vicious – criticism which Walker's work has attracted has come from people who read 'her own story' back into the fiction. Here, for example, is an extract from Philip M. Royster's 'In Search of Our Father's Arms: Alice Walker's Persona of the Alienated Darling':

> Alice Walker cannot afford to allow her protagonists to enjoy male sexuality, not merely because those protagonists believe that males, by nature, are inadequate humans (e.g., Celie's ridiculing of male genitalia along with her image of men as frogs or losers) but also because all the males with the potential for sexual relations with Walker's protagonists may be masks for her father.[8]

Royster's approach is designed to demolish a reputation and discredit a body of work by reducing Walker's womanist politics to 'envy, resentment, or anger' on the grounds of her involvement with white feminism, her representation of lesbianism, and – of course – her criticism of black male violence and abuse; Walker, in short, is only interested in 'dividing the race'.[9] Royster's example is, to be

sure, rather extreme. Part of Walker's reputation as a 'brave' or at
the very least 'controversial' writer comes from her own advertise-
ment of the negative press she has had, notably from African American men. There is exaggeration in this, too: for one, she is certainly
not the only African American woman writer to have incurred the
critical rage of black men – Ntozake Shange's 1977 play *For Colored
Girls Who Have Considered Suicide When the Rainbow Is Enuf* caused
every bit as much of a storm as did *The Color Purple* five years later.[10]
Second, the balance in Walker criticism leans heavily towards uncritical adulation rather than vitriol or dismissal. If anything this
explains why, despite the sheer amount of commentary on her work,
the quality of it is often disappointing: many of the hundreds of articles produced by the Walker critical industry are merely descriptive
or – indeed – biographical rather than offering any analytical insight
into the work. On the other hand, some of the best serious Walker
criticism has been written by African American men such as Henry
Louis Gates Jr, Houston Baker and Calvin Hernton, as well as black
and white feminist critics, and even some white men.

A self-styled writer/activist runs the risk of having her writing
judged by her political (and cultural/spiritual) convictions and by
what she chooses to disclose about her life, as the case of Philip Royster indicates, whereas serious criticism avoids the mistake of conflat-
ing these different dimensions. It is quite possible, in my view, to
admire the activist and find the writer wanting. It is equally possible
to credit the writer and remain critical of her agenda, but such distinctions can only be made once the work of aesthetic analysis *and*
political (cultural/spiritual) reflection has been done. This book has
tried to do that work in order to counter some readers' and critics'
tendencies to either 'buy the whole Walker package' because they
approve of the activist/writer, or to reject the writing because the activism or the persona do not suit. When Walker is dismissed as an
ideologue whose work is a mere vehicle for leftist, racially divisive,
feminist or wacky New Age ideas, the significance of that work as art
and as political/cultural/spiritual intervention is diminished or misrecognised. *But* this does not mean that it does not misfire, at times,
on one, the other, or both fronts. Walker's work, like Walker criticism, is uneven. Where the writing and the activism work together to
the mutual enhancement of both, as in *Meridian*, *The Color Purple*,
'Advancing Luna – and Ida B. Wells', 'Nineteen Fifty-five', 'Looking
for Zora' and 'In Search of Our Mothers' Gardens', to name a few

favourites, there is nothing quite like it in the literary tradition, black and white, to match them as aesthetic and (surreptitiously) didactic achievements. In *Possessing the Secret of Joy* also, the formal precision of the writing as an activist argument against female genital mutilation has to be admired, even if one does not agree with that argument (as I, for one, do not). And where activism and writing don't mesh – in my view in most of the poetry, many of the short stories, in *The Third Life of Grange Copeland* and in large sections of *The Temple of My Familiar*, as well as some of the later autobiographical writings – then it is because the language is trite, narrative and stylistic economy are lost, and the reader is patronised or – worse – denied any room to move and make her own meanings.

Alice Petry's critical assessment of the short stories is a good example of discerning criticism which identifies unevenness in technique and thereby illuminates the texts' failure of political/cultural/spiritual vision. Petry compares the stories of *In Love and Trouble* with those in *You Can't Keep a Good Woman Down* and attributes the unintentionally comic effect of several stories in the latter ('Fame', 'Porn', 'The Lover') to 'Alice Walker's preference for telling over showing [which] suggests a mistrust of her readers, or her texts, or both'.[11] The same misapprehension, on Walker's part, of the comic effect of poor writing mars some of the poetry too; when Walker read a selection of poems from *Anything We Love Can Be Saved* in London in April 1998 to an adoring audience of hundreds, many laughed at 'Natural Star' (a poem about Michael Jackson) and 'A Woman Is Not a Potted Plant', but Walker made it quite clear in her demeanour that she was not trying to be funny – or even ironic.

Petry's comments on this phenomenon are more insightful than David Bradley's similar, but more judgmental appraisal of the same short stories, which he says are flawed by 'unassimilated rhetoric, simplistic politics and a total lack of plot and characterization'.[12] Petry gives a number of textual examples which she analyses closely to show where style and characterisation are off beam, whereas Bradley provides no support for his dismissive appraisal. And when Petry argues that Walker's propensity to hold forth rather than dramatise also applies to 'Advancing Luna – and Ida B. Wells' (where the narrator is indeed intrusive and argumentative), it is possible to disagree with her: in this story I find the narrator's inconsistent perspective and multiple changes of mind (the story has four different endings) highly effective as a way of formally enacting what the story itself is about, that is, the dilemma of a black woman positioning herself between her gender and racial allegiances on the issue of interracial rape. Good criticism like Petry's explains *how* the work works without requiring agreement *that* it does, and in Walker criticism, positive and negative, that distinction is often hard to find. Perhaps it is in any case more easily demonstrable on the literary/technical side of Walker's writing than it is on the political. Another example might clarify how Walker's brand of political/cultural/spiritual activism in writing can backfire stylistically and rhetorically. As we have seen in the preceding chapters, *this* writer's activism in an important sense carries on where the Civil Rights movement left off, but a brief comparison with a political commentator's view of such post-Civil Rights activism can put Walker's stance into perspective. In a recent article in *Race & Class*, the political historian Manning Marable evaluates African American activism in the 1990s in the aftermath of Civil Rights and of black nationalism of the 1960s. Marable does not mention the cultural arena in which many of those 1960s debates have continued (in African American critical theory, in the canon wars, in the Clarence Thomas/Anita Hill and O. J. Simpson cases, in rap music – in short, in the politics of representation generally), but it is clear that his agenda for the 1990s is informed by those debates and not least by African American women's writing. Marable identifies three sites of struggle for black liberation: community, class and gender, in a hard-nosed materialist analysis which acknowledges diversity, refuses essentialism and recognises that 'the primary victims and scapegoats of the Right are women of colour and their children'.[13] Class, Marable notes, has virtually disappeared from mainstream political discourse, but he argues for its continuing importance because history shows 'that the way things are produced and distributed within society, the patterns of ownership and divisions of property, prefigure or set in motion certain consequences which, in turn, impact on everything else'.[14] If we put Marable's analysis next to Walker's politics, their bottom lines would be much the same. The model of local struggle around gender, community and distribution of resources (she tends not to use 'class') have been central to Walker's project as a writer/activist since the 1960s. In *Anything We Love Can Be Saved*, as in the previous essay collections, Walker writes about the United States' boycott of Cuba, the Million Man March, the exclusion of women from certain Native American rituals, female genital mutilation, the mistreatment of animals, dreadlocks and racial pride, and many other issues which have both public/political and personal dimensions. In other words, her writing-as-activism runs the gamut of Marable's concerns but also widens his agenda beyond that of African Americans *per se* and beyond the United States. The example of Cuba serves as a ground of comparison for the United States' treatment of its poor, and her gender activism involves Native American and African women as well as black women living on welfare in the richest country on earth. At the same time, Marable's essay highlights by comparison where *Anything We Love Can Be Saved fails* as activist writing: where Walker writes that Louis Farrakhan 'needed to be forgiven' for his anti-Semitism, Marable does not mince his words and describes him unabashedly as 'homophobic, anti-Semitic and sexist'. And where, as I noted in Chapter 1, Walker writes in her 'Letter to President Clinton' that she 'cares for' him and his family, Marable reminds his readers of Clinton's record regarding approval of the death penalty, a repressive crime bill and welfare cuts 'which will devastate the households of millions of poor women and children'.[15] Not only does Walker's writing here lack the critical edge that its political critique (which is also present in the pieces on Farrakhan and Clinton) demands, but it lapses into sentimentality and an emotive discourse of 'forgiveness' and 'caring' which loses sight of the distinction between interpersonal and political relations altogether. Like Walker herself in the opening lines of this chapter, reading this I 'cringe at the inappropriateness' of this language and at the fact that, as readers, we are presumably invited to 'share' such a spirit of conciliation and concern for the nation's leaders' souls. On these occasions, Walker's autobiographical voice does not fit the ostensible didactic purposes of the political essay; it is intrusive and – well, overblown.

'The' Tradition

Then again, there may be another side to this, which will lead us, as so often, back into 'deep history'. When asked about her relationship with her daughter Rebecca in a recent interview, Walker answered:

> Because of her, I know again the daughter and the mother I was. I've also discovered the world is full of mothers who've done their best and still hurt their daughters; that we have daughters

everywhere. [....] I feel like I have tons of daughters,...and they're in good hands.[16]

Even if Walker was merely referring to her large following of young female readers in this statement, there is nevertheless an audacity in it which few other widely read contemporary women writers would dare to match. In the *history* of women's writing however, such apparent self-aggrandisement is not unprecedented, for Walker echoes – unwittingly perhaps, but maybe not – Sojourner Truth's self-representation as 'mother of all that is here' (which I cited in Chapter 3). Of course, it is easier to accept such a self-proclaimed 'elder' status from a venerable old ex-slave a century ago than it is from a middle-aged, living writer. But the hubris contained in the idea that real mothers all over the world, who have done their best, still hurt their daughters, whereas Walker's global brood are 'in good hands' can only be understood – other than as mere megalo-mania – if we read this in the context of a tradition. This tradition, I suggest, is characterised by a way of speaking and a way of conceiv-ing of individual, spiritual responsibility which has little or nothing to do with Hurston's fiction or Woolf's essays or Southern writing, but links Walker with nineteenth-century African American women who were visionaries, itinerant preachers, abolitionists and femi-nists; women like Sojourner Truth, Rebecca Cox Jackson, Amanda Berry Smith and Jarena Lee.[17] In the twentieth century Fannie Lou Hamer, Ella Baker, Ruby Doris Smith Robinson and other Civil Rights 'community mothers', whose words and works have not been preserved, perhaps represent a more down-to-earth version of it, but the distinctive features Walker shares with her nineteenth-cen-tury foremothers are those of the visionary rhetorical style and sense of mission of the mystic or lay preacher. Truth, Jackson and Lee were, of course, Christians who practised their mission outside the institution of the Church in which women, at that time, were not even allowed to speak; their preaching was in that sense an act of feminist defiance – a form of activism – from the outset. Walker writes about Rebecca Cox Jackson in 'Gifts of Power', an essay that is rarely cited but worth rereading for its resonances with her own work. She asks in that essay what we are to make of Jackson's gnostic beliefs, in which the spirit of Christ is experienced in dreams and visions, not in the institution of the Church, and the resurrection does not happen after death but in life. Jackson, furthermore, believed in a divine Mother as well as in the Father, and Walker likens this to pre-Western Indian and African religious worship of the goddess.[18] What we are to make of this, it would seem, is that somewhere along the line this nonconformist and feminist Christianity is transmuted into Walker's paganism, *via* the intermediate stage of Shug's liberation theology in *The Color Purple* (which still has a god in it, albeit not in church). Henry Louis Gates Jr traces an unwitting connection between Jackson, Hurston and Walker in 'Color Me Zora', and is aware of Walker's conscious revision of Jackson and especially of the scene in *Gifts of Power* where Jackson describes how she was taught to read by divine inspiration: 'Walker . . . makes much of this scene . . . underscoring the fact that "Jackson *was* taught how to read and write by the spirit within her." When Walker dedicates *The Color Purple* "to the Spirit", it is to this spirit which taught Rebecca Jackson to read.'[19] Black women's claim on orality (public speaking) and literacy are thus inscribed in this tradition from the outset and both, of course, are central to the Walker paradigm of a womanist creative tradition which is distinct from, but intersects with, black male and white feminist traditions. In the spiritual development of Walker's work, God first gives way to the Spirit (in *The Color Purple*) and then merges with the Cosmic Mother, who is also Nature, or the goddess (in *The Temple of My Familiar* and onwards from there). *The Great Cosmic Mother*, Monica Sjöö and Barbara Mor's massive study of goddess worship and 'the religion of the earth', is Walker's paganist bible and an important source for much of her cultural/spiritual activism in the later essays and novels. It presents a global survey of pagan and female-centred religions and draws cross-cultural parallels to support the argument that goddess worship was not only anterior but also superior to the current major world religions, and that the time is ripe for Her comeback if the planet is to survive.

For my purposes of outlining an alternative 'visionary' tradition for Walker's later work, their chapter on America is the most illuminating. Sjöö and Mor distinguish between three streams of spiritual thought in eighteenth-century America: colonial Puritanism, the rational–humanist Deism of the writers of the Constitution, and a secular stream which, they say:

> has always been an underground stream: that of wildness, of sensual innocence, of paganism. [. . . .] Not a few European men (this stream was mostly male) did return to wilderness in America: they

joined Indian tribes, or became frontiersmen. [....] This underground stream emerges as the real 'American Dream' – a peculiar
'lust for innocence' which is always sought, never found.[20]

Mor and Sjöö construct paganism as an indigenous 'religion' drawing on America's utopian traditions; they note that various nonconformist groups (Bohemians, hippies, beats) have sought to revive
it – not, coincidentally, in California, where Walker now lives and
where new age thinking has flourished since the 1960s. Whether or
not all this is true is not the question I am concerned with here;
rather, I am suggesting that Sjöö and Mor's analysis makes it possible
for us to see how various strands of religious thought and various
styles of spiritual discourse, which have informed Walker's work in
the past, come together in a utopian paganism which has belief in the
Great Cosmic Mother at its heart. The trajectory I am sketching out
moves from the nineteenth-century women preachers through –
perhaps – Hurston's interest in Hoodoo, to the Civil Rights movement's redemptive ethos and from there (via feminism) to Native
American and African cosmologies, paganism, goddess worship –
and Jung (see Chapters 5 and 6). This rag-bag of cultural and religious traditions, in other words, in recent years has hybridised into
an eclectic wholistic philosophy which enables us to 'locate' Walker's
work and her activist persona as 'mother of all that is here'.

The maternal activist persona has a sense of mission which is con-
sonant with that of her nineteenth-century visionary foremothers,
but also with the modern paganist's well-nigh cosmic responsibility:
'The paganistic return is like the Buddhistic salvation from the world
wheel: nobody really does it unless, until, we all do it', write Sjöö and
Mor.[21]

With this articulation both of the cosmic consciousness-raising task
in hand for the paganist and its anti-rationalist, anti-Puritan and
anti-patriarchal ethos, we arrive at a point where the 'inappropriate'
language of Walker's letter to President Clinton, or her willingness
to mother the world's daughters, come into perspective: maybe they
are less an individual idiosyncrasy than a rhetorical style and a spiritual conviction that have a history and a tradition.

This tradition is very different from the purely literary one in
which Walker's work is usually read; it is older, more eclectic and
speculative and possibly less conscious on her part. But traditions,
as Hortense Spillers reminds us, are made rather than found; they

'survive as *created social events* only to the extent that an audience cares to intersect them'.[22] My suggestion, above, of a visionary tradition intersects, but is by no means incompatible with, the African American tradition of conscious revision that Henry Louis Gates Jr and others have set out.[23] Walker figures prominently in that tradition: besides the 'common bond' with Hurston, critics have also seen her work in dialogue with that of writers as diverse as Richard Wright (*Native Son*/*The Third Life of Grange Copeland*), Frances Ellen Watkins Harper (*Iola Leroy*/*The Color Purple*) and Ralph Ellison (the Trueblood episode in *Invisible Man*/*The Color Purple*).[24] Walker herself has, of course, in her essays created a tradition of her own which includes Jean Toomer, Flannery O'Connor, Langston Hughes and Rebecca Cox Jackson. Notably absent in that self-defined literary lineage are the other women writers of the Harlem Renaissance (Jessie Fauset, Nella Larsen), those later in the century (Ann Petry, Margaret Walker, Gwendolyn Brooks, Lorraine Hansberry) and the African American novelists of the late nineteenth century (Frances Ellen Watkins Harper and Pauline Hopkins). These absences would be striking if they were not so familiar: apart from Larsen, Hopkins and Harper, these writers tend to be much less discussed in African American criticism too, and it may well be that they are less discussed *because* of Walker's impact on the writing of African American women's literary history.

Marjorie Pryse hints at this phenomenon in her introduction to *Conjuring: Black Women, Fiction and Literary Tradition*, where she writes that her and Hortense Spillers's collection 'is intended to free writers like Walker from the necessity of writing critical and biographical work – or at least to encourage others in the task of doing so'.[25] *Conjuring* does contain articles on Petry, Fauset and Margaret Walker too, but the crux of the problem in writing traditions is articulated at the end, when Hortense Spillers exposes the fiction of a monolithic 'African American tradition', or even of a moderately cohesive and continuous tradition of African American women's writing. Noting the divergences between the writing of Hurston on one hand, and Fauset and Larsen on the other, or that between Hurston and Petry, or in the post-war period Paule Marshall and Margaret Walker, Spillers writes that '"tradition" for black women's writing community is a matrix of literary *discontinuities* that partially articulate various periods of consciousness in the history of an African-American people'.[26] Spillers's narrative of discontinuity is helpful, because it works against a critical tendency to homogenise the category of 'black women writers' and to take the notion of 'the' African American tradition – even when defined as a dynamic 'changing same' of revision and dialogue – too far. Besides, but importantly, the discontinuity model can also throw some light on the differences between contemporary African American women writers: Alice Walker, Toni Morrison, Gloria Naylor, Audre Lorde, Gayl Jones, Terry McMillan, Toni Cade Bambara, Paule Marshall, Maya Angelou – to mention only a few of the best known – are often discussed comparatively (or even together, in one breath) despite the fact that they are really very different writers, even if many of them draw on common cultural sources like jazz and blues, Afrocentric thought, the black vernacular, or folklore. In the preceding chapters I have deliberately omitted such comparative discussion, because I wanted to make a case for Walker's particularity within and outside this field of black women's writing. One, or possibly *the* major difference that emerges is Walker's self-inscription as a visionary and a writer/activist.

Of the writers mentioned above, Maya Angelou and Toni Morrison have a large female following, too, and their fans may well construct them as role models or wise women, but they do not style *themselves* as guiding spirits in their readers' lives: they are writers (and, certainly in Angelou's case, also performers), but they are not visionaries or metaphorical mothers. The contrast with Morrison is instructive in another respect as well: her and Walker's shared institutional status as favoured black women novelists, prizewinners and bestsellers has nevertheless produced a very different kind of reception, both in the critical industry and in educational practice. Judging by the volume of 'serious' criticism, Morrison's work seems to invite theoretically informed approaches (psychoanalytic, postmodernist, poststructuralist) in a way that Walker's writing does not, whereas in the classroom *The Color Purple* is regarded as 'easy' next to the 'complexity' of, say, *Beloved* or *Jazz*. There is little to be gained from such a comparison, of course, except in so far as it highlights the tokenism which is writ large in the canonical status of these texts and in the writers' very different critical appeal.

Hortense Spillers identifies a change in the American classroom from a pedagogic practice which valorises 'difficult' texts (credited with 'complexity' and 'ambiguity') to those which maintain 'not only an allegiance to "power to the people", but also "talking" to "the people" in the now familiar accents of representation and mimesis'.[27] In the classroom, as in critical practice, I think that the differential appeal of Morrison and Walker shadows this movement, quite possibly to the detriment of both. If I can roughly translate Spillers's shift as a movement from primarily aesthetic analysis to a more politicised reading, then neither Walker's nor Morrison's reception benefit from a contest between aesthetics and politics which, to quote Walker one last time, 'they did not design'. Comparisons of this kind are invidious, and it is a mark of the institutional power invested in criticism, a power of which this book partakes, that it seems necessary to engage with the Walker/Morrison nexus only to refuse and refute its validity at the end. In making my case for Walker's distinctiveness in the preceding chapters, I hope to have shown that her work comes out of, and responds to, a cultural arena in which there is room for more than just two major black women writers. Perhaps it is more helpful, as a closing gesture, to sum up what Morrison and Walker share both with other African American women writers and with their post-colonial contemporaries. Despite discontinuous traditions and across cultural difference, they share what Françoise Lionnet terms a new universalism:

> They write in the interstices between domination and resistance. [....] They appropriate the concept of universality in order to give it a new valence and to define broader commonalities. [....] Their works de-exoticize the non-West, indicating the centrality of their concerns to the self-understanding of people everywhere.[28]

This, if anything, is Alice Walker's contribution to the 'immense story' of a multi-racial, cross-cultural tradition: no less, and no more.

Postscript: *By the Light of My Father's Smile*

It is, of course, quite impossible to write a concluding chapter about the work of a living writer. *By the Light of My Father's Smile*, however, provides a fitting conclusion to this book, both because it constitutes, in many ways, a reprise of Walker's previous work and because its own ending is so peculiar: on the final page, we witness the death of an author and the burning of her books.

Walker's readers are used to having their credulity – and their patience – stretched, and this latest novel offers no dispensation from that rule. Although the familiar contours of Walker's imaginative landscape are clearly visible here, we get to see it from a most unusual perspective: that of the recently dead, who still have unfinished business to clear up with the living. Set in Mexico and the United States, with a brief sojourn in Greece, the story is narrated by angels, that is, by all the main characters who successively 'cross over', bar the novelist who is the last to die and who, ironically, does not get to tell her own story.

By the Light of My Father's Smile presents a tale of two sisters, Susannah, a novelist, and Magdalena/June, an academic, who grow up in Mexico. They are the daughters of African American anthropologists who, although they are agnostics, have to masquerade as missionaries in order to secure the funding for their research. Their object of study is a mixed African American/Indian tribe called the Mundo, who believe in the continuity between life and death and in telling the truth, because 'it takes only one lie to unravel the world' (81).[1] The sisters' father, however, absorbs enough of the Christian teaching he is hired to merely transmit to begin to live such a lie, when he temporarily forgets his love for his daughter and punishes

Magdalena for her sexual exploits with a Mexican boy, Manuelito. The beating Magdalena receives from her father – administered with Manuelito's silver-studded belt, to add insult to injury – is the cause of her and her sister's estrangement from him, and ultimately also from each other. Susannah sides with her sister against the father she loves and comes to resent Magdalena for it. In the end, however, both the father's trespass and Magdalena's envy of her sister's happiness are forgiven, as each of the dead makes up with the others in the afterlife. This plot, which revolves around two sisters and a childhood trauma (another 'patriarchal wound') that ruins the life of one of them, is instantly recognisable as that of *The Color Purple* and *Possessing the Secret of Joy* rolled into one. Here again we encounter missionaries/anthropologists in a foreign land, who fail to convert or to fully understand an invented tribe (Olinka/Mundo), and a lesbian relationship (between Susannah and her lover, Pauline), in which both the closeness and the distance between sisters, caused by patriarchal intervention, is acted out. Other familiar features of Walker's previous work are woven into this core narrative: the Greek dwarf Irene, who at first lives in a church like Miss Lissie in her temple, acts as a spirit guide to Susannah (an echo of Suwelo). Later, once she has inherited her father's fortune, Irene sails around the world like Mary Ann Haverstock did in *The Temple of My Familiar*, and lives for a while with the Pygmies in Africa – 'little people' like herself. Irene (whose name means 'peace') enlightens Susannah about the ills of Europe, about the persecution of the gypsies and its similarity to the treatment of black people in America, and about worship of the Black Madonna in Greece, as in Africa. She also knows, as Miss Lissie did, of the witch hunts in Europe which meant that in the Middle Ages 'Europe lost . . . its mother. Her strong mother', as a result of which it was made to 'shrink its spirit to half its size' (189). Another spirit guide is Manuelito, a Vietnam veteran who dies in a traffic accident shortly after his reunion with Magdalena. He is the one who instructs Señor Robinson, Magdalena's father, in the Mundo way of life and death. The Mundo believe in 'nonpossession of others' (96), and this lesson the father has yet to learn with regard to his daughters, even from beyond the grave. Manuelito tells him that

> The dead are required to finish two tasks before all is over with them: one is to guide back to the path someone you left behind

who is lost, because of your folly; the other is to host a ceremony so that you and others you have hurt may face eternity reconciled and complete. (150)

For the father, this means that he has to make good with both Magdalena and Susannah, whereas Manuelito's task of reconciliation lies in Vietnam, where he has to face the people he murdered during the war. In a strange reversal of the usual relationship between the dead and the living, then, in this novel it is not the living who have to honour and remember their ancestors, but the other way around: the dead have a duty to help the living, and to atone for the wrongdoings they committed whilst still alive.

This may be interesting as an idea but, to quote one of the novel's many heavy-handed insights, 'ideas are made of blocks. Rigid and hard', whereas 'Stories are the way spirit is exercised' (195–6). In this novel, ideas often have to stand in for narrative development; they are talked through by the characters, or literalised to comic effect in the same flat-footed and discordant way that Alice Petry, in the previous chapter, said some of Walker's short stories misfire: by telling, rather than showing, what she wants to convey. In *By the Light of My Father's Smile* Walker again mistrusts her text, her readers, or both. The way the death of Magdalena is represented is an example. Although her love for Manuelito is in the end requited, her relationship with her father is not resolved and she dies, unfulfilled, from obesity. But rather than letting the grotesque image of a woman who eats herself to death resonate in its own right, Walker allows Magdalena to explain: 'It was as if my memories were lodged in my cells, and needed to be fed. If I lost weight perhaps my memories of Manuelito and my anger at my father would fade away. I felt so abandoned already, I did not want them to go' (125).

This is unnecessary, and indicative of the novel's style as a whole: it holds forth, it doesn't flow, and the dead narrators' all-too-human 'jokes' (such as 'If I were not dead already, I would have killed myself' (83)) are simply embarrassing. Walker's use of names, likewise, is rather crudely 'symbolic' instead of subtly suggestive, and often their significance is explained by the characters themselves: Pauline, Susannah's lover, used to be Lily Paul, a name which combines the free sexuality of the biblical Lilith with the misogyny of St Paul, the church father – a rather dubious coupling for a woman whose sexuality is described as manly and aggressive (albeit from the father's jealous narrative perspective, early on in the narrative). The Lilith of her name then aligns her with Magdalena; both are 'loose women' whose childhoods were ruined by violent men and whose relationship to Susannah is marked by the ambivalence of love and resentment; this ambivalence also is discussed at length by the women themselves. Walker makes it clear in her (now customary) afterword, that this novel is a tribute to Eros, because the ability to experience sexual pleasure, once again, is represented as the thing that makes, or breaks, a person's spirit. Unlike Tashi in *Possessing the Secret of Joy*, of whom she is an incarnation, Magdalena dies defeated by the memory of her father's violence. In childhood the unbroken, 'wild' Magdalena was respected by the Mundo as a 'Changing Woman, a natural one, uninstructed and uninitiated, and therefore very rare'; they name her Mad Dog as an Indian honorific (93). Her father, however, sees her as true to her biblical name: a whore (and Manuelito's wife is – predictably – called Maria to highlight the madonna/whore dichotomy in Christian thinking); after the punishment Magdalena herself chooses June as her name to signify the loss of her 'change purse' with the golden zipper, which symbolises (in heavily Freudian terms) her sexuality. The father himself, however, is ultimately saved by Eros because, as Manuelito recognises, his sexual devotion to his wife Langley keeps the flame of truth alive and wins him the protection of the Mundo elders, who watch and guard him from beyond the grave.

Obviously, then, *By the Light of My Father's Smile* is equally an exploration of Thanatos, the other side of Eros's coin, and potentially the more interesting because more innovative side. Walker allows the dead not just to figure in, but to *tell* this story of 'Requited Love, Crossing Over, and the Sexual Healing of the Soul' which is the novel's subtitle, but – as noted above – the angels' view of life is disconcertingly similar to that of the living. The first of these dead narrators is the father, who in the early chapters reports on one sexual adventure after another, as he is both remembering his own relations with his wife and witnessing Susannah's lovemaking with her husband or her lesbian lover. The latter, in particular, makes for uncomfortable reading because the father's perspective is, by implication, that of the voyeur who clearly resents his daughter's lover; this, in many ways, is a rewrite of 'The Child Who Favoured Daughter', an early short story of Walker's about a father's jealous – and violent – desire to possess his daughter.[2] As a dead narrator/observer of Susannah's sex-life, the father learns, however, to repent for his sins through the intervention of Manuelito, who joins him in the realm of the recent dead. Magdalena, finally, is the third dead narrator; her task is the reconciliation with her sister, which she achieves as she watches Susannah's 'crossing over' in the closing pages of the novel.

Possessing the Secret of Joy already prepared us for the spectre of a dead storyteller; Tashi, after all, begins her tale with the words 'I did not realize for a long time that I was dead. And that reminds me of a story.'[3] But Tashi, as we later find out, is only spiritually, metaphorically dead at this time; her physical death at the end coincides with a spiritual rebirth, as we saw in Chapter 6. In *By the Light of My Father's Smile* this order is reversed and the dead narrators speak, from the beginning, truly 'from the other side' of the crossing place in the river, the Vado, which signifies death and is reminiscent of the river Styx that the ancient Greeks believed they had to cross before arriving in the under- or afterworld. This is one of several cross-cultural parallels between the beliefs of the Mundo (meaning 'world') and those of the ancient Greeks; when Lily Paul tells Susannah that she was raped at fifteen the latter likens her to Persephone, who was raped by the god of the underworld and forced to spend half of each year there, during which time her mother, Demeter, 'turned the earth to winter' because she missed her daughter (105). The *motif* of betrayal, or not, by the mother (which Susannah and Lily Paul are discussing at this point) both echoes and redresses the betrayal of daughters by mothers in *Possessing the Secret of Joy*, for Walker's latest novel is predominantly about fathers, as its title announces; the mother (Langley, again a flamboyant Zora Neale Hurston-type of figure) remains largely in the background. 'By the light of my father's smile' is taken from the Mundo initiation song which Manuelito teaches Señor Robinson, '*por la luz de la sonrisa de mi padre*' (196). This is also the song that Magdalena sings, compulsively, as a child – for she is the one who has 'naturally' absorbed the Mundo world-view, in a way that her father has not. Significantly his voyeuristic preoccupation with surveillance of his daughters' sexuality leads him to mis-learn the refrain of the song as '*por la luz de los ojos de mi padre*', meaning 'by the light of my father's eyes', and Manuelito has to put him straight about that as well: daughters don't need their fathers to watch over them but to give them the light of his smiling approval of whatever it is in their nature to do and to be.

As Jack Forbes's *Africans and Native Americans* again testifies, there is a long history of mixed-race black and Native American presence in Mexico which the Mundo represent here, but apart from this fact there is little in the narrative or in the spiritual vision which the novel promulgates that is specific to Mexico.[4] For those who are familiar with Walker's previous work, this is a novel we have, in a sense, already read; at times it even looks like a parodic condensation of the themes and styles of that previous work. Walker's conception of death is perhaps the only feature of *By the Light of My Father's Smile* which warrants its Mexican references, for, as Octavio Paz observes:

> The opposition between life and death was not so absolute to the ancient Mexicans as it is to us. [...] Life had no higher purpose than to flow into death, its opposite and complement; and death, in turn, was not an end in itself: man fed the insatiable hunger of life with his death. Sacrifices had a double purpose: on the one hand man participated in the creative process, at the same time paying back to the gods the debts contracted by his species; on the other hand he nourished cosmic life and also social life, which was nurtured by the former.[5]

Paz's words have a peculiar resonance not only because this philosophy of continuity obviously informs Walker's text, but more eerily because *By the Light of My Father's Smile* ends, in effect, with a human sacrifice when Susannah the novelist dies along with her books. As the poem, which Magdalena quotes during her vigil, puts it: Susannah has become her own candle, willingly burning herself 'to light up the darkness' around her (221). This final scene is as anachronistic a representation of a writer's aspiration to martyrdom as one could expect to find near the end of the twentieth century. As I noted in the previous chapter, Walker's increasingly visionary inclinations, evident in the essays as in the fiction, align her more with black women preachers of a century ago, or with mediaeval mystics like Margery Kempe. Though obviously – and ironically – Susannah's demise is a literal enactment of 'the death of the author' which I referred to at the beginning of this book, Walker's representation of this writer's self-immolation is no postmodern device to signal her lack of control of, or her abdication of responsibility for, the process of signification. If anything, it is the reverse: Susannah dies, contentedly, of old age – the only character in the book to do so because she has lived a good life. Her refusal to be remembered is a protest against the long tradition in Western culture which holds the author to be immortal *because of* his (and I do mean 'his') writing: 'It is the need to be remembered that has caused most of the trouble in the world, [Susannah] said. Most of the conquering. Destruction of what is natural. War' (220). Walker thus lets her character speak for herself: Susannah's final act is in keeping with the revision of Western thought that runs through all of Walker's writing, and here she articulates her author's views.

At century's end, and on this final page, the question then arises what Susannah's act signifies in relation to Walker's anxiety about the survival of her person and her work that she has expressed elsewhere, and which I discussed in the preceding chapter. Two answers present themselves: either *By the Light of My Father's Smile* articulates a superior wisdom, a spiritual growth in which that anxiety has finally been transcended, *or* it bespeaks a more desperate fear that the light of Alice Walker's imagination has indeed, with this novel, burned itself out. Each of these two readings, in its way, is as disturbing as the other, just as each, in its way, also fits the paradoxical persona that is Alice Walker: author and medium, writer and activist, woman and visionary 'mother of all that is here'. Yet somehow, the idea of continuity between life and death is not enough to reconcile these contradictory readings and identities; somehow, this latest novel does not provide an answer but a further question: having killed off the novelist, what will, or, what *can* Alice Walker do next?

Notes

Chapter 1   Alice Walker's Life and Work: The Essays

1. John O'Brien, 'Alice Walker: an Interview' [1973], in Henry Louis Gates Jr and K. A. Appiah (eds), *Alice Walker: Critical Perspectives Past and Present* (New York: Amistad, 1993), p. 331.
2. Ibid.
3. Ruth-Ellen Boetcher Joeres and Elizabeth Mittman, 'An Introductory Essay', in Ruth-Ellen Boetcher Joeres and Elizabeth Mittman (eds), *The Politics of the Essay: Feminist Perspectives* (Bloomington: Indiana University Press, 1993), p. 16.
4. Roland Barthes, 'The Death of the Author' [1968], in Philip Rice and Patricia Waugh (eds), *Modern Literary Theory: a Reader*, second edition (London: Edward Arnold, 1992), pp. 114–18.
5. Sharon Wilson, 'An Interview with Alice Walker' [1984], in Gates and Appiah (eds), *Alice Walker*, p. 319.
6. Alice Walker, 'The Black Writer and the Southern Experience' [1970], in *In Search of Our Mothers' Gardens: Womanist Prose* (London: Women's Press, 1984), p. 17.
7. Ibid., p. 21.
8. Alice Walker, 'Saving the Life That Is Your Own: The Importance of Models in the Artist's Life', in *In Search of Our Mothers' Gardens*, pp. 3–14; 'The Old Artist: Notes on Mr Sweet', in *Living by the Word: Selected Writings 1973–1987* (London: Women's Press, 1988), p. 38. 'The Revenge of Hannah Kemhuff' and 'To Hell with Dying' are published in Alice Walker, *In Love and Trouble: Stories of Black Women* [1973] (London: Women's Press, 1984).
9. Alice Walker, 'Beauty: When the Other Dancer Is the Self' [1984], in *In Search of Our Mothers' Gardens*, p. 386.
10. Ibid., p. 393.
11. O'Brien, 'Alice Walker: an Interview', p. 327.
12. Alice Walker, 'The Unglamorous But Worthwhile Duties of the Black Revolutionary Artist, or of the Black Writer Who Simply Works and Writes' [1971], in *In Search of Our Mothers' Gardens*, p. 130.
13. O'Brien, 'Alice Walker: an Interview', p. 330.
14. Ibid., p. 329.

15. Alice Walker, 'The Civil Rights Movement: What Good Was It?' [1967], in *In Search of Our Mothers' Gardens*, p. 125.

16. Alice Walker, '"But Yet and Still the Cotton Gin Kept on Working…"' [1970], in *In Search of Our Mothers' Gardens*, p. 28.

17. Alice Walker, 'Breaking Chains and Encouraging Life' [1980], in *In Search of Our Mothers' Gardens*, pp. 287–8.

18. Alice Walker, '*One* Child of One's Own' [1979], in *In Search of Our Mothers' Gardens*, p. 367.

19. O'Brien, 'Alice Walker: an Interview', p. 337.

20. Walker, '*One* Child of One's Own', p. 372.

21. Alice Walker, 'Writing *The Color Purple*' [1982], in *In Search of Our Mothers' Gardens*, p. 357.

22. Alice Walker, 'Coming in from the Cold: Welcoming the Old, Funny-talking Ancient Ones into the Warm Room of Present Consciousness, or, Natty Dread Rides Again!' [1984], in *Living by the Word*, p. 55.

23. Alice Walker, 'In the Closet of the Soul' [1987], in *Living by the Word*, p. 79.

24. Ibid., p. 82.

25. Ibid., p. 87.

26. O'Brien, 'Alice Walker: an Interview', p. 332.

27. Alice Walker, 'The Only Reason You Want to Go to Heaven Is That You Have Been Driven Out of Your Mind (Off Your Land and Out of Your Lover's Arms): Clear Seeing Inherited Religion and the Pagan Self' [*sic*], in *Anything We Love Can Be Saved: A Writer's Activism* (London: Women's Press, 1997), p. 17.

28. Miller's whole *oeuvre* focuses on various forms of child abuse; see, for example, *The Untouched Key: Tracing Childhood Trauma in Creativity and Destructiveness* (London: Virago, 1990) and *Banished Knowledge: Facing Childhood Injuries* (London: Virago, 1991).

29. Alice Walker, '"You All Have Seen": If the Women of the World Were Comfortable, This Would be a Comfortable World', in *Anything We Love Can Be Saved*, p. 31.

30. Alice Walker, 'A Letter to President Clinton' [1996], in *Anything We Love Can Be Saved*, p. 209.

31. Ibid.

32. Wilson, 'An Interview with Alice Walker', p. 320.

33. Alice Walker, 'Getting as Black as My Daddy: Thoughts on the Unhelpful Aspects of Destructive Criticism', in *Anything We Love Can Be Saved*, p. 151.

34. Alice Walker, 'This That I Offer You: People Get Tired; Sometimes They Have Other Things to Do', in *Anything We Love Can Be Saved*, p. 177.

35. Alice Walker, 'Zora Neale Hurston: a Cautionary Tale and a Partisan View' [1979], in *In Search of Our Mothers' Gardens*, p. 92.

36. Diane Sadoff, 'Black Matrilineage: The Case of Walker and Hurston', in Harold Bloom (ed.), *Alice Walker*, Modern Critical Views (New York: Chelsea House, 1989), p. 118.

37. Kadiatu Kanneh, 'Mixed Feelings: When My Mother's Garden is Unfamiliar', in Sally Ledger, Josephine McDonagh and Jane Spencer

(eds), *Political Gender: Texts and Contexts* (London: Harvester Wheat-sheaf, 1994), p. 36.

38. Lillie P. Howard (ed.), *Alice Walker and Zora Neale Hurston: the Common Bond* (London: Greenwood Press, 1993); Molly Hite, 'Romance, Marginality and Matrilineage: *The Color Purple* and *Their Eyes Were Watching God*', in Henry Louis Gates Jr (ed.), *Reading Black, Reading Feminist: a Critical Anthology* (New York: Meridian, 1990), pp. 431–54; Henry Louis Gates Jr, 'Color Me Zora', in Gates and Appiah (eds), *Alice Walker*, pp. 239–60.

39. Gates, 'Color Me Zora', p. 244; Michael Cooke, *Afro-American Literature in the Twentieth Century: the Achievement of Intimacy* (London: Yale University Press, 1984), p. 34.

40. Wilson, 'An Interview with Alice Walker', p. 324.

41. Trudier Harris, 'Our People, Our People', in Howard (ed.), *Alice Walker and Zora Neale Hurston*, p. 32.

42. Alice Walker, 'Saving the Life That Is Your Own: the Importance of Models in the Artist's Life' [1976], in *In Search of Our Mothers' Gardens*, p. 11.

43. Alice Walker, 'Everyday Use', in *In Love and Trouble*, pp. 47–59.

44. Wilson, 'An Interview with Alice Walker', p. 320.

45. O'Brien, 'Alice Walker: an Interview', p. 338.

46. Alice Walker, *In Search of Our Mothers' Gardens*, pp. xi–xii.

47. Tuzyline Jita Allan, *Womanist & Feminist Aesthetics: A Comparative Review* (Athens: Ohio University Press, 1995), p. 6.

48. Ibid., p. 93.

49. Walker, 'Saving the Life That Is Your Own', p. 5.

50. Ibid., p. 14; Alice Walker, 'The River: Honoring the Difficult', in *The Same River Twice*, p. 41.

51. Virginia Woolf, *A Room of One's Own* (New York: Harcourt Brace Jovanovich, 1927), p. 79.

52. Alice Walker, 'In Search of Our Mothers' Gardens' [1974], in *In Search of Our Mothers' Gardens*, p. 234.

53. Ibid., p. 240.

54. Alice Walker, 'Beyond the Peacock: the Reconstruction of Flannery O'Connor' [1975], in *In Search of Our Mothers' Gardens*, p. 43.

55. Alice Walker, 'Alice Walker on the Movie The Color Purple', in *The Same River Twice*, p. 203.

56. Toni Morrison, 'Unspeakable Things Unspoken: the Afro-American Presence in American Literature', *Michigan Quarterly Review* (Winter 1988), p. 11.

57. Woolf, *A Room of One's Own*, p. 52.

58. Virginia Woolf, *Three Guineas* [1938] (Harmondsworth: Penguin, 1977), p. 125.

59. For this kind of internationalism, see, for example, Patricia Hill Collins, *Black Feminist Thought: Knowledge, Consciousness, and the Politics of Empowerment* (London: Routledge, 1991); Carole Boyce Davies, *Black Women, Writing and Identity: Migrations of the Subject* (London: Routledge, 1994) and the two volumes of *Moving Beyond Boundaries*: vol.1, Carole Boyce

Davies and 'Molara Ogundipe-Leslie (eds), *International Dimensions of Black Women's Writing* (London: Pluto, 1995), and vol. 2, Carole Boyce Davies (ed.), *Black Women's Diasporas* (London: Pluto, 1995).

60.   Walker, 'One Child of One's Own', p. 378.
61.   Morrison, 'Unspeakable Things Unspoken', p. 10.
62.   Ibid., p. 9.
63.   Alice Walker, 'Deep Waters', in *The Same River Twice*, p. 216.

Chapter 2   *The Third Life of Grange Copeland*

1.   Alice Walker, *The Third Life of Grange Copeland* [1970], with a new Afterword (London: Women's Press, 1991); all page references are given in the text.
2.   See, for example, Josephine Hendin's review, originally published in *Saturday Review*, 22 August 1970 and Robert Coles's in *The New Yorker*, 27, February 1971, both in Henry Louis Gates Jr and K. A. Appiah (eds), *Alice Walker: Critical Perspectives Past and Present* (New York: Amistad Press, 1993), pp. 3–8.
3.   Klaus Ensslen, 'Collective Experience and Individual Responsibility: Alice Walker's *The Third Life of Grange Copeland*', in Peter Bruck and Wolfgang Karrer (eds), *The Afro-American Novel since 1960* (Amsterdam: Gruner, 1982), p. 194.
4.   Hortense Spillers, 'Afterword: Cross-Currents, Discontinuities: Black Women's Fiction', in Marjorie Pryse and Hortense Spillers (eds), *Conjuring: Black Women, Fiction, and Literary Tradition* (Bloomington: Indiana University Press, 1985), p. 255.
5.   Elliott Butler-Evans, *Race, Gender and Desire: Narrative Strategies in the Fiction of Toni Cade Bambara, Toni Morrison and Alice Walker* (Philadelphia: Temple University Press, 1989), p. 133.
6.   Alice Walker, 'Interview with John O'Brien', in Gates and Appiah (eds), *Alice Walker*, p. 332.
7.   Ensslen, 'Collective Experience and Individual Responsibility', p. 210; p. 212.
8.   Madhu Dubey, *Black Women Novelists and the Nationalist Aesthetic* (Bloomington: Indiana University Press, 1994), p. 112.
9.   Lawrence W. Hogue, 'Discourse of the Other: *The Third Life of Grange Copeland*', in Harold Bloom (ed.), *Alice Walker* (New York: Chelsea House, 1989), p. 113.
10.   Alice Walker, 'From an Interview', in *In Search of Our Mothers' Gardens: Womanist Prose* [1983] (London: Women's Press, 1984), pp. 250–1.
11.   Dubey, *Black Women Novelists and the Nationalist Aesthetic*, p. 115.
12.   Joyce A. Ladner, *Tomorrow's Tomorrow: The Black Woman* [1971] (New York: Doubleday, 1972), p. 40; p. 43.
13.   Robert Staples, 'The Myth of the Black Matriarchy', in *The Black Scholar* (January–February 1970); Toni Cade (ed.), *The Black Woman: an Anthology* (New York: New American Library, 1970).

14. Walker, 'Interview with John O'Brien', p. 335.
15. Sigmund Freud, 'Family Romances' [1909], in *On Sexuality: Three Essays on the Theory of Sexuality and Other Works*, The Pelican Freud Library, vol. 7 (Harmondsworth: Penguin, 1977), p. 221.
16. Ibid., p. 223.
17. Ibid., p. 224.
18. Ibid., p. 221.
19. See, for the Emmett Till story, Studs Terkel, *Race* (London: Minerva, 1992), pp. 19–26 and Cynthia Griggs Fleming, 'African-Americans', in John D. Buenker and Lorman A. Ratner (eds), *Multiculturalism in the United States: A Comparative Guide to Acculturation and Ethnicity* (New York: Greenwood Press, 1992), pp. 20–1.
20. Alice Miller, *Banished Knowledge: Facing Childhood Injuries* [1988: *Das Verbannte Wissen*] (London: Virago, 1991), pp. 1–2.
21. Sigmund Freud, 'The Psychology of Women', in *New Introductory Lectures on Psychoanalysis* [1932] (London: The Hogarth Press and the Institute of Psychoanalysis, 1962), p. 166.
22. Frantz Fanon, *Black Skin, White Masks* [1952] (London: Pluto Press, 1986), pp. 152–3.
23. Carolyn Steedman, *Landscape for a Good Woman: a Story of Two Lives* (London: Virago, 1986), p. 52.
24. Ibid., p. 72.
25. Fanon, *Black Skin, White Masks*, p. 150.
26. Ibid.
27. Linda Ruth Williams, *Critical Desire: Psychoanalysis and the Literary Subject* (London: Edward Arnold, 1995), p. 1.
28. Ibid., p. 17 (original emphasis).
29. Gloria Wade-Gayles, *No Crystal Stair: Visions of Race and Sex in Black Women's Fiction* (New York: Pilgrim Press, 1984), p. 102.
30. Richard Godden, *Fictions of Capital: the American Novel from James to Mailer* (Cambridge: Cambridge University Press, 1990), p. 140.
31. Alice Walker, 'Afterword' to 1991 edition of *The Third Life of Grange Copeland*, p. 251.
32. Len Davis interviewed by Bob Blauner, *Black Lives, White Lives: Three Decades of Race Relations in America* (Berkeley: University of California Press, 1989), p. 30.
33. Melissa Walker, *Down From the Mountaintop: Black Women's Novels in the Wake of the Civil Rights Movement, 1966–1989* (New Haven: Yale University Press, 1991), p. 115.
34. Peter Erickson, '"Cast Out Alone/to Heal/and Recreate Ourselves": Family-based Identity in the Work of Alice Walker', in Bloom (ed.), *Alice Walker*, pp. 5–24.
35. Dubey, *Black Women Novelists and the Nationalist Aesthetic*, p. 112.
36. Sandi Russell, *Render Me My Song: African-American Women Writers from Slavery to the Present* (New York: St Martin's Press, 1990), p. 127; p. 122.
37. Fanon, *Black Skin, White Masks*, p. 142.

Chapter 3   *Meridian*

1. Alice Walker, 'The Civil Rights Movement: What Good Was It?' [1967], in *In Search of Our Mothers' Gardens: Womanist Prose* (London: Women's Press, 1983), pp. 119–29; *Meridian* [1976] (London: Women's Press, 1983); all page references will be given in the text.

2. For the connections between feminism and Civil Rights see, for example, Sara Evans, *Personal Politics: the Roots of Women's Liberation in the Civil Rights Movement and the New Left* (New York: Random House, 1979).

3. David Bradley, 'Telling the Black Woman's Story', *New York Times Magazine* (January 1984), p. 31.

4. For Bearden, see Regenia A. Perry, *Free within Ourselves: African-American Artists in the Collection of the National Museum of American Art* (Washington, DC: National Museum of American Art, Smithsonian Institution, 1992), pp. 29–36; Jean Toomer, *Cane* (New York: Liveright, 1975).

5. 'Alice Walker', in Claudia Tate (ed.), *Black Women Writers at Work* [1983] (Harpenden: Oldcastle Books, 1989), p. 176.

6. Christine Hall, 'Art, Action and the Ancestors: Alice Walker's *Meridian* in Its Context', in Gina Wisker (ed.), *Black Women's Writing* (London: Macmillan, 1993), p. 97.

7. For example, Gloria Wade-Gayles, *No Crystal Stair: Visions of Race and Sex in Black Women's Fiction* (New York: The Pilgrim Press, 1984), p. 211; John F. Callahan, 'The Hoop of Language: Politics and the Restoration of Voice in *Meridian*', in Harold Bloom (ed.), *Alice Walker*, Modern Critical Views (New York: Chelsea House, 1989), p. 157.

8. bell hooks, 'Gangsta Culture – Sexism and Misogyny', in *Outlaw Culture: Resisting Representation* (London: Routledge, 1994), p. 116.

9. 'Maya Angelou Talking with Rosa Guy', in Mary Chamberlain (ed.), *Writing Lives: Conversations Between Women Writers* (London: Virago, 1988), p. 17.

10. Callahan, 'The Hoop of Language', p. 160.

11. Joseph E. Lowery, Methodist minister in Mobile in the 1950s, in Howell Raines, *My Soul Is Rested: Movement Days in the Deep South Remembered* [1977] (New York: Bantam, 1978), p. 66.

12. James Farmer in Raines, *My Soul Is Rested*, p. 134.

13. Bernice Johnson Reagon, 'Women as Culture Carriers in the Civil Rights Movement: Fannie Lou Hamer', in Vicki L. Crawford, Jacqueline Anne Rouse and Barbara Woods (eds), *Women in the Civil Rights Movement: Torchbearers and Trailblazers 1941–1965* [1990] (Bloomington: Indiana University Press, 1993), pp. 103–4.

14. Andrew Ross, 'The Gangsta and the Diva', *The Nation*, 22/29 August 1994, p. 192.

15. bell hooks, 'Ice Cube Culture', in *Outlaw Culture*, p. 136.

16. Alice Walker, *The Temple of My Familiar* (Harmondsworth: Penguin, 1990), p. 262. I use this line also as the conclusion to a chapter

on *Meridian* which presents a different (more psychoanalytic) reading from the one proposed here. See Maria Lauret, *Liberating Literature: Feminist Fiction in America* (London: Routledge, 1994), pp. 124–43.

17. Thulani Davis, *1959* [1992] (London: Penguin, 1993); Toni Cade Bambara, *The Salt Eaters* [1980] (London: Women's Press, 1982).

18. Alan Nadel, 'Reading the Body: *Meridian* and the Archeology of Self', in Henry Louis Gates Jr and K. A. Appiah (eds), *Alice Walker: Critical Perspectives Past and Present* (New York: Amistad, 1993), p. 156.

19. Greil Marcus, 'Review of *Meridian*' [1976], in Gates and Appiah (eds), *Alice Walker*, p. 12.

20. Fannie Lou Hamer, cited in Kay Mills, *This Little Light of Mine: the Life of Fannie Lou Hamer* (New York: Penguin, 1994), p. 79.

21. Dave Dennis in Raines, *My Soul Is Rested*, p. 301.

22. This phrase is cited by Mills in *This Little Light of Mine*, p. 87.

23. Mary Aickin Rothschild, 'White Women Volunteers in the Freedom Summers: Their Life and Work in a Movement for Social Change', *Feminist Studies*, 5:3 (Fall 1979), p. 482.

24. SNCC Members of the Atlanta Project, 'A Position Paper on Race', in Joanne Grant (ed.), *Black Protest: History, Documents, Analyses 1619 to the Present*, second edition (New York: Random House, 1991), p. 453.

25. Howard Zinn, 'The Limits of Non-Violence', in Joanne Grant (ed.), *Black Protest*, pp. 312–17; James Forman, 'Black Manifesto' in the same collection, pp. 443–4.

26. 'Alice Walker', in Tate (ed.), *Black Women Writers at Work*, pp. 179–80.

27. Anne Moody, *Coming of Age in Mississippi* (New York: Doubleday, 1968), p. 328.

28. Dave Dennis, cited by Raines in *My Soul Is Rested*, p. 304; p. 302.

29. Lawrence Guyot in interview with Raines, *My Soul Is Rested*, p. 317.

30. Deborah E. McDowell, 'The Self in Bloom: Walker's *Meridian*', in Gates and Appiah (eds), *Alice Walker*, p. 173.

31. Amy-Jacques Garvey, 'Women as Leaders' [1925], in Gerda Lerner (ed.), *Black Women in White America: A Documentary History* (New York: Panther, 1972) p. 578.

32. Moody, *Coming of Age in Mississippi*, p. 370; p. 371.

33. Marcus, 'Review of *Meridian*', p. 11; Jean Toomer, 'The Blue Meridian' [1925], in Darwin T. Turner (ed.), *The Wayward and the Seeking: A Collection of Writings by Jean Toomer* (Washington, DC: Howard University Press, 1982), pp. 214–34.

34. Sojourner Truth, cited by Lerner in *Black Women in White America*, p. 371.

35. Alice Walker, 'A Name Is Sometimes an Ancestor Saying Hi, I'm With You', in *Living by the Word: Selected Writings 1973–1987* [1986] (London: Women's Press, 1988), p. 97.

36. Jack Forbes, *Africans and Native Americans: the Language of Race and the Evolution of Red-Black Peoples*, second edition (Urbana: University of Illinois Press, 1993), p. 62; p. 189.

37. Ibid., p. 219.
38. Sojourner Truth, 'Convention of the American Equal Rights Association, New York City 1867', in Lerner (ed.), *Black Women in White America*, p. 569.
39. Ibid., p. 370.
40. Hall, 'Art, Action and the Ancestors', pp. 98–9.
41. Martha J. McGowan, 'Atonement and Release in Alice Walker's *Meridian*', *Studies in Modern Fiction*, XXIII:1 (1981), pp. 25–36; Barbara Christian, 'The Black Woman Artist as Wayward', in *Black Feminist Criticism: Perspectives on Black Women Writers* (New York: Pergamon, 1985), p. 89, rpt. in Bloom (ed.), *Alice Walker*, p. 47.
42. Susan Willis, *Specifying: Black Women Writing the American Experience* (Madison: University of Illinois Press, 1987), p. 124.
43. For this kind of critique of women's liberation, see Patricia Hill Collins, *Black Feminist Thought: Knowledge, Consciousness and the Politics of Empowerment*, Perspectives on Gender, vol. 2 (London: Routledge, 1991); Angela Davis, *Women, Race and Class* (London: Women's Press, 1982); bell hooks, *Ain't I a Woman: Black Women and Feminism* (London: Pluto Press, 1982); and my own *Liberating Literature*, which draws on these sources.
44. Toni Morrison, *Beloved* (New York: Signet, 1987).
45. Rhetaugh Graves Dumas, 'Dilemmas of Black Females in Leadership', in LaFrances Rodgers-Rose (ed.), *The Black Woman* (London: Sage, 1980), p. 210.
46. Ibid., p. 207.
47. See Ann Standley, 'The Role of Black Women in the Civil Rights Movement', in Crawford et al. (eds), *Women in the Civil Rights Movement*, p. 197.
48. Ella Baker, 'Developing Community Leadership', in Lerner (ed.), *Black Women in White America*, pp. 345–52.
49. Lawrence Guyot, interviewed in Raines, *My Soul Is Rested*, p. 261.
50. Ibid.
51. Alice Walker, 'The Right to Life: What Can the White Man . . . Say to the Black Woman?', *The Nation*, 22 May 1989, in Katrina Vanden Heuvel (ed.), *The Nation: Selections from the Independent Magazine of Politics and Culture 1865/1990* (London: Pluto Press, 1991), pp. 462–3.
52. I have written elsewhere of the way in which interracial rape is treated contextually in *Meridian* and in the short story 'Advancing Luna – and Ida B.Wells', which is usefully read as its companion piece; Lauret, *Liberating Literature*, pp. 131–3.
53. Gloria T. Hull, Patricia Bell Scott and Barbara Smith (eds), *All the Women Are White, All the Men Are Black, But Some of Us Are Brave: Black Women's Studies* (Old Westbury: The Feminist Press, 1982).
54. Hall, 'Art, Action and the Ancestors', p. 105.
55. Walker, 'The Civil Rights Movement: What Good Was It?', p. 120.
56. Ibid.
57. Franklin McCain, interviewed by Raines in *My Soul Is Rested*, p. 79.

58. Fannie Lou Hamer, cited by Bernice Johnson Reagon, 'Women as Culture Carriers: Fannie Lou Hamer', in Crawford et al. (eds), *Women in the Civil Rights Movement*, p. 216.

Chapter 4 *The Color Purple*

1. Sally Placksin, *Jazzwomen 1900 to the Present: Their Lives and Music* [1982] (London: Pluto Press, 1985), p. 20.
2. Alice Walker, 'Looking for Zora' [1975], in *In Search of Our Mothers' Gardens: Womanist Prose* [1983] (London: Women's Press, 1984), pp. 93–116.
3. Alice Walker, *The Color Purple* (London: Women's Press, 1982); all page references are given in the text.
4. Some of this debate is documented in Walker's collection *The Same River Twice: Honoring the Difficult. A Meditation on Life, Spirit, Art and the Making of the Film The Color Purple Ten Years Later* (London: Women's Press, 1996). For reception of the film, see also Jacqueline Bobo, '*The Color Purple*: Black Women as Cultural Readers', in E. Deirdre Pribram (ed.), *Female Spectators: Looking at Film and Television* (London: Verso, 1988), pp. 90–109.
5. Alan Sinfield, contribution to Brighton LTP (Literature Teaching Politics) Group, *Problems of the Progressive Text: The Color Purple by Alice Walker* (Brighton: LTP, 1985), p. 117.
6. bell hooks, 'Writing the Subject: Reading *The Color Purple*', in Harold Bloom (ed.), *Alice Walker, Modern Critical Views* (New York: Chelsea House, 1988), p. 215. Also published as 'Reading and Resistance: *The Color Purple*', in Henry Louis Gates Jr (ed.), *Reading Black, Reading Feminist: a Critical Anthology* (New York: Penguin, 1990), pp. 454–71; and in Henry Louis Gates Jr and K. A. Appiah (eds), *Alice Walker: Critical Perspectives Past and Present* (New York: Amistad, 1993), pp. 284–95.
7. Lauren Berlant, 'Race, Gender and Nation in *The Color Purple*', in Gates and Appiah (eds), *Alice Walker*, p. 212.
8. Darryl Pinckney, 'Black Victims, Black Villains', *The New York Review of Books*, 29 January 1987, p. 17.
9. bell hooks, 'Writing the Subject: Reading *The Color Purple*', in Bloom (ed.), *Alice Walker*, p. 217.
10. Melissa Walker, *Down from the Mountaintop: Black Women's Writing in the Wake of the Civil Rights Movement, 1966–1989* (New Haven and London: Yale University Press, 1991), p. 63; p. 71.
11. See, for example, Charles Proudfit, 'Celie's Search for Identity: a Psychoanalytic Developmental Reading of Alice Walker's *The Color Purple*', *Contemporary Literature*, 32:1 (Spring 1991), pp. 12–37; Daniel W. Ross, 'Celie in the Looking Glass: the Desire for Selfhood in *The Color Purple*', *Modern Fiction Studies*, 34:1 (1988), pp. 69–84; John J. Hiers, 'Creation Theology in Alice Walker's *The Color Purple*', *Notes on*

Contemporary Literature, XIV:4 (September 1984), pp. 2–3; Delores S. Williams, 'Black Women's Literature and the Task of Feminist Theology', in Clarissa W. Atkinson, Constance H. Buchanan and Margaret R. Miles (eds), *Immaculate & [sic] Powerful: the Female in Sacred Image and Social Reality* (Boston: Beacon Press, 1985), pp. 88–110.

12. Wendy Wall, 'Lettered Bodies and Corporeal Texts', in Appiah and Gates (eds), *Alice Walker*, p. 271.

13. See, for example, Michael Awkward, *Inspiriting Influences: Tradition, Revision and Afro-American Women's Novels* (New York: Columbia University Press, 1989), p. 139; Valerie Babb, '*The Color Purple*: Writing to Undo What Writing Has Done', *Phylon*, XLVII:2 (June 1986), pp. 107–16; Berlant, 'Race, Gender, and Nation in *The Color Purple*', p. 228; King-Kok Cheung, '"Don't Tell": Imposed Silences in *The Color Purple* and *The Woman Warrior*', *PMLA*, 103:2 (March 1988), pp. 162–74; Karla F. C. Holloway, *Moorings and Metaphors: Figures of Culture and Gender in Black Women's Literature* (New Brunswick: Rutgers University Press, 1992), p. 28.

14. See, for example, Awkward, *Inspiriting Influences*, p. 138; Marjorie Pryse, 'Introduction: Zora Neale Hurston, Alice Walker, and the Ancient Power of Black Women', in Marjorie Pryse and Hortense J. Spillers (eds), *Conjuring: Black Women, Fiction, and Literary Tradition* (Bloomington: Indiana University Press, 1985), p. 15.

15. Maya Angelou, *I Know Why the Caged Bird Sings* [1969] (London: Virago, 1984).

16. Christine Froula, 'The Daughter's Seduction: Sexual Violence and Literary History', *Signs*, 11:4 (Summer 1986), pp. 621–44.

17. Molly Hite, *The Other Side of the Story: Structures and Strategies of Contemporary Feminist Narrative* (London: Cornell University Press, 1989), p. 110.

18. Elizabeth Fifer, 'Alice Walker: the Dialect and Letters of *The Color Purple*', in Catherine Rainwater and William J. Schweick (eds), *Contemporary American Women Writers: Narrative Strategies* (Lexington: University Press of Kentucky, 1985), p. 163.

19. Linda Abbandonato, 'Rewriting the Heroine's Story in *The Color Purple*', in Gates and Appiah (eds), *Alice Walker*, pp. 296–308.

20. Henry Louis Gates Jr, *The Signifying Monkey: a Theory of African-American Literary Criticism* (Oxford: Oxford University Press, 1989), p. xvi; Wall, 'Lettered Bodies and Corporeal Texts', p. 272.

21. Anonymous, 'The Signifying Monkey' [1964], in Paul Lauter et al. (eds), *The Heath Anthology of American Literature*, vol. 2 (Lexington: D. C. Heath, 1990), pp. 202–3.

22. See Gates, *The Signifying Monkey*, pp. 51–5 and passim.

23. For these functions see, for example, Geneva Smitherman, *Talkin' and Testifyin': the Language of Black America* (Boston: Houghton Mifflin, 1977), pp. 119–20.

24. Marjorie Pryse, 'Introduction: Zora Neale Hurston, Alice Walker and the Ancient Power of Black Women', in Pryse and Spillers (eds), *Conjuring*, p. 19.

25. Calvin C. Hernton, *The Sexual Mountain and Black Women Writers: Adventures in Sex, Literature, and Real Life* (New York: Doubleday, 1987), p. 6.
26. Houston A. Baker Jr, *Workings of the Spirit: the Poetics of Afro-American Women's Writing* (London: University of Chicago Press, 1991), p. 42.
27. Harriet Jacobs, *Incidents in the Life of a Slave Girl, Written by Herself*, ed. Lydia Maria Child [1861], ed. and intro. Jean Fagan Yellin (London: Harvard University Press, 1987).
28. Gates, *The Signifying Monkey*, p. 52.
29. See for these points Walter J. Ong, *Orality and Literacy: the Technologizing of the Word*, New Accents Series [1982] (London: Routledge, 1989).
30. Christine Hall, 'Art, Action and the Ancestors: Alice Walker's *Meridian* in Context', in Gina Wisker (ed.), *Black Women's Writing* (London: Macmillan, 1993), p. 102; p. 104.
31. Anne Bradstreet, 'The Prologue', in Lauter et al. (eds), *The Heath Anthology of American Literature*, vol. 1, pp. 258–9; Charlotte Perkins Gilman, *The Yellow Wallpaper* [1892] (London: Virago, 1985); Virginia Woolf, *A Room of One's Own* [1929] (New York: Harcourt Brace Jovanovich, 1957); Tillie Olsen, *Silences* (London: Virago, 1980); Hélène Cixous, 'Sorties' and 'The Laugh of the Medusa', in Elaine Marks and Isabelle de Courtivron (eds), *New French Feminisms: an Anthology* (Brighton: Harvester Press, 1981), pp. 90–9; pp. 245–64.
32. Tamar Katz, '"Show Me How to Do Like You": Didacticism and Epistolary Form in *The Color Purple*', in Bloom (ed.), *Alice Walker*, pp. 185–93.
33. Graham Connah, *African Civilizations, Precolonial Cities and States in Tropical Africa: An Archaeological Perspective* (Cambridge: Cambridge University Press, 1987), p. 101; and map of precolonial trade routes and commodities in West Africa, p. 118.
34. Frances D. Gage/Sojourner Truth, 'Reminiscences of Frances D.Gage of Sojourner Truth, for May 28–29, 1851', in Lauter et al. (eds), *The Heath Anthology of American Literature*, vol. 1, p. 1912; Frederick Douglass, 'What to the Slave is the Fourth of July?' [1852], in the same volume, pp. 1704–23.
35. Billie Holiday, 'I've Got a Right to Sing the Blues' (Harold Arlen/Ted Koehler), recorded 25 August 1955 in Los Angeles, on *The Essential Billie Holiday* (Polygram: 1992).
36. LeRoi Jones, *Blues People: Negro Music in White America* (New York: Morrow Quill, 1963), p. 12.
37. Houston A. Baker Jr, *Blues, Ideology and Afro-American Literature: a Vernacular Theory* (Chicago: Chicago University Press, 1984), p. 8.
38. Placksin, *Jazzwomen*, p. xv.
39. Angela Davis, 'Black Women and Music: a Historical Legacy of Struggle', in Joanne M. Braxton and Andrée Nicola McLaughlin (eds), *Wild Women in the Whirlwind: Afra-American Culture and the Contemporary Literary Renaissance* (London: Serpent's Tail, 1990), p. 7.
40. Frederick Douglass, *Narrative of the Life of an American Slave*, in Nina Baym et al. (eds), *The Norton Anthology of American Literature*, vol. I, third edition (New York: W. W. Norton, 1979), pp. 1887–8.

41. Billie Holiday, 'My Man' (Yvain/Charles/Willemetz/Pollock) and 'Good Morning Heartache' (Higginbotham/Drake/Fisher), both MCA Ltd and recorded on Decca between 1944 and 1950, on *Billie Holiday: the Essential Recordings* (MCA Records: 1993).

42. Cora Kaplan, 'Keeping the Colour in *The Color Purple*', in *Sea Changes: Essays in Culture and Feminism* (London: Verso, 1986), pp. 177–87.

43. For a thoughtful account of problems in teaching *The Color Purple*, see also Alison Light, 'Fear of the Happy Ending: *The Color Purple*, Reading, and Racism', in Linda Anderson (ed.), *Plotting Change: Contemporary Women's Fiction* (London: Edward Arnold, 1990), pp. 85–98, and June Jordan, 'Nobody Mean More to Me Than You and the Future Life of Willie Jordan', in *Moving Towards Home: Political Essays* (London: Virago, 1989), pp. 175–89.

44. Walker, *The Third Life of Grange Copeland*, p. 148.

45. Alice Walker, *Meridian* (London: Women's Press, 1982), p. 128.

46. Ray Pratt, *Rhythm and Resistance: Explorations in the Political Uses of Popular Music* (New York: Praeger, 1990), p. 83.

47. Alice Walker, 'Nineteen Fifty-five', in *You Can't Keep a Good Woman Down* (London: Women's Press, 1982), pp. 3–20.

48. Ibid., p. 4.

49. Ibid., p. 8.

50. Ibid., p. 13.

51. Alice Walker, 'Everyday Use', in *In Love and Trouble* [1973] (London: Women's Press, 1984), pp. 47–59.

52. Jones, *Blues People*, p. 93.

53. Hortense J. Spillers, 'Interstices: a Small Drama of Words', in Carole S. Vance (ed.), *Pleasure and Danger: Exploring Female Sexuality*, second edition (London: Pandora, 1992), p. 87.

54. Bessie Smith, 'I'm Wild at That Thing' (Williams) and 'You've Got to Give Me Some' (Williams) (n.d.) on *Blue Spirit Blues* (Tring International plc: n.d.)

55. Henry Louis Gates Jr, 'Color Me Zora', in Gates and Appiah (eds), *Alice Walker*, p. 255; Sharon Wilson, 'A Conversation with Alice Walker', *Kalliope*, 6:2 (1984), p. 38.

56. Ethel Waters with Charles Samuels, *His Eye Is on the Sparrow: an Autobiography* [1951] (New York: Da Capo, 1992), p. 93.

57. Ibid., p. 55.

58. Zora Neale Hurston, *Their Eyes Were Watching God* [1937] (London: Virago, 1987).

59. Waters, *His Eye Is on the Sparrow*, p. 240.

60. For what I have here called the blues discourse, see Elizabeth Schultz's article 'To Be Black and Blue: the Blues Genre in Black American Autobiography', in Albert E. Stone (ed.), *The American Autobiography: A Collection of Critical Essays* (Englewood Cliffs: Prentice Hall, 1981), pp. 109–32.

61. Waters, *His Eye Is on the Sparrow*, p. 1.

62. Michele Russell, 'Black-Eyed Blues Connections: Teaching Black Women', in Gloria T. Hull et al. (eds), *All the Women Are White, All the*

Men Are Black, But Some of Us Are Brave: Black Women's Studies (Old
Westbury: The Feminist Press, 1982), p. 202.

63. Michele Russell, 'Slave Codes and Liner Notes', in Hull et al. (eds), *But Some of Us Are Brave*, p. 131.
64. Pratt, *Rhythm and Resistance*, p. 85.
65. June Jordan, 'Nobody Mean More to Me Than You and the Future Life of Willie Jordan', p. 176.
66. Ibid., p. 177.
67. Ethel Waters, 'My Man' (Yvain/Charles/Willemetz/Pollock). In her introduction, Waters says she sings it as she did in 1924, but the actual recording date is unknown. On *Who Said Blackbirds Are Blue?* (Sandy Hook Records: 1981).
68. Deanna Campbell Robinson et al.(eds), *Music at the Margins: Popular Music and Global Cultural Diversity* (London: Sage, 1991), p. 44.
69. Patricia Hill Collins, *Black Feminist Thought: Knowledge, Consciousness and the Politics of Empowerment* (New York and London: Routledge, 1991), p. 102.
70. I thank John Moore for alerting me to the French origin of this song.
71. Paul Gilroy, *The Black Atlantic: Modernity and Double Consciousness* (London: Verso, 1993), p. 99.
72. Alice Walker, 'Saving the Life That Is Your Own: the Importance of Models in the Artist's Life' [1976], in *In Search of Our Mothers' Gardens: Womanist Prose* (London: Virago, 1984), p. 5.
73. Gilroy, *The Black Atlantic*, p. 106.
74. Missy Dehn Kubitschek, 'Subjugated Knowledge: Towards a Feminist Exploration of Rape in Afro-American Fiction', in Joel Weixlmann and Houston A. Baker Jr (eds), *Black Feminist Criticism and Critical Theory* (Greenwood: Penkevill, 1988), p. 45; p. 48.
75. Jordan, 'Nobody Means More to Me Than You and the Future Life of Willie Jordan', p. 175.
76. Babb, '*The Color Purple*: Writing to Undo What Writing Has Done'.

Chapter 5   *The Temple of My Familiar*

1. Alice Walker, *The Temple of My Familiar* [1989] (London: Penguin, 1990); all page references will be given in the text.
2. Lillie P. Howard, 'Benediction: A Few Words About *The Temple of My Familiar*, Variously Interpreted, and *Possessing the Secret of Joy*', in Howard (ed.), *Alice Walker and Zora Neale Hurston: The Common Bond* (London: Greenwood Press, 1993), p. 141; p. 142.
3. Alice Walker, 'Writing *The Color Purple*' [1982], in *In Search of Our Mothers' Gardens: Womanist Prose* (London: Women's Press, 1984), pp. 355–60.
4. Gloria Anzaldúa, *Borderlands/La Frontera: The New Mestiza* (San Francisco: Aunt Lute Books, 1987), pp. 69–70.

5. C. G. Jung, 'Approaching the Unconscious', in C. G. Jung et al. (eds), *Man and His Symbols* [1964] (London: Picador, 1978), p. 6.

6. Anthony Storr, *Jung* (London: Fontana, 1986), p. 13.

7. Jung, 'Approaching the Unconscious', p. 84.

8. For Jung's approach to the unconscious via a dialogue with one's 'inner cast of characters' see also Demaris S. Wehr, *Jung & Feminism: Liberating Archetypes* (London: Routledge, 1990), p. 58.

9. Ngũgĩ wa Thiong'O, *Decolonising the Mind: the Politics of Language in African Literature* (London: James Currey, 1986), pp. 56–7.

10. Carol Iannone, 'A Turning of the Critical Tide?', *Commentary*, 88:5 (November 1989), pp. 57–9.

11. Larry J. Zimmerman, *Native North America*, Living Wisdom Series (London: Macmillan, 1996), p. 7.

12. I take this formulation from J. Laplanche's *New Foundations for Psychoanalysis*, trans. David Macey (Oxford: Basil Blackwell, 1989), p. 118, but unfortunately he gives no reference to Jung for this concept.

13. C. G. Jung, 'Some Aspects of Modern Psychotherapy', in *The Practice of Psychotherapy: Essays on the Psychology of the Transference and Other Subjects*, second edition, trans. R. F. C. Hull (London: Routledge, 1993), p. 35.

14. C. G. Jung, 'The Aims of Psychotherapy', in *The Practice of Psychotherapy*, p. 52.

15. Alice Walker, *The Color Purple* [1982] (London: Women's Press, 1983), p. 243; p. 244.

16. J. M. Coetzee, [Review of *The Temple of My Familiar*] [1989 *New York Times Book Review*] in Henry Louis Gates Jr and K. A. Appiah (eds), *Alice Walker: Critical Perspectives Past and Present* (New York: Amistad, 1993), p. 26.

17. Ursula K. LeGuin, [review of *The Temple of My Familiar*] [1989 *San Francisco Review of Books*] in Gates and Appiah (eds), *Alice Walker*, p. 23.

18. Robert O. Stephens, *The Family Saga in the South: Generations and Destinies* (London: Louisiana State University Press, 1995), p. 6.

19. Hazel Carby, 'The Politics of Fiction, Anthropology, and the Folk: Zora Neale Hurston', in Géneviève Fabre and Robert O'Meally (eds), *History & Memory in African-American Culture* (New York: Oxford University Press, 1994), p. 38.

20. Eudora Welty, cited by Stephens in *The Family Saga in the South*, p. 7.

21. Terry Dehay, 'Narrating Memory', in Amritjit Singh, Joseph T. Skerrett Jr and Robert E. Hogan (eds), *Memory, Narrative and Identity: New Essays in Ethnic American Literatures* (London: Northeastern University Press, 1996), p. 33.

22. Ibid., p. 31.

23. Eva Lennox Birch, *Black American Women's Writing: A Quilt of Many Colours* (London: Harvester Wheatsheaf, 1994), p. 236.

24. Toni Morrison, 'Unspeakable Things Unspoken: The Afro-American Presence in American Literature', *Michigan Quarterly Review* (Winter 1988), p. 32.

25. Paul Gilroy, *The Black Atlantic: Modernity and Double Consciousness* (London: Verso, 1993) p. 2.

26. Kwame Anthony Appiah, *In My Father's House: Africa in the Philosophy of Culture* (Oxford: Oxford University Press, 1992), p. viii.

27. Wolfgang Karrer, 'Nostalgia, Amnesia, and Grandmothers: The Uses of Memory in Albert Murray, Sabine Ulibarri, Paula Gunn Allen, and Alice Walker', in Singh et al. (eds), *Memory, Narrative and Identity*, p. 142.

28. Alice Walker, 'Saving the Life That Is Your Own', in *In Search of Our Mothers' Gardens* (London: Women's Press, 1984), p. 5.

29. Jung, 'The Aims of Psychotherapy', p. 50.

30. Susan Willis, 'Memory and Mass Culture', in Fabre and O'Meally (eds), *History & Memory in African-American Culture*, p. 179.

31. Bessie Head, 'Notes on Novels' [1978], in *A Woman Alone: Autobiographical Writings* (London: Heinemann, 1990), p. 64.

32. Ngũgĩ, 'The Language of African Literature', in *Decolonising the Mind*, p. 64.

33. Coetzee [review of *The Temple of My Familiar*], p. 26.

34. Birch, *Black American Women's Writing*, p. 230.

35. Merlin Stone, *When God Was a Woman* (London: Harcourt Brace Jovanovich, 1976), p. 33.

36. Coetzee [review of *The Temple of My Familiar*], p. 24; LeGuin [review of *The Temple of My Familiar*], p. 22.

37. Stone, *When God Was a Woman*, p. 20.

38. Martin Bernal, *Black Athena: the Afro-Asiatic Roots of Classical Civilization. Volume I. The Fabrication of Ancient Greece 1785–1985* [1987] (London: Vintage, 1991), pp. 51–2; p. 70.

39. Ibid., p. 2.

40. See Sander Gilman, 'Black Bodies, White Bodies: Toward an Iconography of Female Sexuality in Late Nineteenth Century Art, Medicine and Literature', in Henry Louis Gates Jr (ed.), *'Race', Writing and Difference* (London: University of Chicago Press, 1986), p. 257.

41. The best-known source on Ishi's life is Theodora Kroeber, *Ishi in Two Worlds: A Biography of the Last Wild Indian in North America* (Berkeley: University of California Press, 1961).

42. Alice Walker, 'Turquoise and Coral: The Writing of *The Temple of My Familiar*', in *Anything We Love Can Be Saved: A Writer's Activism* (London: Women's Press, 1997), pp. 111–17.

43. Patricia Hearst told her own story in *Every Secret Thing* (Garden City, NY: Doubleday, 1982). It is discussed as a captivity narrative in Christopher Castiglia, *Bound and Determined: Captivity, Culture-Crossing, and White Womanhood from Mary Rowlandson to Patty Hearst* (London: University of Chicago Press, 1996), pp. 87–105 and in Joan Didion, 'Girl of the Golden West', in *After Henry* (London: Simon & Schuster, 1992), pp. 95–109.

44. For extracts from the diaries and notes of these women travellers see, for example, Mary Morris (ed.), *The Virago Book of Women Travellers* (London: Virago, 1994); Rebecca Stefoff, *Women of the World: Women Travellers and Explorers* (Oxford: Oxford University Press, 1992) and

Jane Robinson (ed.), *Unsuitable for Ladies: An Anthology of Women Travellers* (Oxford: Oxford University Press, 1994).

45. Appiah, *In My Father's House*, p. 130; see also, for example, V. Y. Mudimbe, *The Idea of Africa* (London: James Currey, 1994) and *The Invention of Africa* (Bloomington: Indiana University Press, 1988) on this point.

46. Toni Morrison, 'The Site of Memory', in William Zinsser (ed.), *Inventing the Truth: The Art and Craft of Memoir* (Boston: Houghton Mifflin, 1987), p. 111.

47. Fabre and O'Meally (eds), *History & Memory in African-American Culture*, p. 7.

48. Pierre Nora, 'Between Memory and History: *Les Lieux de Mémoire*', in ibid., p. 284.

49. Ibid., p. 285.

50. See Peter Nicholls, 'The Belated Postmodern: History, Phantoms, and Toni Morrison', in Sue Vice (ed.), *Psychoanalytic Criticism: A Reader* (Oxford: Polity Press, 1996), pp. 50–74.

51. For the contrast between Freud and Jung on this point, see Jean Laplanche and J. B. Pontalis, *The Language of Psychoanalysis* (New York: Norton, 1973), pp. 112–13 and Laplanche, *New Foundations for Psychoanalysis*, p. 118.

52. Nora, 'Between Memory and History', p. 300.

53. Howard Zinn, *A People's History of the United States* [1980] (New York: Harper Collins, 1990), p. 9.

Chapter 6   *Possessing the Secret of Joy*

1. Eva Lennox Birch, *Black American Women's Writing: A Quilt of Many Colours* (London: Harvester Wheatsheaf, 1994), p. 238.

2. Alice Walker, *Possessing the Secret of Joy* (London: Women's Press, 1992); all page references will be given in the text.

3. Kadiatu Kanneh, *African Identities: Race, Nation and Culture in Ethnography, Pan-Africanism and Black Literatures* (London: Routledge, 1998), p. 110.

4. Alice Walker, '*One* Child of One's Own: A Meaningful Transgression within the Work(s)' [1979], in *In Search of Our Mothers' Gardens: Womanist Prose* (London:Women's Press, 1984), p. 373.

5. Ibid., p. 361.

6. Ibid., p. 362.

7. Alice Walker and Pratibha Parmar, *Warrior Marks: Female Genital Mutilation and the Sexual Blinding of Women* (London: Jonathan Cape, 1993), p. 18.

8. Ibid., p. 307.

9. Walker, '*One* Child of One's Own', p. 379.

10. Ibid., p. 377.

11. Ibid., p. 379.

12. Ibid., p. 365.
13. See, for example, Patricia Hill Collins, *Black Feminist Thought: Knowledge, Consciousness and the Politics of Empowerment* (London: Routledge, 1991).
14. Walter J. Ong, *Orality and Literacy: the Technologizing of the Word* [1982] (London: Routledge, 1988), p. 41.
15. Nawal El Sadaawi, *The Hidden Face of Eve: Women in the Arab World* (London: Zed Books, 1980), p. 8.
16. Ama Ata Aidoo, 'Ghana: To Be a Woman', in Robin Morgan (ed.), *Sisterhood Is Global: The International Women's Movement Anthology* (New York: Doubleday, 1984), p. 258.
17. Ibid., p. 262.
18. I owe this reference to Gina Dent, 'Black Pleasure, Black Joy: An Introduction', in Gina Dent (ed.), *Black Popular Culture* (Bay Press: Seattle, 1992), p. 19 and to Angeletta K.M.Gourdine, 'Postmodern Ethnography and the Womanist Mission: Postcolonial Sensibilities in *Possessing the Secret of Joy*', *African American Review*, 30:2 (1996), p. 238.
19. Margaret Kent Bass, 'Alice's Secret', *CLA Journal*, XXXVIII:1 (September 1994), p. 5.
20. W. E. B. DuBois, *The Souls of Black Folk* [1903], rpt. in *Three Negro Classics* (New York: Avon, 1965), p. 215.
21. Walker and Parmar, *Warrior Marks*, p. 270.
22. Ibid., p. 19.
23. James Clifford, *The Predicament of Culture: Twentieth Century Ethnography, Literature and Art* (London: Harvard University Press, 1988), p. 10; p. 11.
24. El Sadaawi, *The Hidden Face of Eve*, p. 9.
25. Thiam quotes here from *La Cité Magique et Magie en Afrique Noire* by Jacques Lantier; Awa Thiam, *Black Sisters, Speak Out: Feminism and Oppression in Black Africa* [1978, *La Parole aux Négresses*] (London: Pluto Press, 1986), p. 58.
26. On this point see also Gay Wilentz's review 'Healing the Wounds of Time', *Women's Review of Books*, 10:5 (1993), p. 16.
27. Thiam, *Black Sisters, Speak Out*, p. 58.
28. Jomo Kenyatta, *Facing Mount Kenya: The Tribal Life of the Gikuyu* [1938] (London: Secker & Warburg, 1961), p. 162. Margaret Kent Bass also rereads this text in 'Alice's Secret'.
29. Ibid., p. 133.
30. Ibid., p. 146.
31. Ibid., p. xix.
32. John Mbiti, *African Religions & Philosophy* (London: Heinemann, 1969), p. 123.
33. Ibid., p. 57.
34. For a related discussion of Clifford and Walker, see Gourdine, 'Postmodern Ethnography and the Womanist Mission'.
35. Clifford, *The Predicament of Culture*, p. 46; p. 40.
36. Ibid., p. 60; p. 89.
37. Ibid., p. 60.

38.   For a critical examination of animus and anima see Anthony Storr,
      'Archetypes and the Collective Unconscious', in *Jung*, Fontana
      Modern Masters (London: Harper Collins, 1973), pp. 39–61.
39.   C. G. Jung, *Analytical Psychology: Its Theory and Practice (The Tavistock
      Lectures)* [1935] (London: Routledge, 1986), p. 155.
40.   Ibid., p. 165.
41.   Ibid., p. 166.
42.   See, for example, Sander L.Gilman, 'Black Bodies, White Bodies:
      Toward an Iconography of Female Sexuality in Late Nineteenth Cen-
      tury Art, Medicine and Literature', in Henry Louis Gates Jr (ed.),
      'Race', Writing and Difference (London: University of Chicago Press,
      1986), p. 257.
43.   Jung, *Analytical Psychology*, p. 166.
44.   Ibid., p. 181.
45.   Ibid., p. 183.
46.   Ibid., p. 172.
47.   Ibid., p. 186.
48.   Charles R. Larson, [review of] *'Possessing the Secret of Joy'* [5, July 1992,
      The Washington Post Book World] in Henry Louis Gates Jr and K. A.
      Appiah (eds), *Alice Walker: Critical Perspectives Past and Present* (New
      York: Amistad, 1993), pp. 27–9; Birch, *Black American Women's Writ-
      ing*, p. 237.
49.   Kimberley Joyce Pollock, 'A Continuum of Pain: a Woman's Legacy in
      Alice Walker's *Possessing the Secret of Joy*', in Elizabeth Brown-Guillory
      (ed.), *Women of Color: Mother–Daughter Relationships in 20th Century Lit-
      erature* (Austin: University of Texas Press, 1996), p. 38; p. 50 and Tina
      McElroy Ansa, [review of *Possessing the Secret of Joy*] [5 July 1992, *The
      Los Angeles Times Book Review*] in Gates and Appiah (eds), *Alice Walker*,
      p. 34.
50.   Bass, 'Alice's Secret', p. 10; p. 9.
51.   Kadiatu Kanneh, 'Feminism and the Colonial Body', in Bill Ashcroft,
      Gareth Griffiths and Helen Tiffin (eds), *The Post-colonial Studies Reader*
      (London: Routledge, 1995), p. 347.
52.   For a similar analysis of 'the' Third World woman in Western feminist
      scholarly discourse, see Chandra Talpade Mohanty's seminal essay
      'Under Western Eyes: Feminist Scholarship and Colonial Discourses',
      in Patrick Williams and Laura Chrisman (eds), *Colonial Discourse and
      Post-colonial Theory: A Reader* (London: Harvester Wheatsheaf, 1993),
      pp. 196–220.
53.   Wilentz, 'Healing the Wounds of Time', p. 16.
54.   Gourdine, 'Postmodern Ethnography and the Womanist Mission',
      p. 242.
55.   Victoria Moyston, 'Women Warriors' [an interview with Pratibha Par-
      mar], *Black Film Bulletin*, 1:3/4 (Autumn/Winter 1993–94), p. 12.
56.   Asma El Dareer, *Woman, Why Do You Weep? Circumcision and Its Conse-
      quences* (London: Zed Press, 1982). The copy whose marginal notes I
      quote is in Sussex University library, should anyone want to check.
57.   Dent, 'Black Pleasure, Black Joy', p. 4.

Chapter 7   *A Writer's Activism: Alice Walker, Her Critics, and 'the' Tradition*

1. Alice Walker, 'Recording the Seasons' [1976], in *In Search of Our Mother's Gardens: Womanist Prose* (London: Women's Press, 1983), p. 225.
2. Tillie Olsen, 'The Strike', in Charlotte Nekola and Paula Rabinowitz (eds), *Writing Red: an Anthology of American Women Writers, 1930–1940* (New York: The Feminist Press, 1987), pp. 245–51; also 'Political Silences', in *Silences* (London: Virago, 1980), pp. 143–4.
3. Alice Walker, 'Introduction', to *Anything We Love Can Be Saved: A Writer's Activism* (London: Women's Press, 1997), p. xx.
4. Alice Walker, 'Acknowledgements', in *Anything We Love Can Be Saved*, p. ix.
5. Marjorie Pryse, 'Introduction: Zora Neale Hurston, Alice Walker, and the "Ancient Power" of Black Women', in Marjorie Pryse and Hortense J. Spillers (eds), *Conjuring: Black Women, Fiction, and Literary Tradition* (Bloomington: Indiana University Press, 1985), pp. 3–4.
6. Alice Walker, 'Preface' to *Her Blue Body Everything We Know: Earthling Poems 1965–1990 Complete* (London: Women's Press, 1991), p. xv; 'Author's Preface' to *The Complete Stories* (London: Women's Press, 1994), p. ix.
7. Libby Brooks, 'Nobody's Darling', *Guardian*, 29 April 1998, p. 7.
8. Philip M. Royster, 'In Search of Our Father's Arms: Alice Walker's Persona of the Alienated Darling', *Black American Literature Forum*, 20:4 (Winter 1986), p. 367.
9. Ibid., p. 357; p. 361.
10. See, for example, Robert Staples on Shange and Michelle Wallace in 'The Myth of Black Macho: a Response to Angry Black Feminists', *The Black Scholar* (March–April 1979), pp. 24–33; Mel Watkins, 'Sexism, Racism and Black Women Writers', *New York Times Book Review*, 15 June 1986, pp. 1–3; and Darryl Pinckney, 'Black Victims, Black Villains', *The New York Review of Books*, 29 January 1987, pp. 17–20.
11. Alice Hall Petry, 'Walker: the Achievement of the Short Fiction', in Henry Louis Gates Jr and K. A. Appiah (eds), *Alice Walker: Critical Perspectives Past and Present* (New York: Amistad, 1993), p. 204.
12. David Bradley, in an otherwise thoughtful article, 'Telling the Black Woman's Story', *New York Times Magazine* (January 1984), p. 32.
13. Manning Marable, 'Rethinking Black Liberation: Towards a New Protest Paradigm', *Race & Class*, 38:4 (April–June 1997), p. 10.
14. Ibid., p. 9.
15. Alice Walker, 'What That Day Was Like For Me: the Million Man March' and 'A Letter to President Clinton', both in *Anything We Love Can Be Saved*, p. 106; p. 209. Marable, 'Rethinking Black Liberation', p. 7; p. 5.
16. Brooks, 'Nobody's Darling', p. 7.

17. Sojourner Truth did not write, but her *Narrative of Sojourner Truth* was recorded by Olive Gilbert; *The Life and Religious Experiences of Jarena Lee, a Colored Lady* and *An Autobiography: The Story of the Lord's Dealings with Mrs Amanda Smith, the Colored Evangelist* have both been published in the Schomburg Library of Nineteenth Century Black Women Writers, and Rebecca Cox Jackson's writings have been collected and edited by Jean McMahon Humez as *Gifts of Power: the Writings of Rebecca Jackson, Black Visionary, Shaker Eldress* (Amherst: University of Massachusetts Press, 1981).

18. Alice Walker, 'Gifts of Power: the Writings of Rebecca Jackson' [1981], in *In Search of Our Mother's Gardens*, pp. 78–9.

19. Henry Louis Gates Jr, 'Color Me Zora', in Gates and Appiah (eds), *Alice Walker*, p. 243.

20. Monica Sjöö and Barbara Mor, *The Great Cosmic Mother: Rediscovering the Religion of the Earth*, second edition (San Francisco: Harper, 1991), p. 335.

21. Ibid., p. 336.

22. Hortense J. Spillers, 'Afterword: Cross-Currents, Discontinuities: Black Women's Fiction', in Pryse and Spillers (eds), *Conjuring*, p. 250.

23. Henry Louis Gates Jr, 'Introduction', to Henry Louis Gates Jr (ed.), *Reading Black, Reading Feminist: A Critical Anthology* (New York: Meridian, 1990), p. 7.

24. See, for example, Lillie P. Howard (ed.), *Alice Walker and Zora Neale Hurston: the Common Bond* (London: Greenwood Press, 1993); on Walker and Wright, Spillers, 'Afterword: Cross-Currents, Discontinuities', pp. 254–6; on Walker and Harper, Deborah E. McDowell, '"The Changing Same": Generational Connections and Black Women Novelists', in Gates (ed.), *Reading Black, Reading Feminist*, pp. 91–115; on Walker and Ellison David Wyatt, 'Alice Walker', in Wyatt, *Out of the Sixties: Storytelling and the Vietnam Generation* (Cambridge: Cambridge University Press, 1993), pp. 122–37.

25. Pryse and Spillers (eds), *Conjuring*, p. 21.

26. Spillers, 'Afterword: Cross-Currents, Discontinuities', p. 251.

27. Ibid., p. 259.

28. Françoise Lionnet, *Postcolonial Representations: Women, Literature, Identity* (London: Cornell University Press, 1995), p. 5.

Postscript: *By the light of My Father's Smile*

1. Alice Walker, *By the Light of My Father's Smile: A Story of Requited Love, Crossing Over, and the Sexual Healing of the Soul* (London: Women's Press, 1998); all page references will be given in the text.

2. Alice Walker, 'The Child Who Favoured Daughter', in *In Love and Trouble: Stories of Black Women* [1973] (London: Women's Press, 1984), pp. 35–46.

3. Alice Walker, *Possessing the Secret of Joy* (London: Women's Press and Jonathan Cape, 1992), p. 3.

4. Jack D. Forbes, *Africans and Native Americans: The Language of Race and the Evolution of Red-Black Peoples* (Urbana and Chicago: University of Illinois Press, 1993), p. 165; see also Chapter 5.

5. Octavio Paz, *The Labyrinth of Solitude: Life and Thought in Mexico*, trans. Lysander Kemp [1959 *El Laberinto de la Soledad*] (Harmondsworth: Penguin, 1983), p. 46.

Select Bibliography

Works by Alice Walker

Walker, Alice, *The Third Life of Grange Copeland* [1970] rpt. with a new Afterword (London: Women's Press, 1991).
——, *In Love and Trouble: Stories of Black Women* [1973] (London: Women's Press, 1984).
——, *Meridian* [1976] (London: Women's Press, 1983).
——, (ed.), *I Love Myself When I Am Laughing...And Then Again When I Am Looking Mean and Impressive: A Zora Neale Hurston Reader* (New York: The Feminist Press, 1979).
——, *The Color Purple* [1982] (London: Women's Press, 1983).
——, *You Can't Keep a Good Woman Down* (London: Women's Press, 1982).
——, *In Search of Our Mothers' Gardens: Womanist Prose* [1983] (London: Women's Press, 1984).
——, *Living by the Word: Selected Writings 1973–1987* (London: Women's Press, 1988).
——, *To Hell with Dying* (London: Harcourt Brace, 1988).
——, 'The Right to Life: What Can the White Man...Say to the Black Woman?', *The Nation* 22 May 1989, rpt. in Katrina Vanden Heuvel (ed.), *The Nation: Selections from the Independent Magazine of Politics and Culture 1865/1990* (London: Pluto Press, 1991), pp. 460–3.
——, *The Temple of My Familiar* [1989] (Harmondsworth: Penguin, 1990).
——, *Finding the Green Stone* (London: Hodder & Stoughton, 1991).
——, *Her Blue Body Everything We Know: Earthling Poems 1965–1990 Complete* (London: Women's Press, 1991).
——, *Possessing the Secret of Joy* (London: Women's Press, 1992).
—— (and Pratibha Parmar), *Warrior Marks: Female Genital Mutilation and the Sexual Blinding of Women* (London: Jonathan Cape, 1993).
——, *The Complete Stories* (London: Women's Press, 1994).
——, *The Same River Twice: Honoring the Difficult. A Meditation on Life, Spirit, Art and the Making of the Film The Color Purple Ten Years Later* (London: Women's Press, 1996).
——, *Anything We Love Can Be Saved: A Writer's Activism* (London: Women's Press, 1997).
——, *By the Light of My Father's Smile* (London: Women's Press, 1998).

Secondary Texts

Abbandonato, Linda, 'Rewriting the Heroine's Story in *The Color Purple*', in Gates and Appiah (eds), *Alice Walker*, pp. 296–308.

Aidoo, Ama Ata, 'Ghana: To Be a Woman', in Robin Morgan (ed.), *Sisterhood Is Global: The International Women's Movement Anthology* (New York: Doubleday, 1984), pp. 258–65.

Allan, Tuzyline Jita, *Womanist & Feminist Aesthetics: A Comparative Review* (Athens: Ohio University Press, 1995).

Anzaldúa, Gloria, *Borderlands/La Frontera: The New Mestiza* (San Francisco: Aunt Lute Books, 1987).

Appiah, Kwame Anthony, *In My Father's House: Africa in the Philosophy of Culture* (Oxford: Oxford University Press, 1992).

Awkward, Michael, *Inspiriting Influences: Tradition, Revision and Afro-American Women's Novels* (New York: Columbia University Press, 1989).

Babb, '*The Color Purple*: Writing to Undo What Writing Has Done', *Phylon*, XLVII:2 (June 1986), pp. 107–16.

Baker, Houston A. Jr, *Blues, Ideology and Afro-American Literature: A Vernacular Theory* (Chicago: Chicago University Press, 1984).

——, *Workings of the Spirit: The Poetics of Afro-American Women's Writing* (London: University of Chicago Press, 1991).

Bass, Margaret Kent, 'Alice's Secret', *CLA Journal*, XXXVIII:1 (September 1994), pp. 1–10.

Berlant, Lauren, 'Race, Gender and Nation in *The Color Purple*', in Gates and Appiah (eds), *Alice Walker*, pp. 211–39.

Birch, Eva Lennox, *Black American Women's Writing: A Quilt of Many Colours* (London: Harvester Wheatsheaf, 1994).

Bloom, Harold (ed.), *Alice Walker: Modern Critical Views* (New York: Chelsea House, 1988).

Bobo, Jacqueline, '*The Color Purple*: Black Women as Cultural Readers', in E. Deirdre Pribram (ed.), *Female Spectators: Looking at Film and Television* (London: Verso, 1988), pp. 90–109.

Boetcher Joeres, Ruth-Ellen and Elizabeth Mittman (eds), *The Politics of the Essay: Feminist Perspectives* (Bloomington: Indiana University Press, 1993).

Bradley, David, 'Telling the Black Woman's Story', *New York Times Magazine* (January 1984), pp. 24–37.

Braxton, Joanne M. and Andrée Nicola McLaughlin (eds), *Wild Women in the Whirlwind: Afra-American Culture and the Contemporary Literary Renaissance* (London: Serpent's Tail, 1990).

Brighton LTP (Literature Teaching Politics) Group, *Problems of the Progressive Text: The Color Purple by Alice Walker* (Brighton: LTP, 1985).

Brooks, Libby, 'Nobody's Darling', *Guardian*, 29 April 1998, pp. 6–7.

Butler-Evans, Elliott, *Race, Gender and Desire: Narrative Strategies in the Fiction of Toni Cade Bambara, Toni Morrison and Alice Walker* (Philadelphia: Temple University Press, 1989).

Callahan, John F., 'The Hoop of Language: Politics and the Restoration of Voice in *Meridian*', in Bloom (ed.), *Alice Walker*, pp. 153–84.

Carby, Hazel, 'The Politics of Fiction, Anthropology, and the Folk: Zora Neale Hurston', in Fabre and O'Meally (eds), *History & Memory in African-American Culture*, pp. 28–44.

Cheung, King-Kok, '"Don't Tell": Imposed Silences in *The Color Purple* and *The Woman Warrior*', *PMLA*, 103:2 (March 1988), pp. 162–74

Christian, Barbara, *Black Feminist Criticism: Perspectives on Black Women Writers* (New York: Pergamon, 1985).

——, 'Fixing Methodologies: *Beloved*', in Elizabeth Abel, Barbara Christian and Hélène Moglen (eds), *Female Subjects in Black and White: Race, Psychoanalysis, Feminism* (Berkeley: University of California Press, 1997), pp. 363–70.

Clifford, James, *The Predicament of Culture: Twentieth Century Ethnography, Literature and Art* (London: Harvard University Press, 1988).

Collins, Patricia Hill, *Black Feminist Thought: Knowledge, Consciousness, and the Politics of Empowerment* (London: Routledge, 1991).

Cooke, Michael, *Afro-American Literature in the Twentieth Century: The Achievement of Intimacy* (London: Yale University Press, 1984).

Crawford, Vicki L., Jacqueline Anne Rouse and Barbara Woods (eds), *Women in the Civil Rights Movement: Torchbearers and Trailblazers 1941–1965* [1990] (Bloomington: Indiana University Press, 1993).

Davies, Carole Boyce, *Black Women, Writing and Identity: Migrations of the Subject* (London: Routledge, 1994).

——, (ed.), *Moving Beyond Boundaries: Vol. 2, Black Women's Diasporas* (London: Pluto, 1995).

——, and 'Molara Ogundipe-Leslie (eds), *Moving Beyond Boundaries: Vol. 1, International Dimensions of Black Women's Writing* (London: Pluto, 1995).

Davis, Angela, *Women, Race and Class* (London: Women's Press, 1982).

Dehay, Terry, 'Narrating Memory', in Singh et al. (eds), *Memory, Narrative and Identity*, pp. 26–44.

Dent, Gina (ed.), *Black Popular Culture* (Bay Press: Seattle, 1992).

Dixon, Melvin, 'The Black Writer's Use of Memory', in Fabre and O'Meally (eds), *History & Memory in African-American Culture*, pp. 18–27.

Dubey, Madhu, *Black Women Novelists and the Nationalist Aesthetic* (Bloomington: Indiana University Press, 1994).

El Dareer, Asma, *Woman, Why Do You Weep? Circumcision and Its Consequences* (London: Zed Press, 1982).

El Sadaawi, Nawal, *The Hidden Face of Eve: Women in the Arab World* (London: Zed Books, 1980).

Ensslen, Klaus, 'Collective Experience and Individual Responsibility: Alice Walker's *The Third Life of Grange Copeland*', in Peter Bruck and Wolfgang Karrer (eds), *The Afro-American Novel since 1960* (Amsterdam: Gruner, 1982), pp. 189–218.

Eriksson, Peter, '"Cast Out Alone/to Heal/and Recreate Ourselves": Family-based Identity in the Work of Alice Walker', in Bloom (ed.), *Alice Walker*, pp. 5–24.

Evans, Mari (ed.), *Black Women Writers: Arguments and Interviews* (London: Pluto, 1985).

Evans, Sara, *Personal Politics: the Roots of Women's Liberation in the Civil Rights Movement and the New Left* (New York: Random House, 1979).

Fabre, Géneviève and Robert O'Meally (eds), *History & Memory in African-American Culture* (New York: Oxford University Press, 1994).

Fanon, Frantz, *Black Skin, White Masks* [1952] (London: Pluto Press, 1986).

Fifer, Elizabeth, 'Alice Walker: the Dialect and Letters of *The Color Purple*', in Catherine Rainwater and William J. Schweick (eds), *Contemporary American Women Writers: Narrative Strategies* (Lexington: University Press of Kentucky, 1985), pp. 155–71.

Forbes, Jack, *Africans and Native Americans: The Language of Race and the Evolution of Red-Black Peoples*, second edition (Urbana: University of Illinois Press, 1993).

Freud, Sigmund, 'Family Romances' [1909], in Sigmund Freud, *On Sexuality: Three Essays on the Theory of Sexuality and Other Works*, The Pelican Freud Library, vol. 7 (Harmondsworth: Penguin, 1977).

Froula, Christine, 'The Daughter's Seduction: Sexual Violence and Literary History', *Signs*, 11:4 (Summer 1986), pp. 621–44.

Gates, Henry Louis Jr, *The Signifying Monkey: A Theory of African-American Literary Criticism* (Oxford: Oxford University Press, 1989).

——, (ed.), *Reading Black, Reading Feminist: A Critical Anthology* (New York: Meridian, 1990).

——, 'Color Me Zora', in Gates and Appiah (eds), *Alice Walker*, pp. 239–60.

——, and K. A. Appiah (eds), *Alice Walker: Critical Perspectives Past and Present* (New York: Amistad, 1993).

Gilroy, Paul, *The Black Atlantic: Modernity and Double Consciousness* (London: Verso, 1993).

Gourdine, Angeletta K. M., 'Postmodern Ethnography and the Womanist Mission: Postcolonial Sensibilities in *Possessing the Secret of Joy*', *African American Review*, 30:2 (1996), pp. 237–44.

Hall, Christine, 'Art, Action and the Ancestors: Alice Walker's *Meridian* in Its Context', in Gina Wisker (ed.), *Black Women's Writing* (London: Macmillan, 1993), pp. 96–110.

Hernton, Calvin C., *The Sexual Mountain and Black Women Writers: Adventures in Sex, Literature, and Real Life* (New York: Doubleday, 1987).

Hiers, John J., 'Creation Theology in Alice Walker's *The Color Purple*', *Notes on Contemporary Literature*, XIV:4 (September 1984), pp. 2–3.

Hite, Molly, *The Other Side of the Story: Structures and Strategies of Contemporary Feminist Narrative* (London: Cornell University Press, 1989).

——, 'Romance, Marginality and Matrilineage: *The Color Purple* and *Their Eyes Were Watching God*', in Gates (ed.), *Reading Black, Reading Feminist*, pp. 431–54.

Hogue, Lawrence W., 'Discourse of the Other: *The Third Life of Grange Copeland*', in Bloom (ed.), *Alice Walker*, pp. 97–114.

Holloway, Karla F. C., *Moorings and Metaphors: Figures of Culture and Gender in Black Women's Literature* (New Brunswick: Rutgers University Press, 1992).

hooks, bell, *Ain't I a Woman: Black Women and Feminism* (London: Pluto Press, 1982).

hooks, bell, *Outlaw Culture: Resisting Representation* (London: Routledge, 1994).
Howard, Lillie P. (ed.), *Alice Walker and Zora Neale Hurston: The Common Bond* (London: Greenwood Press, 1993).
Hull, Gloria T., Patricia Bell Scott and Barbara Smith (eds), *All the Women Are White, All the Men Are Black, But Some of Us Are Brave: Black Women's Studies* (Old Westbury: The Feminist Press, 1982).
Iannone, Carol, 'A Turning of the Critical Tide?', *Commentary*, 88:5 (November 1989), pp. 57–9.
Jones, Leroi, *Blues People: Negro Music in White America* (New York: Morrow Quill, 1963).
Jordan, June, *Moving Towards Home: Political Essays* (London: Virago, 1989).
Jung, Carl G., *Analytical Psychology: Its Theory and Practice (The Tavistock Lectures)* [1935] (London: Routledge, 1986).
——, *The Practice of Psychotherapy: Essays on the Psychology of the Transference and Other Subjects*, second edition, trans. R. F. C. Hull (London: Routledge, 1993).
——, et al. (eds), *Man and His Symbols* [1964] (London: Picador, 1978).
Kanneh, Kadiatu, 'Mixed Feelings: When My Mother's Garden is Unfamiliar', in Sally Ledger, Josephine McDonagh and Jane Spencer (eds), *Political Gender: Texts and Contexts* (London: Harvester Wheatsheaf, 1994), pp. 28–36.
——, 'Feminism and the Colonial Body', in Bill Ashcroft, Gareth Griffiths and Helen Tiffin (eds), *The Post-colonial Studies Reader* (London: Routledge, 1995), pp. 346–8.
——, *African Identities: Race, Nation and Culture in Ethnography, Pan-Africanism and Black Literatures* (London: Routledge, 1998).
Kaplan, Cora, 'Keeping the Colour in *The Color Purple*', in *Sea Changes: Essays in Culture and Feminism* (London: Verso, 1986), pp. 177–87.
Karrer, Wolfgang, 'Nostalgia, Amnesia, and Grandmothers: The Uses of Memory in Albert Murray, Sabine Ulibarri, Paula Gunn Allen, and Alice Walker', in Singh et al. (eds), *Memory, Narrative and Identity*, pp. 128–44.
Katz, Tamar, '"Show Me How to *Do* Like You": Didacticism and Epistolary Form in *The Color Purple*', in Bloom (ed.), *Alice Walker*, pp. 185–93.
Kubitschek, Missy Dehn, 'Subjugated Knowledge: towards a Feminist Exploration of Rape in Afro-American Fiction', in Joel Weixlmann and Houston A. Baker Jr (eds), *Black Feminist Criticism and Critical Theory* (Penkevill: Greenwood, 1988), pp. 43–56.
Lauret, Maria, *Liberating Literature: Feminist Fiction in America* (London: Routledge, 1994).
Lerner, Gerda (ed.), *Black Women in White America: A Documentary History* (New York: Panther, 1972).
Light, Alison, 'Fear of the Happy Ending: *The Color Purple*, Reading, and Racism', in Linda Anderson (ed.), *Plotting Change: Contemporary Women's Fiction* (London: Edward Arnold, 1990), pp. 85–98.
Lionnet, Françoise, *Postcolonial Representations: Women, Literature, Identity* (London: Cornell University Press, 1995).
Mbiti, John, *African Religions & Philosophy* (London: Heinemann, 1969).

McDowell, Deborah E., '"The Changing Same": Generational Connections and Black Women Novelists', in Gates (ed.), *Reading Black, Reading Feminist*, pp. 91–115.

——, 'The Self in Bloom: Walker's *Meridian*', in Gates and Appiah (eds), *Alice Walker*, pp. 168–78.

McGowan, Martha J., 'Atonement and Release in Alice Walker's *Meridian*', *Studies in Modern Fiction*, XXIII:1 (1981), pp. 25–36.

Miller, Alice, *The Untouched Key: Tracing Childhood Trauma in Creativity and Destructiveness* (London: Virago, 1990).

——, *Banished Knowledge: Facing Childhood Injuries* (London: Virago, 1991).

Mohanty, Chandra Talpade, 'Under Western Eyes: Feminist Scholarship and Colonial Discourses', in Patrick Williams and Laura Chrisman (eds), *Colonial Discourse and Post-colonial Theory: A Reader* (London: Harvester Wheatsheaf, 1993), pp. 196–220.

Moody, Ann, *Coming of Age in Mississippi* (New York: Doubleday, 1968).

Morrison, Toni, 'The Site of Memory', in William Zinsser (ed.), *Inventing the Truth: The Art and Craft of Memoir* (Boston: Houghton Mifflin, 1987), pp. 101–24.

——, 'Unspeakable Things Unspoken: the Afro-American Presence in American Literature', *Michigan Quarterly Review* (Winter 1988), pp. 1–34.

Moyston, Victoria, 'Women Warriors' [an interview with Pratibha Parmar], *Black Film Bulletin*, 1:3/4 (Autumn/Winter 1993–94), pp. 12–13.

Nadel, Alan, 'Reading the Body: *Meridian* and the Archeology of Self', in Gates and Appiah (eds), *Alice Walker*, pp. 155–67.

Nora, Pierre, 'Between Memory and History: *Les Lieux de Mémoire*', in Fabre and O'Meally (eds), *History and Memory in African-American Culture*, pp. 284–300.

O'Brien, John, 'Alice Walker: an Interview' [1973], in Gates and Appiah (eds), *Alice Walker*, pp. 326–46.

Ong, Walter J., *Orality and Literacy: the Technologizing of the Word*, New Accents Series [1982] (London: Routledge, 1989).

Paz, Octavio, *The Labyrinth of Solitude* [1959 *El Laberinto de la Soledad*] trans. Lysander Kemp (Harmondsworth: Penguin, 1983).

Petry, Alice Hall, 'Walker: The Achievement of the Short Fiction', in Gates and Appiah (eds), *Alice Walker*, pp. 193–210.

Pinckney, Darryl, 'Black Victims, Black Villains', *The New York Review of Books*, 29 January 1987, pp. 17–20.

Placksin, Sally, *Jazzwomen 1900 to the Present: Their Lives and Music* [1982] (London: Pluto Press, 1985).

Pollock, Kimberley Joyce, 'A Continuum of Pain: a Woman's Legacy in Alice Walker's *Possessing the Secret of Joy*', in Elizabeth Brown-Guillory (ed.), *Women of Color: Mother–Daughter Relationships in 20th Century Literature* (Austin: University of Texas Press, 1996), pp. 38–56.

Pratt, Ray, *Rhythm and Resistance: Explorations in the Political Uses of Popular Music* (New York: Praeger, 1990).

Proudfit, Charles, 'Celie's Search for Identity: A Psychoanalytic Developmental Reading of Alice Walker's *The Color Purple*', *Contemporary Literature*, 32:1 (Spring 1991), pp. 12–37.

Pryse, Marjorie and Hortense J. Spillers (eds), *Conjuring: Black Women, Fiction, and Literary Tradition* (Bloomington: Indiana University Press, 1985).

Ross, Daniel W., 'Celie in the Looking Glass: the Desire for Selfhood in *The Color Purple*', *Modern Fiction Studies*, 34:1 (1988), pp. 69–84.

Royster, Philip M., 'In Search of Our Father's Arms: Alice Walker's Persona of the Alienated Darling', *Black American Literature Forum*, 20:4 (Winter 1986), pp. 347–70.

Russell, Sandi, *Render Me My Song: African-American Women Writers from Slavery to the Present* (New York: St Martin's Press, 1990).

Sadoff, Diane F., 'Black Matrilineage: The Case of Walker and Hurston', in Bloom (ed.), *Alice Walker*, pp. 115–34.

Schultz, Elizabeth, 'To Be Black and Blue: the Blues Genre in Black American Autobiography', in Albert E. Stone (ed.), *The American Autobiography: a Collection of Critical Essays* (Englewood Cliffs: Prentice Hall, 1981), pp. 109–32.

Singh, Amritjit, Joseph T. Skerrett Jr and Robert E. Hogan (eds), *Memory, Narrative and Identity: New Essays in Ethnic American Literatures* (London: Northeastern University Press, 1996).

Sjöö, Monica and Barbara Mor, *The Great Cosmic Mother: Rediscovering the Religion of the Earth*, second edition (San Francisco: Harper, 1991).

Smitherman, Geneva, *Talkin' and Testifyin': the Language of Black America* (Boston: Houghton Mifflin, 1977).

Staples, Robert, 'The Myth of Black Macho: a Response to Angry Black Feminists', *The Black Scholar* (March–April 1979), pp. 24–33.

Stephens, Robert O., *The Family Saga in the South: Generations and Destinies* (London: Louisiana State University Press, 1995).

Stone, Merlin, *When God Was a Woman* (London: Harcourt Brace Jovanovich, 1976).

Storr, Anthony, *Jung* (London: Fontana, 1986).

Tate, Claudia (ed.), *Black Women Writers at Work* [1983] (Harpenden: Oldcastle Books, 1989).

Thiam, Awa, *Black Sisters, Speak Out: Feminism and Oppression in Black Africa* [1978, *La Parole aux Négresses*] (London: Pluto Press, 1986).

Thiong'O, Ngũgĩ wa, *Decolonising the Mind: the Politics of Language in African Literature* (London: James Currey, 1986).

Wade-Gayles, Gloria *No Crystal Stair: Visions of Race and Sex in Black Women's Fiction* (New York: Pilgrim Press, 1984).

Walker, Melissa, *Down From the Mountaintop: Black Women's Novels in the Wake of the Civil Rights Movement, 1966–1989* (New Haven: Yale University Press, 1991).

Wall, Wendy, 'Lettered Bodies and Corporeal Texts', in Gates and Appiah (eds), *Alice Walker*, pp. 261–74.

Watkins, Mel, 'Sexism, Racism and Black Women Writers', *New York Times Book Review*, 15 June 1986, pp. 1; 35–7.

Wehr, Demaris S., *Jung & Feminism: Liberating Archetypes* (London: Routledge, 1990).

Wilentz, Gay, 'Healing the Wounds of Time', *Women's Review of Books*, 10:5 (1993), pp. 16–17.

Williams, Delores S., 'Black Women's Literature and the Task of Feminist Theology', in Clarissa W. Atkinson, Constance H. Buchanan and Margaret R. Miles (eds), *Immaculate & Powerful: The Female in Sacred Image and Social Reality* (Boston: Beacon Press, 1985), pp. 88–110.

Williams, Linda Ruth, *Critical Desire: Psychoanalysis and the Literary Subject* (London: Edward Arnold, 1995).

Willis, Susan, *Specifying: Black Women Writing the American Experience* (Madison: University of Illinois Press, 1987).

——, 'Memory and Mass Culture', in Fabre and O'Meally (eds), *History & Memory in African-American Culture*, pp. 178–87.

Wilson, Sharon, 'An Interview with Alice Walker' [*Kalliope*, 6:2 (1984)], rpt. in Gates and Appiah (eds), *Alice Walker*, pp. 319–25.

Winchell, Donna Haisty, *Alice Walker* (New York: Twayne, 1992).

Wisker, Gina (ed.), *Black Women's Writing* (London: Macmillan, 1993).

Wyatt, David, 'Alice Walker', in David Wyatt, *Out of the Sixties: Storytelling and the Vietnam Generation* (Cambridge: Cambridge University Press, 1993), pp. 122–37.

Zinn, Howard, *A People's History of the United States* [1980] (New York: Harper Collins, 1990).

Zinsser, William (ed.), *Inventing the Truth: The Art and Craft of Memoir* (Boston: Houghton Mifflin, 1987).

Index

Note: Main entries are indicated in bold.

248   *Index*